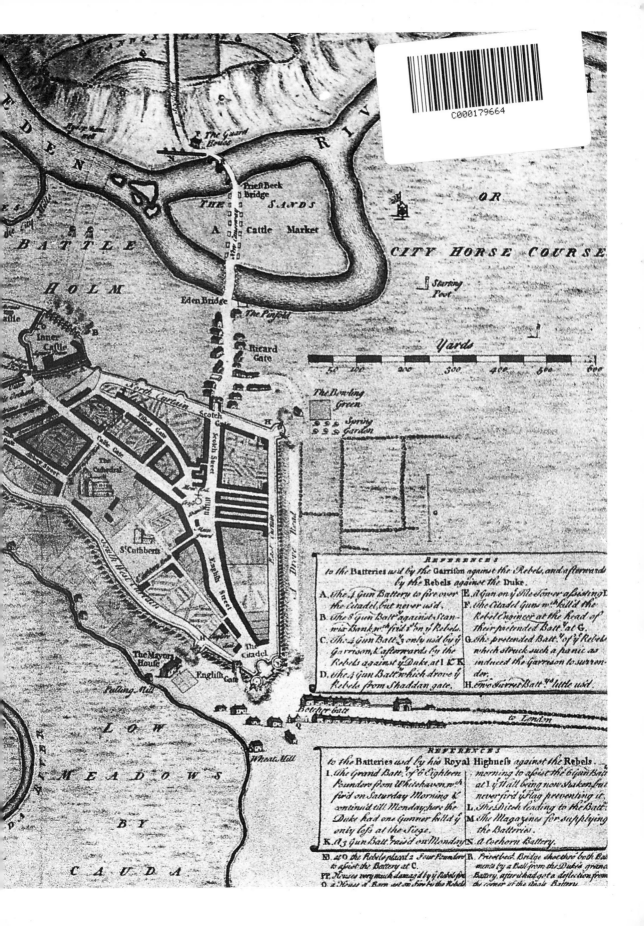

A History of
CARLISLE

Elizabethan Carlisle.

A History of
CARLISLE

Sydney Towill

Phillimore

1991

Published by
PHILLIMORE & CO. LTD
Shopwyke Hall, Chichester, Sussex

© Sydney Towill, 1991

ISBN 0 85033 742 9

Phototypeset by Intype, London
Printed and bound in Great Britain by
STAPLES PRINTERS ROCHESTER LIMITED
Love Lane, Rochester, Kent.

Contents

List of Illustrations vii
Acknowledgements ix
Introduction 1

1. Roman Carlisle 3
2. Dark Age Carlisle 9
3. The Rebirth of Carlisle 17
4. Medieval Carlisle 26
5. Tudor Carlisle 41
6. Carlisle in the Stuart Era 53
7. Eighteenth-Century Carlisle 63
8. The Industrial Revolution in Carlisle 77
9. The Social Consequences of the Industrial Revolution 91
10. The Mature City 107
11. Twentieth-Century Carlisle 123

Appendices 133
Notes 139
Bibliography 148
Index 151

List of Illustrations

Frontispiece: Map of Elizabethan Carlisle

1. Tombstone of Antigonus Papias 7
2. Siege of Carlisle, 1173 20
3. Carlisle Cathedral, king's head 27
4. Charter of Edward II, 1316 31
5. Carlisle Cathedral, Miserere seat 37
6. Shoemakers' Guild regalia 40
7. The Guildhall 40
8. Medieval paintings 42
9. Carlisle Cathedral, Renaissance screen 42
10. Twin-towered citadel 44
11. Carlisle Castle, half-moon battery, *c*.1540 44
12. Lady's Walk 47
13. The Dormont Book 51
14. John Speed's map of Carlisle in the 17th century 55
15. Lord Lonsdale's 'mushrooms' 64
16. Hutchinson's map of Carlisle, 1790 66
17. Carlisle, a walled city, *c*.1770 69
18. Eighteenth-century Carlisle from the west 69
19. Carlisle from the north, 1795 69
20. Regulator stage coach notice, 1819 71
21. Priest Beck bridge 73
22. Drove Lane 73
23. The Town Hall, 1780 75
24. Carlisle Cathedral, *c*.1800 75
25. The cottage-based textile industry 79
26. The factory-based textile industry 82
27. Ferguson's Holme Head works, *c*.1854 84
28. Langthwaite Mill 86
29. Shaddon Mills 86
30. Carlisle canal share certificate 88
31. The canal basin, 1835 89
32. Ships berthed in the canal basin 90
33. Plan from the Reid report, 1845 92
34. Plan from the Reid report, 1845 92
35. Slum property, 19th and 20th centuries 94
36. Dr. Heysham 97
37. Carlisle dispensary notice, 1783 98
38. City gates, *c*.1800 105
39. Subscription newsroom and library, *c*.1830 106
40. Newcastle and Carlisle Railway 108
41. Newcastle and Carlisle Railway: notice of initial services and a draconian trespass warning 109

42. Port Carlisle Dandy 111
43. Carr's biscuit works, *c*.1834 114
44. Advertisement for Hudson Scott's printing and engraving business 116
45. Green Market, late 19th century 119
46. Working-class housing 120
47. 'Genteel' housing 121
48. The Town Hall and street market, late 19th century 126/7
49. General Strike, 1926 129
50. Globe Lane, *c*.1980 131
51. The 'Lanes' shopping precinct 132

Acknowledgements

An author of a study covering a period of nearly two millennia owes an immeasurable debt to those who have researched in the field before him. Indebtedness is expressed, however inadequately, by specific references in the text and indirectly in the bibliography. I wish, however, to be more explicit; to thank individuals who have helped me directly in this work. To Dr. John Stedman and Dr. John Walton who have read my manuscripts and made invaluable criticisms and suggestions. To Bruce Jones, former Cumbria County Archivist and staff of the Cumbria Record Office; Stephen White and E. R. Wilkinson, present and former local history librarian of the Cumbria County Library; Harry Horton, formerly of Manchester Central Reference Library, who all have far exceeded the call of duty in searching out information in answer to my incessant requests.

My thanks are also due to Denis Perriam, who has generously shared his immense knowledge of the buildings of Carlisle; to Mike McCarthy, city archaeologist; David Clarke, curator, and other staff of Tullie House, for the help they have given me; to Guy Pawle for his expert reproduction of prints; and to Simon Fletcher, my editor. I also wish to express my appreciation to Dr. Graeme White and Dr. Tom Driver for their friendship and encouragement over many years and to Liz Skinner for her skill in deciphering my rough drafts to produce neat typescripts.

Above all I wish to thank my wife, Dorothy, for her encouragement, and for her forbearance during the long periods I have, from necessity, spent in my study researching and writing this book.

Introduction

Our earliest history of Carlisle concerns Luguvalium, a frontier town in the extreme north-west of the Roman province of Britain. Carlisle, in truth, was on the edge of all things, a place too obscure to feature in classical literature, yet it was important to Roman military forces. The knowledge we have of Carlisle comes largely from the archaeologist, and that knowledge is being notably augmented at present.

For centuries after the Roman withdrawal from Britain *c.*A.D. 410, Carlisle's history becomes indistinct, little being firmly documented until the seventh and eighth centuries.

An etymological study of the name 'Carlisle', and its transformations from Luguvalium to Luelcestre to Caerluel, gives some indication of racial complexity and of the dominant ruling race at different periods. The documentary sources, apart from Bede, are indirect and sparser than we would wish. Zosimus (at the beginning of the sixth century) and Gildas (second quarter of the sixth century) give information of the Roman withdrawal. For later periods we have to rely on material collected some three hundred years later by Nennius. In his *Historia Brittonum* he wrote that *'Ego autem coacervavi omne quod inveni'* ('I have made a heap of all that I have found'). His scraps include material relating to northern British Kingdoms of the sixth and seventh centuries, in particular to Rheged, thought to include land on both sides of the Solway Firth. In the seventh and eighth centuries the emergence of literate scribes, pre-eminent among whom was Bede, places the history of Carlisle on much firmer ground. In the 10th and 11th centuries Carlisle was at risk of total destruction by the Vikings but a nihilistic interpretation of events can be countered by impressive sculptural evidence, and by indirect evidence from the *Anglo-Saxon Chronicle* that Carlisle was incorporated in Strathclyde, which with Scottish and Viking allies was potent enough to present a threat to the English kingdom. The history of Carlisle from the Normans through to the Tudors and Stuarts is excellently documented and provides material for a commentary that in vitality and colour can stand comparison with any city in the country. In this period the most abundant historical sources, whether they are state documents or monastic chronicles, are not primarily written with Carlisle or its people at their focus of attention, but notwithstanding they shed a great deal of light on the fortunes of the city. There is a massive growth of source material and documentation in the mid-18th century. For the present purpose this has been allocated arbitrarily to 1745, the year that demarcated the end of border warfare and marked the early stages of the industrial revolution in Carlisle. The flood of information henceforth available from local historians, travellers, commissioners charged to enquire into the lowest and most humble sections of society, and increasingly from newspapers, was palpably different in scope to anything that had happened before. But an even more fundamental change occurs in the 20th century when the historian has increasingly direct access to events. These sources, complex and of different degrees of authenticity, are the building blocks with which to reconstruct nearly two millennia of history, that is Carlisle's proud heritage.

Chapter One

Roman Carlisle

The first written sources to mention the Carlisle area are the accounts of the Roman campaigns in Britain by the Roman historian Tacitus (A.D. 55-120). Before this date the region was part of the lands of the Brigantes, who were a Celtic tribe. Petilius Cerealis, one of Vespasian's generals, made the first assault on their territory. Tacitus gave a brief account of the campaign:

> Petilius Cerealis at once struck terror into their hearts by attacking the state of the Brigantes, which is said to be the most populous in the whole province. After a series of battles, some of them by no means bloodless, Petilius had overrun, if not actually conquered the major part of the territory.[1]

It is thought that Petilius founded the first timber fort at Carlisle, on the Annetwell Street site, during his campaign of A.D. 71-4, before the Roman governor Agricola took up his command in A.D. 77. A fine site was selected for this fort. Its position on the confluence of three rivers and its close proximity to the Solway Firth; its easy access via the valleys of the Irthing and Tyne to the east coast, over upland not exceeding 500 ft.; and the route via the Eden valley and Stainmore to the fortress at York all made the fort an ideal base for the control of the native population and for future operations north into Scotland. Agricola's campaign of A.D. 79 established Roman control of Britain up to the Tyne-Solway isthmus, approximately the boundary of the Brigantian kingdom. Subsequent campaigns culminated in the defeat of the Caledonians at Mons Graupius in A.D. 84, a battle vividly described by Tacitus.[2] Never again, however, were the Romans within sight of the complete conquest of Britain. At the moment of his triumph Agricola was recalled to Rome, and the army in Britain was further weakened by the removal of Legio II Adiutrix to the Danube. The era of expansion was over, and the Roman forces withdrew to the Clyde-Firth isthmus.

In Emperor Hadrian's reign, further contraction of Roman occupied territory was considered expedient, and Hadrian's Wall was constructed from the Tyne to the Solway between 122 and 128. The western end of the wall, considered the most vulnerable because of the presence of hostile tribes to the north, received the major mobile force of the northern frontier, the Ala Petriana.[3] Its commanding officer was the senior officer of the whole wall garrison. The establishment of a line of signalling stations from the command headquarters at Petriana (Stanwix) to York is an example of the professionalism of the Roman army.

Hadrian died in 138 and a new policy was adopted by his successor, Antoninus Pius. Lollius Urbicus, his general, reconquered southern Scotland and consolidated his gains by building a turf wall – the Antonine Wall – from the Clyde to the Forth, between 139 and 143. The strategy was initially successful. Hadrian's Wall was opened at various points to allow the rapid deployment of forces, so policing of the hostile tribes between the two walls was possible. Deprived of help from their northern allies, the Brigantes were subjugated, and for a short time a more peaceful way of life ensued.

Such stability could not be maintained throughout the second century. The Brigantes, only temporarily subdued, rose in a revolt that necessitated a change in Roman strategy. The Antonine Wall was abandoned c.184, and forces were withdrawn to Hadrian's Wall. All traces of Roman occupation to the north disappeared, except for a few isolated forts

such as Netherby and Bewcastle. Roman influence was more subtly maintained in the
abandoned territory by the creation of buffer states, who, in return for local autonomy,
created a barrier between the Caledonians from the highlands and the Brigantes.

The period of stability for Luguvalium (the Romano-British name for Carlisle, used as
early as 103)[4] and adjacent territory was interrupted abruptly in 192 when Clodius Albinus,
Governor of Britain, withdrew troops from Britain in order to stake his claim to the imperial
throne. He was unsuccessful, and was executed by Emperor Severus. In the interim, the
Maeatae, Caledonii and Brigantes rebelled, and Hadrian's Wall was extensively damaged.
Severus regained control, and rebuilt long sections of the wall and forts; their reoccupation
was completed by 207. Thereafter the British frontier was to remain peaceful until 296.

The physical remains of Roman Carlisle, after the accumulation of the debris of sixteen
centuries, are now buried, and most of it is inaccessible because of modern development.
Since 1977, however, archaeologists have made a number of exciting discoveries in Annetwell Street, Blackfriars Street, Castle Street and the Lanes. A number of articles have been
published which contain interim rather than final assessments, but their importance cannot
be over-estimated.

The most spectacular discovery, in 1977-9, was undoubtedly the southern rampart and
gate of a Flavian fort in Annetwell Street.[5] In the words of Mike McCarthy, the city
archaeologist:

> Miss Dorothy Charlesworth excavating for the Department of the Environment behind Abbey Street
> uncovered the remains of part of perhaps the best preserved Roman timber fort ever unearthed in
> Britain. Not only was the rampart standing nearly a metre high but the wooden gateway and the
> foundations of the gate towers, guard chambers and associated features were still largely intact.
> Wet ground conditions, that excluded bacterial action, guaranteed the survival of the timber work
> for 1,900 years.[6]

The extent of the fort has yet to be determined by excavation, but a typical Roman fort
covered five and a half acres and measured 600 ft. by 400 ft. Stretching north from Annetwell Street this would have covered most of the castle promontory. The fort can be dated
from coin evidence to A.D. 78-9, and thus may be attributed to Agricola. Its well-chosen
site would have appeared rather more formidable in Roman times than it does today, after
the bifurcation of the River Eden and the subsequent filling-in of the southern channel.
The river used to skirt the castle promontory, while the adjacent land was marshy and a
defile separated the castle and cathedral sites. A civilian settlement serving and dependent
upon the fort, the 'vicus', occupied the western portion of the present city centre. It was
aligned north-south on Blackfriars Street, with the fort entrance to the north and the
Roman approach road along the present Botchergate and London Road to the south. An
opportunity to investigate this area occurred when Marks and Spencer extended their store
across Blackfriars Street. The remains of wooden buildings, almost exactly contemporary
with the fort, were interpreted by McCarthy as artisan dwellings primarily serving the
Roman forces, the front sections being shops, living areas (with raised floors) behind, and
possibly kitchens, or areas for small-scale industrial activity at the rear (with earthen floors
and hearths). Blackfriars Street has a long occupation history; in reverse chronological
order the archaeologists revealed nearly two hundred skeletons associated with the medieval
Blackfriars, artefacts associated with a Saxon monastery, traces of Dark Age buildings, and
finally layers of Roman buildings from the three centuries of occupation.

During the erection of new buildings at Tullie House in 1893, a great timber platform
was discovered. It was traced for 220 ft. west to east from Abbey Street to Castle Street,
and was 40 ft. wide.[7] It fits awkwardly into the complex of fort and vicus, and its purpose

is still a subject of speculation. Shaw believed it to be the rampart of the fort and, because of its massive dimensions, capable of mounting ballistae.[8] The site of the fort, however, is now seen to be some distance to the north. Ferguson suggested that it was a drill hall or riding school.[9] Later writers believe it to have been a granary, located outside the Flavian fort, although the floor was packed solid and not suspended as is usual for a granary.[10] All authorities agree that a building on this scale must have had a military rather than a civilian purpose, but all hypotheses leave difficult interpretative problems. Why was an important military building outside the protective area of the fort? And why should it be between the fort and the main road to the south, Blackfriars Street?

At present the function of the cathedral site in Roman Carlisle remains an enigma, although the recent dig (in 1988) may eventually shed light on the subject. Situated between fort and vicus it must have been a prime site, as today. Could the forum have been situated there? McCarthy writes:

> No public buildings have been excavated though their presence is clearly implied by the size and status of Carlisle as well as by some nineteenth century discoveries of architectural fragments. An obvious possible location for major public buildings is the Cathedral precinct.[11]

A strong case can also be made for the positioning of the forum in the market cross area of the modern city, perhaps extending into the Lanes area, which, it will be argued, became the hub of the Roman street network after the second-century reconstruction.

The Lanes is a new five-acre shopping complex in the east of central Carlisle. The controversy and delay associated with the development of this site had the highly beneficial windfall of permitting a four-year exploration period for the archaeologists. Among the many finds, the remains of two major buildings were discovered, both massive structures of timber, and dating from before 150. The long rectangular building, 34 ft. wide and a minimum of 180 ft. long, ran north and south parallel to Scotch Street, and 33 ft. to the east of it. It appears to have been a long range of rooms, the central one of monumental proportions. The walls were clad with a double layer of wattling, woven into prefabricated panels and supported by substantial wooden uprights. A military or official purpose is suggested by the building's size and construction, but the weakness of its defences argues against it being part of the military enclave, which was centred on the Flavian fort and was replaced by a succession of structures until at least the fourth century. Caruana believes it might have been the praetorium, house of an important field commander, but perhaps the biggest puzzle is that the building only had a very short life before it was demolished and most of the timber was taken away. The uncovering of many pounds of molten lead, presumably from the building's roof, testifies to its substantial construction. Some 130 ft. to the east of the 'praetorium' is the other major building, roughly contemporary and again a massive wooden structure. Caruana suggests it was a temple, and produces a speculative isometric reconstruction which shows a classical-style cella (inner chamber) and a peristyle colonnaded court to the rear.

After the demolition of the 'praetorium', timber buildings were constructed in the Lanes area, which by their position and orientation seem to reflect the line of modern Scotch Street, leading to the crossing of the Eden and to Stanwix.[12] Caruana argues that this Roman river crossing was substantially in the same place as the medieval Eden bridges which crossed the floodplain between Stanwix and Carlisle.[13]

The comparatively recent discovery of the remains of a Roman road running through the grounds of Tullie House, past the east end of the cathedral, adds to the evidence that the market cross area was the centre of the town and the location of the forum. The road leads to the market-place in one direction, and in the other to the west gate of the city and the entrance to the Flavian fort. Excavations in Castle Street have revealed timber buildings on stone piles fronting onto this cambered and metalled road.[14] Supplementary evidence includes the road to the river crossing and Petriana, and the significant widening of the road network in the market cross area.

The second century saw major changes in both city and fortress. A detachment of a Roman legion was established in the fort, the defences were reorganised and stone barracks were built. Substantial new buildings were erected in Blackfriars Street, while the discovery of hypocausts in the Lanes indicates that comparatively wealthy Roman citizens settled there. The limits of the town are easily defined partly because of the Roman prohibition of burials in their urban areas. Graves have been discovered to the east at the bowling green, Spring Garden Lane, and to the west the scarp along West Walls is a natural boundary. The fort and the River Eden provide another natural boundary to the north. In fact the area of the Roman town was remarkably similar to that surrounded by the medieval town walls, except that the citadel protrudes to the south of the Roman town.[15]

The intervention of Emperor Severus in the third century began a period of stability and growth for Britain in general, and Luguvalium in particular. By mid century the military rule in the Pennines was relaxed, with a transition to civilian-organised territories made possible by an increasing community of interests between the military and the native populations. Epigraphic evidence from milestones and a tombstone shows that at this time Luguvalium became the 'Civitas Carvetiorum', that is the administrative centre for the Carvetii, a subdivision of the Brigantes.[16] References to the town in the *Antonine Itinerary* and in the *Ravenna Cosmography* show that it was an important communications centre.[17] Charlesworth argues for the prominence but also the limitations of the Civitas Carvetiorum, and supports the hypothesis that the forum was located in the market cross area:

> . . . although the Civitas Carvetiorum prospered it may not produce the lavishly decorated town homes of the other towns of the same status in Britain. But there are indications of substantial stone buildings, the wide north end of English Street with its market cross may reflect the forum. It was not an insecure jerry built frontier town.[18]

Luguvalium was, at this time, an administrative, market and social centre which served both military and civilian settlements. The remains of wide metalled roads and relatively ostentatious stone public buildings testify to a substantial town. The museum at Tullie House contains fragments of stone columns and capitals, and costly and elaborate grave monuments suggest that many people were relatively wealthy. A considerable number of writing tablets have been discovered, which suggest the presence of a literate element among the citizens. Eloquent support for these contentions is given by the Latin inscription on a tombstone found on Gallows Hill, which refers to a Greek, presumably a trader, who settled in the town. An English translation reads:

> To the spirits of the departed
> Flavius Antigonus Papias
> a citizen of Greece, lived
> 60 years more or less, and
> gave back to the fates his
> soul lent for that time,
> Septima Do. (   ) set this up.[19]

Archaeological evidence points towards the dismantling of the Flavian fort in the Trajan period (A.D. 98-117), but rebuilding took place and a military enclave was present in

1. Tombstone of Antigonus Papias. A memorial, with Latin inscription,
to a Greek trader who died in Carlisle during the Roman period.

Luguvalium throughout the second and third centuries. With the establishment of the
frontier on the Clyde-Forth isthmus the fort and the vicus were downgraded. Nevertheless
military communications between the Solway and Tyne were consolidated by the construction of a road known today by its medieval name, Stanegate. Later, when the over-extended
Roman forces retreated to the Tyne-Solway line, the strengthening of the fortress at
Luguvalium was both necessary and permitted by the release of manpower.

The building of Hadrian's Wall and, later, the Antonine Wall, did not make the fort at
Luguvalium redundant, and there is no evidence that it was downgraded again. The walls
were not inviolate barriers, and the defensive system of the western frontier was underpinned
by the garrison at Luguvalium, which from the second or third century consisted of élite
detachments of a legion.

The Roman occupation of northern Britain was largely one of success for the imperial
armies, and of imposed peace, rising prosperity and the status of a regional administration
centre for the people of Luguvalium. They were introduced to the trappings of Roman
civilisation, fine public buildings and, for the favoured few, the delights of the hypocaust
to temper the cold northern climate. As the third century drew to a close, however, the
peace of the province was disturbed by the ambitions of provincial rulers, and Luguvalium
increasingly was threatened. The usurper Carausius, and his murderer and successor,
Allectus, ruled Britain from 286 to 296, before Allectus was defeated by imperial forces
under Constantius Chlorus. The revolt of the army in Britain was not without its dire
consequences for the forces on the northern frontier. When Allectus withdrew his troops
south to resist invasion in 293, the wall was pierced in places. But the situation was
redeemed by Constantius who brought Britain back to legitimate Roman control, and
repaired the wall. On the death of Constantius in York, in 306, he was succeeded by his
son Constantine who, in spite of being proclaimed emperor, returned to Britain many times
before his death in 337. The revival of Roman power and stability was short-lived. From

henceforth the archaeological evidence points to the decline of Luguvalium in the fourth and fifth centuries; even the stone buildings in the fort appear to have fallen into disuse. Only in the Blackfriars area is there convincing evidence for continued occupation, but significantly, when we come to consider the evidence for the survival of the town through the Dark Ages, the Roman road to the fort entrance remained in use until the early Middle Ages. The archaeological evidence for this period of decline is consistent with and complements documentary records. By mid-century, the Roman world was in turmoil, due to the attacks by barbarians on the frontiers of an overstretched empire, compounded by the political ambitions of usurpers to the imperial throne. The withdrawing of forces from Britain was disastrous, particularly for the northern frontier. Attacks by Picts and Scots on the wall were recorded in 350, during the reign of another usurper, Magnentius. A further attack occurred in 360, when the land around Hadrian's Wall was ravaged. The greatest disaster took place in 367. Picts, Saxons, Scots and the tribes of the Attacotti made what appeared to be a concerted attack, breaching the wall and flooding into the Midlands. The situation was temporarily resolved when Count Theodosius, sent to Britain by Emperor Valentinian in 368, succeeded in defeating the enemy forces. After this Britain secured, for the next 15 years, its last period of peace and stability under Roman rule.

An unresolved problem in the study of Luguvalium is whether it was a walled town. The evidence is conflicting. Excavation at 'The Lanes' did not produce unequivocal evidence of a stone Roman wall to the east of the town: 'Defences have been seen on West Tower Street and they certainly incorporate Roman masonry, but it is far from clear whether these are Roman or medieval. It seems possible that the civilian community was undefended'.[20] The western walls of the town are clearly medieval, but again they incorporate Roman masonry. Present archaeological opinion is that the existence of a Roman wall is, at best, doubtful. Bede, however, refers to Cuthbert being conducted around the walls on his visit to the town in 685.[21] When it became the Civitas Carvetiorum in the third century, Luguvalium was both an administrative and a trading centre. In the fourth century, when Hadrian's Wall was breached repeatedly as a series of usurpers withdrew their troops for military adventures on the continent, it is almost inconceivable that Luguvalium remained unprotected: Hadrian's Wall may have retained military value after it was rebuilt and remanned, but its protective value for an important regional centre was minimal. There are certain times when the building or restoration of the town's defences seems probable, for example when Count Theodosius restored Roman authority in 367. Frere draws attention to the strengthening of the defences of British towns at this time, when he refers to '... the recently established fact that in about 369 many, if not all, of the town walls of Roman Britain were modernised by the addition of ballista towers and the strengthening of their ditch systems'.[22] It is possible that Luguvalium shared in this policy.

There is archaeological evidence that Luguvalium survived into the fifth century, but not as part of the Roman system. The drying-up of coin and pottery evidence in the 390s is consistent with the departure of the military, but other evidence shows that Luguvalium was still habitable. McCarthy reports that finds in Blackfriars Street indicate that building continued to the end of Roman rule, late Roman houses continued to be reconstructed during the fifth century and the building alignment of Blackfriars Street was retained for some time.[23] He draws attention to the position of St Cuthbert's church at the north-western end, and at right angles to Blackfriars Street – that is, conforming to the Roman alignment of Blackfriars Street but out of true with the usual Christian west-east alignment of the Augustinian priory and the Dominican friary to its north and south.[24] One may speculate that St Cuthbert's is on the site of an early Saxon church that had to be built within the constraints of the Roman street pattern.

Chapter Two

Dark Age Carlisle

With the decay of Roman rule in Britain in the late fourth century, Carlisle all but disappeared from documentary history, apart from a brief but significant reappearance in 685. The history of Carlisle in the Dark Ages is largely that of north-west England, as it was successively dominated by British, English, Scandinavian, Scottish and Norman overlords. The task of assessing the fate of Carlisle in this era of ever-changing political allegiances is difficult, as the relatively abundant consumer goods and money of the Roman era ceased to circulate, thus depriving the archaeologist of artefacts, and there is limited documentary evidence. The problem is compounded by the partiality of sources, whether Gildas' gloom and animosity towards the Anglo-Saxons, the antipathy of Bede to the British, or the fixation of Nennius' sources on the epic deeds of British chieftains. The effect of the turmoil on the town could not have been other than traumatic, as its former position in the Roman economy as an administrative and trading centre was no longer viable. It is debatable whether Carlisle survived throughout the Dark Ages, albeit on a reduced scale with a much depleted economic base, or whether it was physically destroyed during the repeated invasions. There were two periods when Carlisle was critically at risk: *c.*410, after the Romans had withdrawn, and during the invasion of the Norwegian Vikings *c.*910.

British Carlisle

The security of Luguvalium was threatened in the late fourth century by the increasing barbarian threat to the Roman Empire and by power struggles as a series of usurpers attempted to wrest power from the legitimate emperors. Three revolts were of particular moment to Luguvalium and the border regions. The first took place in 383, when Magnus Maximus crossed the channel to establish himself as emperor in Gaul and Spain, taking with him the larger part of his army in Britain. The venture ended in disaster, and was followed by attacks on southern England by the Picts, emphasising both their mobility and their choice of land for plunder. The second revolt took place after Emperor Honorius sent his general, Stilicho, to reorganise the defence of Britain. In 399 Stilicho made a punitive expedition against the Irish, Picts and Saxons, but in the following year he was withdrawn, along with a large part of the remaining garrison, to meet an urgent threat to the Roman heartland. Constantine III was the final usurper to intervene on the continent. His failure left the legitimate Roman authority in Britain discredited and virtually powerless.

Events in early fifth-century Britain and Gaul are described by the Greek historian Zosimus. Although not a direct contemporary, he derived much of his material from earlier sources. Zosimus describes how a weakened Roman army was unable to withstand incursions from barbarians beyond the Rhine, and the Britons and some of the Celtic nations were left to defend themselves:

> The Britons themselves took up arms and incurred many dangerous enterprises for their own protection until they had freed their cities from the barbarians who had besieged them. Thus happened this revolt or defection of Britain and the Celtic nations when Constantine usurped the Empire, by whose negligent government the barbarians were emboldened to commit such destruction.[1]

Emperor Honorius recognised the desperate situation and 'sent letters to the cities of Britain counselling them to be watchful of their own security'.[2] This bleak instruction served as an official withdrawal of the Roman law that prohibited barbarians from possessing arms.

Bede (673-735), an Englishman, threw a less favourable light on the British. If Carlisle's fate was linked to the Roman wall its outlook was dismal:

> On the departure of the Romans, the Picts and Scots, learning that they did not mean to return were quick to return themselves and became bolder than ever, occupied all the Northern and outpart of the Island up to the Wall as if it belonged to them. Here a dispirited British garrison stationed on the fortifications pined in terror night and day, while from beyond the wall the enemy constantly harrassed them with hooked weapons, dragging the cowardly defenders down from their wall and dashing them to the ground. At length the Britons abandoned their cities and wall and fled in disorder pursued by their foes.[3]

Bede's main source for fifth-century events was the sixth-century British ecclesiastic Gildas. His work, *De excidio et conquesta Britanniae* ('Concerning the ruin and conquest of Britain'), was essentially a moral exhortation, of which the historical narrative formed a subordinate element.[4] Gildas' failure to establish a credible sequence of events was to cause confusion for later historians, but was the inevitable result of relying on a fifth-century oral tradition which paid no heed to chronology.

After relating the disasters that befell the British after the Roman withdrawal, Gildas recounts the appeal to Aetius:

> Again, therefore, the remaining British sent a lamentable petition to Aetius (a person of great authority in the Roman state) as follows:
>   To Aetius, thrice Consul
>   The Groans of the British
>   The Barbarians drive us to the sea, the sea again to the Barbarians, thus between two deaths we perish either by the sword or by water.[5]

According to Gildas the appeal was turned down, and the Britons were left to their fate. He did not have all the information available to later historians, however. The appeal did not immediately follow the Roman withdrawal; it could not have pre-dated, indeed, Aetius' third consulship which began in 446. It was, in fact, a sequel to the British struggle with the Saxons who had been invited to south-east England as mercenaries *c*.430 who, after a further influx of their countrymen, turned on their masters. Thus the source on which Bede relies for evidence of the destruction of the walls, and by inference the town, of Luguvalium after the Roman withdrawal, is severely compromised. There is no evidence to suggest that the town was physically destroyed, but good reason to believe that an economic decline took place. This could have begun in the fourth century when troops were withdrawn to the continent.

In the absence of hard fact, apart from Carlisle's emergence into the limelight in 685, there are circumstantial reasons for discounting the destruction hypothesis. Carlisle became part of the British kingdom of Strathclyde, and was not on the frontier against the Picts and Scots, who found it more rewarding to attack southern England from the sea. Important contributory factors towards border peace, but difficult to quantify, were the strong revival of the Christian church, which had been established for two centuries in Roman Britain, and the evangelising zeal of British missionaries in Scotland and Ireland. The Carlisle area had connections with two of the outstanding early Christian leaders, St Ninian and St Patrick. Ninian (fl. early fifth century) built a church at Whithorn (Candida Casa) and his widespread diocese seems to have extended from Glasgow to the borders of Westmorland. Bede tells us that his work among the southern Picts caused them to abandon the errors of idolatry and accept the true faith,[6] so the cessation of Pictish raids in the early fifth century may have been influenced by Ninian's work. The second great churchman who had a profound effect on the border country was St Patrick, who was born *c*.410 at either Birdoswald or possibly Bewcastle, and spent his early days in or near Carlisle. It is possible that the suspension of major Scottish and Irish incursions may be connected with his work in Ireland, but paganism was not finally banished from the north west. In *c*.573 the great battle of Ardderyd (Arthuret, a small parish about eight miles north of Carlisle) was fought between Britons who had retained the Christian faith and those who had relapsed into their old pagan ways.[7] The Christians were victorious and their leader, Rederech, became king of the Britons. It is possible that the tribes of the western coast were brought together into a kingdom called Strathclyde, which stretched from the Clyde to the Mersey, with its capital at Dumbarton, but the emergence of a federation of petty kingdoms would appear to be a more sustainable hypothesis. In the aftermath of the battle, a British chieftain named Urien seized Rheged, from his powerbase at Catraeth (Catterick). Rheged was a region on both sides of the Solway Firth which was possibly coterminous with the Civitas Carvetiorum.

The written evidence in the sixth and much of the seventh century relates to the Christian kingdom of Rheged. Sources include Nennius' *Historia Brittonum* and the highly-developed poetical literature of Canu Taliesin, in which warfare eclipses all other activities.[8] A court that certain scholars have connected with Carlisle is mentioned in these sources, which present two very different aspects of sixth- and seventh-century life. The first is of an heroic age where the bard sings his panegyric poems of valour and daring in an autocratic world, where British kings fight against Pictish, Irish and Anglo-Saxon intruders. *Historia Brittonum* tells us that Urien was the greatest leader of the Britons ever to wage war on the Angles of Bernicia under Theoderic, *c*.588. The Christian society, in which Urien's sons, Rhun and Owain, played a distinguished rôle, is also described. In the *Historia* there is a curiously-worded passage that links Rhun with Paulinus, archbishop of York, who baptised King Edwin of Northumbria and twelve thousand of his subjects. It is reasonable to accept that Rhun was a man of learning who attained a high position in the British Church just as the English kingdom of Northumbria emerged from paganism. The connection between the two kingdoms continued with Rhun's granddaughter, who married into the Northumbrian royal house. Like his brother, Owain was a man of distinction, and was one of the great heroes in the early Welsh poems.

Nennius' *Historia* concerns a British kingdom which had a close political relationship with Anglian Northumbria. The hypothesis that the north Cumbrian plain bordering on the Solway, with Carlisle at its heart, was the centre of Rheged is supported by the inclusion of Carlisle in chapter 66 of the *Historia*. This is entitled 'These are the names of all cities in the whole of Britain, 28 in number', and lists Anglo-Saxon, British and Welsh towns. No other centre of population is given in Rheged.[9]

English Carlisle
By the beginning of the seventh century there was increasing English pressure on British territories in the west and north. Bede states that in 603 King Ethelfrith of Northumbria 'ravaged the Britons more cruelly than all other English leaders, overran a great area exterminating or enslaving the inhabitants and making their lands either tributary to the English or ready for English settlement'.[10] Further expansion across the Pennines followed in the reigns of Oswald and Oswy (641-70). Jackson argues that England and southern Scotland, west of the Pennines, north of the Ribble and all round the Solway had been absorbed by Northumbria between 650 and 676.[11]

There is evidence, however, that the transition in Cumbria was peaceful. The links between Northumbria and Rheged have been mentioned already, and Oswy, who married Rhun's granddaughter, became king both of Northumbria and Rheged. Oswy's son, Ecgfrith, left his queen in the safety of a convent in Carlisle when he led an expedition against the Picts in 685. St Cuthbert was opposed to this, and prophesied disaster. Bede wrote:

> Cuthbert set off to Carlisle to speak to the Queen who had arranged to stay in her sister's convent to await the outcome of the war. The day after his arrival the citizens conducted him round the city walls to see a remarkable Roman fountain that was built into them. He was suddenly disturbed in spirit. He leaned heavily on his staff, turned his face dolefully to the wall, then straightening himself up and looking up into the sky he sighed deeply and said almost in a whisper 'Perhaps at this moment the battle is being decided'.

Cuthbert hurried back to the queen and spoke to her in secret:

> Tomorrow being Sunday you cannot travel. Monday morning at daybreak leave in your chariot for the Royal city. Enter quickly for perhaps the King has been slain. Tomorrow I have been invited to a neighbouring monastery to dedicate the chapel but as soon as the dedication is over I shall follow you.

Two days later a fugitive from the battle arrived, his tale of woe confirming Cuthbert's dark forebodings: 'The same day, nay the same hour that Cuthbert received the message as he stood by the fountain the King and all his bodyguards had been slaughtered by the enemy'.[12] The anonymous author of the earliest life of St Cuthbert authenticates this significant event in the history of Carlisle: 'Cuthbert, leaning on his staff, was listening to Wagga the reeve of Carlisle explaining to the Queen the Roman Wall of the city'.[13]

Bede's commentary confirms that much of the fabric of the town had survived since the Roman withdrawal. Carlisle was the centre of an ordered and settled community, civically organised, with a convent and a nearby monastery. The inhabitants were aware of the town's heritage, and this is illustrated by Cuthbert's visit to the Roman fountain. Carlisle did not stand in isolation, but was the natural economic, political and ecclesiastical centre for the region, sharing in the artistic revival that flowered in the north in the late seventh and early eighth centuries. This was the era of great Anglian sculpture exemplified by the Bewcastle Cross and its counterpart at Ruthwell. At Bewcastle the church's dedication to St Cuthbert may indicate a connection with his preaching journeys in the diocese; the cross providing a Christian focus centuries before the church was built. Pevsner writes that the crosses 'are the greatest achievement of their date in the whole of Europe'.[14] They exhibit technical mastery, with their naturalistic sculptured figures and scrolls of foliage inhabited with birds and beasts, while the Latin and runic inscriptions show a degree of literacy and monastic learning that is at odds with our usual conception of the Dark Ages.

Carlisle became part of the See of Lindisfarne c.685. Symeon of Durham records that King Ecgfrith of Northumbria bestowed upon Cuthbert the city of Luguballia with the lands fifteen miles around it.[15] This is perhaps represented by the old parish of St Cuthbert Without.

The half-century between the death of Ecgfrith and the death of Bede was a golden age in the history of Carlisle.[16] In 731 Bede summarised the 'present state of all Britain':

> At the present time the Picts have a treaty of peace with the English, and are glad to be united in Catholic peace and truth to the universal church. The Scots who are living in Britain are content with their own territories, and do not contemplate any raids or stratagems against the English. The

Britons for the most part have a national hatred for the English, and uphold their own bad customs against the true Easter of the Catholic church, however they are opposed by the power of God and man alike, and are powerless to obtain what they want. For although they are independent, they have been brought in part under subjection to the English. As such peace and prosperity prevail in these days, many of the Northumbrians, both noble and simple, together with their children have laid aside their weapons preferring to receive the tonsure and to take monastic vows rather than study the arts of war. What the results of this will be the future will show.[17]

For the next century and a half Carlisle continued under English rule, with no evidence to suggest other than an ordered and settled life. A harbinger of things to come, however, was recorded in the Anglo-Saxon Chronicle, in 793:

In that year terrible portents appeared in Northumbria, and miserably afflicted the inhabitants; these were exceptional flashes of lightning and fiery dragons were seen flying in the air, and soon after in the same year the harrying of the heathen miserably destroyed God's church in Lindisfarne by rapine and slaughter.[18]

The Danish Invasions

During the ninth century the Danes began to settle in the conquered lands of eastern England. In 867 they defeated the Northumbrians and occupied York; they moved into northern Northumbria in 875. The Chronicle records that 'in this year went the host from Repton, and Halfdan went with a part of the host into Northumbria and took winter quarters on the river Tyne; and the host overran that land and made frequent raids against the Picts and against the Strathclyde Britons'.[19]

Since Roman withdrawal, Carlisle had been shielded from the major invasions by its favourable geographical position. After eastern England was first ravaged by the pagan Anglo Saxons there was an interval of at least two centuries before the Angles, from Northumbria, reached the Solway Plain. By that time they had reached a more tolerant relationship with their British neighbours. The Danes arrived in north-west England nearly a century after the first brutal pirate raids on Lindisfarne, but with the fall of Northumbria, Carlisle was exposed to the full force of the invasion. It is debatable, however, whether the blow fell in 876 or in the following century, and to what extent the town was devastated.

The pessimistic conclusion is that Carlisle was destroyed and deserted, judging by the absence of entries in the Chronicle between 875 and 1092. Florence of Worcester alleged that Carlisle was left ruined, remaining deserted for 200 years. This assertion was reiterated by Symeon of Durham.[20] Symeon's references to Bishop Eardulf of Lindisfarne and Abbot Eadred of Carlisle, however, are not consistent with the town's destruction. The first reference to Eardulf is in 856, when he is praised for having bestowed as much of his pastoral solicitude on Luel, then named Carleol, a remote part of his diocese, as upon Lindisfarne itself. In 875, when fleeing from the Danes, the same bishop carried the relics of St Cuthbert through the district of Carlisle, before embarking for Ireland from Derwentmouth (Workington) c.877. After the death of Halfdan, the Danish leader, Abbot Eadred, who had accompanied Eardulf, returned to his monastery in Carlisle in 883. One may suppose, therefore, that the monastery, and by inference Carlisle, had not been destroyed by the Danes between 873 and 883. It was also at Carlisle that Cuthbert appeared to Eadred in a vision, and from there that the abbot was sent to proclaim to the Danes that Guthred, son of Hardacanute, should be their king. The entreaty was successful, and the Danish host acclaimed him as their king, swearing upon the body of St Cuthbert that they would keep the peace. That the English abbot of Carlisle advised the Danes who should be their king is strange, but the reference would be inconceivable if the Danes had devastated the town.

The Viking Presence

By the late ninth century, Northumbria had been dismembered by the Danish armies. The lands of the Danelaw, East Anglia, parts of Mercia and the Northumbrian kingdom based on York, had been divided and settled by soldiers turned farmers. What evidence there is, though, seems to point to the survival of the part of the Northumbrian kingdom north of the Tyne and west of the Pennines, which remained subject to the rule of English ealdormen. At the turn of the century Norwegian Vikings, the Norsemen who had established a kingdom in Ireland, directed their aggression to the previously sheltered western seaboard of England. Their mode of aggression was soon to be changed from acts of pillage and destruction to that of settlement on conquered territory, and in the early tenth century settlements were founded on the western coast from the Wirral to the Solway. Within a short period, a succession of Norwegian adventurers attacked the Danish kingdom based at York, where their leader, Raegnald, established himself as king in 919. Symeon records that a princeps (nobleman) bearing the English name Eardulf, who ruled to the west of the Pennines c.910-15, was driven eastwards across the mountains by an invasion of pirates.[21]

It can be asserted confidently that the Norse immigration was very extensive, and evidence is given below to support this assertion, but the political status of north-west England in the anarchy of this period is more speculative. Ekwall writes:

> It is a prevalent opinion that as a result of the downfall of Northumbria, Cumberland again became a British territory, forming part of the British kingdom of Strathclyde. This theory is not supported by sufficient evidence but it is very plausible. Though such an event may have reversed the relative positions of the Anglian and the British element, there is no reason to believe that it carried along with it the extermination or expulsion of the Anglian population.[22]

After an English occupation that had lasted the greater part of three centuries, Carlisle had become once more part of a British kingdom, albeit one with a considerable number of Scandinavian settlers and a pervasive Scandinavian influence. In the absence of documentary records the most permanent reminder of Norse settlement is in place-names: these provide indisputable evidence for the colonisation of north-west England by Norwegians. This area is a land of fells and becks, of thwaites and dales, terms which could only have been introduced by Norwegian settlers.[23] Three examples of thwaites in close proximity to Carlisle are Southwaite, Calthwaite and Curthwaite. There is more subtle evidence that shows that the Norwegians only settled after they had lived in Ireland and absorbed some of the Gaelic culture. This is the fact that they adapted Gaelic syntax in the formation of compound place-names, by placing the defined term first. Thus the town of Aspatria, which means ash tree Patric, is the Gaelic version of an English compound meaning Patric's ash tree. In this case there is also the characteristic use of the Irish, Goidelic, personal name in the compound.[24] Kirkandrews, Kirkbride and Kirkoswald are similar examples of Irish/Norse place-names in the vicinity of Carlisle: Kirk is derived from the Old Norse *kirkja*, meaning church. The general argument is not affected if, as Fellows Jensen and Bailey both suggest, the Goidelic signature arrived in Cumbria secondhand; via Scotland (Galloway) where the Irish influence may predate the formation of a Viking colony.[25] The evolution of the word for Carlisle from Luguvalium (Luguvalo's town – Roman British) to Luelcestre (Luel's town – English) to Caerluel (town of Luel – Irish/Norwegian) is an indication of racial dominance.

Carlisle was now part of Strathclyde, with a strong Norse presence. Its history henceforth was dominated by English hostility and aggression, and the town's fate must be inferred from the contingencies of racial warfare in the border regions. Within a decade of Eardulf's precipitous flight there is evidence of a complete reversal in the relationship of the Norsemen to the Cumbrians. Throughout the tenth century the Vikings, Strathclyde Britons, Scots and the Bamburgh Northumbrians were tacit allies who banded together against the aggressive expansionism of the English under the Wessex kings. This is evident from entries in the Anglo-Saxon Chronicle:

> 924 In this year King Edward was accepted as 'father and lord' by the King of the Scots and his people, by King Raegnald [the Viking] and all the Northumbrians, also by the King of the Strathclyde Welsh and all his subjects.

> 926 In this year the fiery rays of light appear in the northern sky. Sihtric [Norse King of Northumbria with his capital at York] died and King Athelstan annexed the Kingdom of Northumbria, he brought into submission all the Kings of the island . . . They established a covenant of peace with pledges and oaths at a place called Eamont Bridge on 12 July, they forbid all idolatrous practices and thus separated in concord.[26]

The kings who submitted included King Constantine of the Scots, King Eugenius of Strathclyde, the Welsh kings and the Northumbrian king of Bamburgh. There are two significant facts in this entry. Firstly, as it was customary for a king to receive formal submission on the boundary of his kingdom, the northern boundary of the English kingdom was on the Eamont, and Carlisle, some twenty miles to the north, was deep within the British kingdom of Strathclyde. Secondly, the idolatrous practices in lands that had long been Christian must have referred to the actions and beliefs of the Norsemen.

Strathclyde, and Cumbria in particular, continued to be harassed throughout the tenth century as English kings attacked, and played off one adversary against another. In 945, 'King Edmund ravaged all Cumberland and gave it all to Malcolm, King of the Scots, on the condition that he be his ally, both at sea and land'. Dunmail, King of Strathclyde, was humiliated and his sons blinded on Edmund's orders, but nevertheless he was reigning in Cumbria again within a few years. At the end of the century the Chronicle records: '1000: In this year the King [Ethelred] marched into Cumberland and laid waste nearly the whole of it'. The dynasty of Strathclyde became extinct c.1015 on the death of Owen the Bald, and the Carlisle region passed to the king of the Scots. This was only for a few decades, before the resurgence of English power under the Danish kings Canute and Harthacanute (1016-42). The Dane Siward held the earldom of Northumbria from 1041 until 1053, and after defeating the Scots established an overlordship of the lands between the Solway and the Derwent. Subsequently Gospatric, a scion of the royal house of Bamburgh, was appointed as Lord of Allerdale and Dalston, to hold his estate 'in all the lands that were Cumbria' from Earl Siward.[27] Carlisle once again came under Scottish rule when it was seized by Malcolm III shortly before the Norman Conquest. The exclusion of these lands from the Domesday Survey implies that it was not part of the English kingdom in 1086.

Several lines of reasoning support the survival of Carlisle in the 10th and 11th centuries. The land of Carlisle was a component part of Strathclyde, which was allied with Viking and Scottish forces. The fact that it was repeatedly under attack implies that it was seen as a persistent threat to the English kingdom. Secondly, the Normans accepted the Celtic name Caerluel, rather than building a new town with a new name, as they would have done if the town had been destroyed during the Scandinavian invasions. Physical survival is also supported by the sculptural evidence. There is a continuity of sculptural expression, albeit with a coarsening of style, from the Anglian to the Scandinavian period, which suggests co-existence and integration of races. During the two centuries following the Anglian artistic peak of the Bewcastle and Ruthwell crosses the style hardened into the late ninth-century Danish geometric interlaced patterns of the Dacre and Irton crosses.

The style closely conforms to the Anglian custom, however, as neither the Danes nor their successors, the Norwegian Vikings, had stone sculptural traditions, and these crosses would have been the work of English sculptors. In the early tenth century, the arrival of the Vikings had a more radical effect, as English craftsmen adopted the motifs of a pagan or secular world. Patterns were convoluted and included animals and human figures – doll-like and unrealistic. A fine example of Anglo-Norse sculpture is the Gosforth cross, which includes pagan carving but also retains Christian symbolism. Pevsner points out that Cumbria is full of crosses and cross fragments of the late tenth century, with notable examples at Penrith and Dacre, and also numerous Viking hogback tombs, for example those at Appleby, Aspatria, Lowther and Penrith.[28] The tradition of native English stone carving in Cumbria did not merely continue into the Viking period, but was enthusiastically taken up and adapted. It is this continuity of culture that gives ground to believe that the Danish and Viking invaders were absorbed into the native population. It suggests that the invaders did not wantonly destroy their new homeland, but Carlisle had lost its political, strategic and economic importance because of other factors, such as the relocation of the English frontier on the River Eamont and Cumbria's absorption into Strathclyde. This loss of its former importance was echoed by the lack of sculptural remains in Carlisle. As Bailey writes:

> Carlisle was not a dominant economic/social centre in the 10th century and early 11th century on the basis of sculpture . . . It is clearly significant that whilst every other site in northern England which produced sculpture from its pre-Viking monasteries, produced yet more (under secular patronage) in the Viking period, Carlisle actually had less.[29]

A great deal is known of Roman and medieval Carlisle, but until recently little archaeological evidence has been available to bridge the gap between these periods. The Roman road that ran from the market-place to the west gate appears to have remained in use into the Norman period, the evidence that suggests this consisting of four Anglo-Saxon coins, three stycas (ninth and tenth-century coins) and a penny of Edgar (959-75), all found in the rubble of Roman buildings. As Caruana states, 'there is no structural evidence to accompany these, but it is clear that the road remained in use'.[30] The evidence may appear scanty but, with the collapse of industry at the end of the Roman period, the coin supply dried up. More positive evidence for the survival of Carlisle in the Saxon and Scandinavian periods comes from the 1988 excavations preparatory to the construction of an underground cathedral treasury, to the west of the nave. The interim report on this small 31.5 x 23ft. site excavation claims that there is evidence of a 'continuous sequence of activity from the mid-Roman period to the twentieth century'. A late Saxon/Scandinavian cemetery was found containing 41 graves together with a fine group of artefacts which suggests strongly the existence of an early church on the cathedral site. The interim report concludes:

> The post-Roman structure and, particularly, the Saxon/Scandinavian cemetery are thus of prime importance for this city's archaeology. The obscure hints from Saints' lives and chronicles can be fleshed out by positive evidence for a settlement, thriving at least in the late Saxon period. In particular we can now be sure that a church existed on the site before the Cathedral was founded. Indeed it can be argued that there had been a church here since the post-Roman period. That, however, cannot be proved without further excavation.[31]

Chapter Three

The Rebirth of Carlisle

For seven centuries Carlisle had been a victim of border warfare and of clashes between English and Celtic kingdoms. It had been ravaged by Viking invaders and seized by Scottish kings, but had not been abandoned and was still populated. In 1092 the town was restored to the English kingdom by William Rufus. The Anglo-Saxon Chronicle records:

> In this year King William went north to Carlisle with great levies and restored the town, and built the castle. He drove out Dolfin who had formerly ruled that district, and garrisoned the castle with his men. Thereafter he returned hither southwards, sending very many peasants thither with their wives and livestock to settle there and till the soil.[1]

The period 1092-1272, the formative years of a reborn Carlisle, were amongst the most crucial and unpredictable in Carlisle's history.

Carlisle's place in the English-Scottish power struggle

The border between England and Scotland in 1092 was undefined. Carlisle had been in Strathclyde, which stretched from the Clyde into Cumbria, almost continuously from 1018. To the east was Bernicia, formerly extending to the Firth of Forth, but under increasing pressure from the Scottish-Pictish kingdom who wanted to expand towards the Tyne and Stainmore, the gateway to the west.

The purposeful exercise of military strength by early Norman kings to protect their territory brought them into conflict with an expansionist Scottish kingdom, and the seeds were sown for renewed border warfare. William Rufus stopped at the Solway, leaving Annandale, Eskdale and Liddesdale in Scottish hands, but also built fortresses to protect his kingdom. A castle at Carlisle complemented the New Castle upon the Tyne, built in 1080.

The settlement at Carlisle

The castle was built in 1092. Peasants were brought in from far afield to till the land around William's plantation town, which replaced the settlement that had become ruinous.[2] They counterbalanced the racial and cultural background of the indigenous natives who, in the previous century alone, had been under British, English and Scottish rule. John Denton (d. 1617) and Hugh Todd (1657-1728), two of Carlisle's earliest antiquarians, give details of the settlement pattern in the city. They assert that Frenchmen, the Flemings, the Irish and the English were all assigned to their several quarters.

> The English, the best and principal citizens were placed in the principal places of this citty [*sic*] near to the market place and the church, and also in Richard-gate and in Botchardgate. The Irish placed in the Vicus Hibernensium, dwelt there in cottages when it was waste, (the gate at the end of the street is called the Irishgate). The Flemings dwelt in Shaddongate (Shadwinggate) in the area called Vicus Flandrensis. The Frenchmen, or Normans dwelt in Castle St. (Vicus Francorum).[3]

The districts or streets named above are shown in Jones' plan of 13th-century Carlisle.[4]

The pervasive influence of the Norman conquerors and the traces of Scandinavian occupation can be seen in Carlisle and its neighbourhood in the ubiquitous compound place-names. These link the Scandinavian '-by' with a Norman personal name. Clearly the extra-mural area around the town had been given to Norman overlords: Etterby (Etard), Rickerby (Ricard, or Richard), Aglionby (Agyllum), Botcherby (Botchard), Upperby, Harraby (Henry) and Tarraby.

William II's plans for the building of the castle, town walls and church were incomplete at the time of his death, and the work was continued by Henry I who, according to Todd, replaced the Flemings and Dutch (sending them to North Wales and Anglesey) with English families from Kent, Essex and Middlesex.

The king's fortress

Carlisle Castle was sited in a naturally strong position, protected on one side by the River Eden and on the other side by its tributaries, the Petteril and Caldew. The castle, standing some sixty feet above river level, was probably a palisaded wooden building. In 1112 Henry I (1100-35) found it expedient to appoint a Norman nobleman, Ranulf Meschin, to the lordship of the territory, who moved the centre of his domain to Appleby. A castle was built there, and two baronies were created, at Burgh-by-Sands to control the Solway coast, and at Liddel to protect the border region from Scottish incursions. Ranulf's responsibility for Carlisle was terminated when he succeeded to the earldom of Chester after his cousin Earl Richard perished in the 'White Ship' in 1120, together with William the Aetheling and several of the Norman nobility. At this stage Carlisle was taken directly into the king's hands. Henry visited the town in 1122 and ordered its fortification with a castellum and towers.[5] The word 'towers' in the plural suggests that they were towers on the town wall, and it is unlikely that the massive keep, as we see it today, was Henry's work. The evidence is that it was erected by the Scottish King David, who controlled Carlisle from 1135 to 1153, and also heightened the walls of the city. This contention is reasonable in the light of his reputation as a builder of monasteries on a magnificent scale, and because square or rectangular keeps belong stylistically to the mid or late 12th century.

The Church

The foundation of the priory at Carlisle is attributed to Walter, a wealthy Norman who came to England with the Conqueror. It was Henry I, however, and not William, who enfeoffed Walter with the manors of Linstock and Carleton, and it was by Henry's licence that Walter assumed the religious habit in the priory of St Mary's, Carlisle, and endowed the house with his worldly possessions, c.1102. At this time Henry increased the endowment with six churches and their chapels, namely those of Newcastle upon Tyne, Newburn, Warkworth, Rothbury, Whittingham and Corbridge. The foundation of the Augustinian priory can thus be dated to before 1122, the year when Henry visited Carlisle and took direct control away from Ranulf Meschin. Henry looked upon Carlisle as a permanent part of his kingdom, but he might have had some doubts regarding the loyalty of its inhabitants, especially as up to this time the larger portion of Cumbria had been under the control of Scottish and Irish bishops. Even in 1122 John, Bishop of Glasgow, performed pontifical duties in Cumberland, although he did not recognise Henry as his sovereign. Thus the establishment of the diocese of Carlisle in 1133 was motivated by political considerations. Prior Adelulf of the priory at Carlisle, an ex-officio canon of York and once Henry's confessor, was elected as first bishop of the new see, and was consecrated by Archbishop Thurston of York.

Adelulf was an Englishman, judging by his name, and his appointment in an age when Normans were almost universally entrusted with the key positions of state is particularly noteworthy.[6] It is equally remarkable that he retained his position when Carlisle reverted to Scottish rule under David. Adelulf was clearly a man of ability, described as wise, able and devout in the Chronicle of Hexham, but his position under the Scottish Crown (1136-57) must have been anomalous.[7]

Adelulf's cathedral was a modestly-sized Norman building, with an eight-bay nave and a short two-bay choir ending in an apse. The 26 canons had their stalls in the crossing and in the two eastern bays of the nave, as the choir was large enough only for the sanctuary. The construction of this austere Norman church began under Henry I, and probably continued into Henry II's reign. It is fortunate for Carlisle that the cathedral's construction surmounted the vicissitudes of the national political struggles.

In the early 13th century, the elegance of Early English architecture was all but obligatory for major churches, with its rib vaults, pointed arches and large windows. In the more settled reign of Henry III the change in architectural fashion coincided with practical needs and the availability of resources. The canons abandoned the apsidal plan, and rebuilt the choir, extending it from two to seven bays, and adding a short chancel. This separated them from the parishioners in the nave, and provided more space for altars and shrines. Today only two complete bays of the nave remain, but a trace of the Norman east end is still visible: standing in the present choir and looking west, the Norman roof line and the trace of an arch can be seen to the right of the organ.

At this time Dominican and Franciscan friars came to England from the continent. They brought with them their rule of evangelical poverty, which meant that they lived and preached in the community. Walter Mauclerk, Bishop of Carlisle from 1223, was a patron of the Dominicans (also known as Blackfriars or friar-preachers) and it was under his sanction that both groups established themselves in Carlisle, in 1223. The Franciscans (also known as Greyfriars or friars-minor) settled in Carlisle only nine years after the order had reached England. They were given a house within the walls of the city, where Friars Court, off Devonshire Street, now stands. The Dominicans occupied the land bounded on the east and west by Blackfriars Street and West Walls, on the north by Heads Lane, and extending to the south as far as the present citadel. At the time of the dissolution the priory consisted of the church and churchyard, the community's living quarters, large gardens and an orchard. In 1235 Henry III gave the Franciscans timber for their church, and presented the Dominican friars with 10 oaks in 1239 and six more in 1244 for the same purpose. Implicit royal support continued in the next reign, when Edward I and his family took up residence with the Dominicans, while he was engaged in the Scottish wars. During the 13th century the friars became very popular as preachers, which antagonised some of the secular clergy. They resented the mendicants coming into their parishes to preach and hear the parishioners' confessions.

Carlisle's involvement in the Anglo-Scottish power struggle

Carlisle, because of its strategic position, became a pawn in the struggle between the Anglo-Norman and Scottish kingdoms. The impact of this on the city was disastrous. Many citizens fought on the Scottish side in 1138, resisted the Scots when they besieged the city in 1173 and, in the barons' revolt at the end of John's reign, connived at Alexander's Scottish take-over. Corresponding confusion surrounded the attitudes of churchmen, for example when the cathedral canons were accused by Henry III of disloyalty. It was only after the English and Scottish reconciliation in 1235 that Carlisle became, finally and unambiguously, an English city.

When Henry I died in 1135, the succession was disputed by Stephen, grandson of William I, and Henry's daughter, Matilda. King David of Scotland invaded northern England, ostensibly to uphold Matilda's succession, and then retained the province with the acquiescence of Stephen. David retained control of England as far south as the Tees and Ribble even after his defeat at the Battle of the Standard in 1138. Many Cumbrians fought with the Scots at that battle, and it was to Carlisle that the army withdrew after defeat. This would explain, perhaps, how the see of Carlisle survived, and the castle and cathedral continued to develop, despite the apparently traumatic political events. During this period, Carlisle became David's favourite residence and a meeting place for the court; David died there in 1153. The region was a stable, and seemingly permanent, part of the Scottish kingdom. The foundation of Holm Cultram abbey in 1150, some fifteen miles west of Carlisle, either by David or his son, implies a feeling of confidence and security.

The situation on the borders was transformed by the death of David, his son Henry, and Ranulf (formerly ruler of the region) in 1153, and of King Stephen in 1154. Stephen's successor, Henry II, wrested back the English border territory from Malcolm, the boy-king of Scotland. Under Henry, England became part of a vast empire. By marriage, diplomacy and war the house of Anjou had accumulated possessions that included all of western France. The empire of Henry II stretched from the Pyrenees to the Solway Firth.

Although it was now securely in English hands, the king treated Carlisle with circum-spection. Aware of its citizens' divided loyalties, Henry visited the town, first in 1158, and again in 1163 and 1186. A royal charter granted to the abbey of Holm Cultram appears to belong to this period. In 1173 there was a baronial revolt, but Henry responded decisively, and was able thereafter to keep his barons under control. William the Lion of Scotland, who had succeeded Malcolm in 1165, misread the situation, however, and decided to attack the northern counties. After trying his fortune in Northumberland, without success, he directed his attention towards Cumberland. After surprise attacks, William took Liddel Castle, and the king's castles at Appleby and Brough under Stainmore, but besieged Carlisle for three months without success. A vivid but partial account of this is

2.   The siege of Carlisle in 1173, as pictured in Holinshed (1577). Extra-mural citizens make haste to seek refuge within the city walls.

given in Jordan Fantosme's metrical 'Chronicle of War'. Credit is ascribed to Robert de Vaux, the governor, who, together with the baronage of the county who garrisoned the castle, resisted the repeated assaults of a prolonged siege:

> Great was the noise at the beginning of the combat
> The swords resound and the steel crashes
> Scarcely a hauberk or helmet there remained whole
> That day the garrison were knights
> With their swords they made holes in many a shield
> Enough of them they leave stretched beside the walls
> Whom they have no time to pick up
> Henceforth it is fitting for those within to help themselves
> To endure the combat and injure the shields,
> To hold and defend their barbican:
> No coward would have any use there.
> At the gate there was a great assault:
> On both sides there was great fury.
> There you might see so many blood-stained knights,
> So many good vassals in angry mood.
> The swords clash and intermingle   .
> Robert de Vaux defended himself bravely:
> Fitz Odard in no way failed him
> For his lord he undertook great deeds of daring
> In maintaining himself against so many people –
> Forty thousand, if Fantosme tells the truth.[8]

Repulsed from the city's defences, the Scots heard of the approach of an English army and retreated in disorder to Roxburgh. The undisciplined army desecrated churches and ravaged baronial estates on its way, disregarding the king's order to respect the sanctuary of the Church.

Fantosme tells a tale of valour and heroism on the part of the English, but there was another, less welcome, aspect of that ethos. Old border laws stated that disputes, whether homicide or a quarrel, were to be settled by a trial of single combat. In 1237, the clergy of England complained to Otho, a papal legate, that this applied to abbots and priors as well as laymen. Playing physical strength against piety and learning must have seemed to churchmen to be a pernicious aspect of the 'age of chivalry'.

The subsequent capture of King William at Alnwick brought the hostilities between England and Scotland to a close. The period of peace that followed was brought to an end during the later years of a discredited king, whose inept behaviour created unrest in the whole kingdom. King John, who inherited the vast Angevin empire, lost Normandy and Anjou in 1203-4, while his exorbitant demands at home led to a baronial revolt and curtailment of the Crown's powers at Runnymede. When John contrived with the Pope and his legate to repudiate Magna Carta, the barons called for the armed intervention of Prince Louis of France and Alexander II of Scotland, the latter in return for Carlisle. A letter was sent by 'the English barons to the good men of Carlisle against King John regarding the surrender of Carlisle to the King of the Scots', which urged the citizens to rebel. They did not appear unsympathetic to this, and there is a record of 'Amicable composition between the prior of Carlisle and the King of Scotland regarding the marches of Penrith and Soureby'.[9] When Alexander crossed the border and laid siege to Carlisle, the city did not put up its characteristic stubborn resistance, but surrendered to the Scots. The heaviest blows fell on the surrounding countryside, as undisciplined bands attacked the monastery of Holm Cultram, ironically founded by David, and pillaged the whole area, contrary to Alexander's command. Retribution followed swiftly, though. As the Scots retreated across the Eden estuary they were caught by the tide, and 1,900 men were drowned in an hour.

The death of John in 1216 averted a civil war, and the barons proclaimed their loyalty to the young King Henry III. The canons of Carlisle Cathedral, though, found themselves in deep trouble: despite the papal interdict they had elected a Scottish bishop. The anger of the Pope and Henry is clear from an entry in the Papal Register dated 2 July 1217:

> Mandate to the same to examine and make necessary deposition touching a matter about which the King, the archbishops of Dublin and York, and the bishops of London, Winchester, Bath and Worcester have written to the pope, praying him to remove the canons regular of Carlisle, who have publicly communicated with the disturbers of the King and realm who were excommunicated by the pope and the legate, and have celebrated divine offices in places under the interdict, and have also voluntary submitted themselves to the King of Scotland, who is fighting against his Liege Lord, and therefore excommunicate, and at his instance presumed to elect a bishop. He is to place these canons in other regular churches, to declare null the election attempted by them, to appoint to that church persons faithful to the King, to distribute the possessions and rents of the church between the bishops and canons to be appointed, the King and the said bishops attesting that such measures would lead to tranquility, as the church of Carlisle, being on the border, exercises much influence either for or against the King and his realm.[10]

The Scottish occupation of Carlisle did not last long. Alexander was ordered by Henry III to restore the castle, all the lands he had seized and all prisoners to Robert de Vipond. Peace was secured and Carlisle was restored to the English kingdom. In 1235, following an initiative of Pope Gregory, a lasting peace was established between the English and Scottish kingdoms. After accepting the homage of fealty to the English throne, Alexander and his heirs received, in 1242, the manors of Langwathby, Salkeld, Scotby, Castle Sowerby and Carlatton, and land worth £60 in the manor of Penrith.

Carlisle: the town and its government

Medieval Carlisle was surprisingly similar to the modern city.[11] The main thoroughfares of English Street, Scotch Street and Fisher Street radiated from the central market-place. Castle Street, though, was different. The old Roman road from the market-place to the west gate was still in use, and was resurfaced in the 13th century. After the great fire of 1292, which destroyed a large portion of the town, the Roman road was diverted to the comparatively new outer gatehouse of the medieval castle. Then the dog-leg of Castle Street, Paternoster Row and Abbey Street would have been constructed to connect the market-place to the west gate, along with a new east-west perimeter road: Finkle Street and Annetwell Street. At this time the road to Scotland was via Eden Bridge, across the former south channel, then on the line of Etterby Street to Etterby and Rockcliffe, before crossing the Esk to Gretna. An alternative route is suggested by Jones, via Caldew Bridge and across Willow Holme, and crossing the Eden at Etterby.[12] The road to Newcastle and the east went through Stanwix and along the Old Brampton Road.

Upkeep of the wooden Eden Bridge was an onerous duty, and the burden was shared between the king, Church and citizens. In 1382, the king granted pontage for four years to John de Bakhous, Robert Rosegill and Robert de Dalman in aid of the repair of Eden and Caldew Bridges. Frequent bequests are recorded in the wills of clerics and laymen, while in 1356 Bishop Welton published 'an indulgence of 40 days to all that contribute towards the repair to the bridge over the Eden between the City of Carlisle and Stanwix'.[13]

Complementary to the growth of the physical structure of Carlisle was the evolution of its government and administration. The city's development as a self-governing entity, independent of county and feudal magnates and held in fief direct from the king, changed its rôle from a military bastion against the Scots to a civic community which was able to pursue its own economic interests.

When Carlisle reverted to the Crown in 1120 the king's sheriff became responsible for collecting rents and profits from the royal demesne, and providing for the defence of the city. A more significant step was taken when the citizens were given permission to rent the city direct from the king for a fixed payment to the exchequer of £60 p.a. In return they were ceded the rights to the city mills, fishing rights upon the Eden and freedom from tolls in the county. A clear distinction had now been established between the city and the county: in the county the strict manorial system was in force, where labour service was paid to the lord of the manor and the rule of the manorial court was enforced. The city was taxed as a unit and city courts developed in due course. Individual citizens, however, farmed outside the walls in the manor, so had not entirely escaped from the manorial system.

The next step in the emancipation of the city was the Second Charter, of 1251. It gave permission for the formation of a free merchant guild to promote Carlisle's trading interests; this guild eventually became part of the ruling body of the city, the 'mayor and commonalty of Carlisle', so named in the 1292 Quo Warranto of Edward I. The third charter of Edward I was quite specific in the economic concessions that it granted: freedom from tolls, passage, pontage and all customs belonging to the king, reasonable estover (the right to wood) in the forest of Carlisle (Inglewood), together with the confirmation of the merchant guild. The king retained the city defences of the castle and walls, while the land in Carlisle was allocated to lords of manors and baronies in Cumberland, and to religious establishments, with the king remaining as ground landlord. The people of Carlisle had not entirely shaken off their feudal bonds.

A study of documentary sources has brought to light the names of Carlisle's tenants-in-chief, and also the fact that many of the gentry had houses in the city in the early Middle Ages.[14] In 1300 the lords of Liddell had six burgages, from which they derived an annual rent of 40s. The de Tilliots of Scaleby were owners of a 'baronia' in Scotch Street, and the Dentons of Cardew and Musgraves of Edenhall also owned property in the city. The Dacres and the Aglionbys owned houses, and the Earl of Northumberland had a house with a central gateway which later became the entrance to Barwise Court. Houses in a fortified city were secure: the de Boyvilles had a burgage on the east side of English Street, to which William de Boyville's widow, Joan, reserved the right of lodging when threatened in her Thursby home by marauding Scots. The priors of Carlisle held much land in the city, and Holm Cultram Abbey, and Wetheral and Lanercost Priories also owned Carlisle property. This all became part of the dean and chapter's estate after the Reformation.

The 1316 charter of Edward II was particularly important for the development of Carlisle because it recognised that the defence of the city could be more effectively undertaken if the responsibility for it was given to the citizens themselves. Economic resources to do this were given by allowing the city to acquire the rights to property within its boundary. This was an economic necessity, as revenue from tolls fell, continually diminished by exemption. The charter stated that 'any void places within the city and suburbs be granted to the citizens that they and their successors may build upon them or assign them to others for profit'.[15] Thus the civic body became a landlord; the licence to build on vacant land was an important asset in a medieval society. The mayor, bailiffs and commons constituted a perpetual borough landowner that could never die or be taken into profitable wardship by king or feudal lord.

The location of the 'void places' given to the city, and presumably resulting from the fire of 1292, has been traced by Nanson.[16] He concluded that the cullery tenures named in the city records refer to land that the city acquired through the charter. This was subsequently rented out to individual burgesses, and in time the tenancies became tenant rights. The tenures applied to property grouped around the open market, such as the Moot Hall, Redness Hall, the former Baxter Row and the Shambles, and on the land formerly occupied by the ditch between the city and castle, subsequently recovered for burgage plots.[17]

The economic development of Carlisle

There is strong evidence of a growth in trade and rising prosperity in Carlisle in the 12th and 13th centuries. The servicing of the castle garrison, the priory monks and the administration of the diocese from 1133 all provided a stable economic base for the city burgesses. An unprecedented building programme was initiated, to construct the massive city wall and castle fortifications, and the priory and cathedral. On the negative side, trade was hindered by border disputes and warfare, remoteness and difficulties of communication, while Carlisle's growth as a market was retarded by the restrictions placed upon the usage of potentially good agricultural land. To the south, stretching from Carlisle to Penrith, was Inglewood Forest, the king's hunting preserve. To the north, the Anglo-Scottish border created an artificial division between people of essentially the same stock and culture, and border warfare further limited the usefulness of the land. Where farming did develop, arable land was given over to barley and oats, but pasture was more important in the rural economy: wool and hides were sold in the markets of Carlisle in the early 13th century. It seems that the city burgesses passed from a subsistence economy to specialisation and trade during the 12th century, working the wool into cloth which was then sold at the fair. Grants for the levying of tolls show that wood and potash for dying were brought into the city, to finish the process. It seems probable that Carlisle had market and fair rights, and a free guild, confirmed by Henry II's charter, which has now been lost. Carlisle was not self-sufficient in grain, but by the mid-13th century, commercial ties had been established with Ireland. In 1235, the priory was licensed to buy food there, and by the end of the century had its own ship to import supplies. Carlisle Castle did the same, and in 1222 imported 500 quarters of wheat and 40 hogsheads of wine, no doubt originating in the king's province of Gascony. In return, the traders of Carlisle exported cloth and leather goods to Ireland. These trading links served the Crown well when Edward I had to provision his armies during the Scottish wars.

Considerable trading links were forged with Scotland too. Scottish cattle were driven through Carlisle on their way to English markets, and the murage grant of 1261 suggests that corn, salt, fish, garlic, dyestuffs, leather, wine and cloth could have been bought in Carlisle's market. (The murage grant lists goods that were sold in the city, on which toll was paid.) Salt was manufactured along the shores of the Solway from the 12th century. The religious houses were particularly active in this industry, especially Lanercost, Wetheral, Holm Cultram and Carlisle Priory. The last-named had four saltpans in the Burgh marsh locality.

A rather more remarkable enterprise was undertaken by a group of Carlisle entrepreneurs. They acquired a silver mine at Alston for which, in 1130, they paid the Crown a rent of 100s., and subsequently they opened the Carlisle Mint. Durant, who struck the earliest Carlisle coinage, was the first moneyer to operate locally, while Erebald, the head of a wealthy family who held the lease of the Cumberland Silver Mine, plied his trade at the end of Henry II's reign, and continued to do so under Stephen, David and Henry III. In 1243, when the coinage system was reformed, the mint had a staff of four moneyers, four keepers of the dies, two essayers and one clerk.

An optimistic view could be taken of Carlisle's future by the mid-13th century. Trade was thriving, there was a free guild, a city court (probably from the 12th century but certainly by the 13th), and a charter of civic rights. A persuasive testimony to the peace that had settled upon the border lands is given in the letter of 'Sir Thomas Lascelles and others' to Henry III, c.1257, which reported that 'We found the castle in very bad repair'.[18] A very detailed account of the decay of the walls, towers and internal buildings is given in the 'Calendar of Documents relating to Scotland', for 1255.[19]

In 1272, at the time of Henry III's death, England and Scotland were similar kingdoms living at peace with one another. At the end of the 13th century, however, all hopes of further peace and stability were shattered. Edward I was no longer preoccupied with fighting France, and looked to Scotland as an increasingly wealthy and attractive prize. Edward was an energetic and able warrior and administrator, and by the 1280s he had completed the conquest of the last independent part of Wales. At this time the death of Alexander III brought the direct line of Scottish kings to a sudden end, and a relentless war opened a new and turbulent chapter in Anglo-Scottish relations, with Carlisle in the front line.

Chapter Four

Medieval Carlisle

Edwardian Grandeur

For a period of three decades Carlisle witnessed scenes of pageantry never before experienced in a grim and impoverished border region. Geographical position determined that the city should be the military headquarters of Edward I's Scottish wars, and nobility and great churchmen came to support their king. Carlisle became one of the centres for the meetings of the king's councils, the first step towards the constitutional development of a representative national parliament.

Edward was crowned in 1272 and received homage from Alexander III of Scotland. When Alexander died in 1286 Edward adjudicated in the succession crisis. His commission rejected Robert Bruce in favour of John Balliol, who was duly elected in November 1293. John Halton, Bishop of Carlisle, who was a member of the commission, entertained the great magnates of the land on a massive scale at his castle at Linstock and palace at Rose, and was called upon to act at the highest level as churchman, king's envoy, plenipotentiary and military commander.

In May 1292 Carlisle was devastated by a fire, an eyewitness account of which appears in the *Chronicle of Lanercost*. It was started reputedly by a man who was attempting to revenge his disinheritance:

> [He] set fire to his father's house outside the town at the west end of the cathedral church, and this, escaping notice at first, soon spread over the whole town, and what is more, it speedily consumed the neighbouring hamlets to a distance of two miles beyond the walls, and afterwards the streets of the city, with the churches and collegiate buildings, none being able to save any but very few houses. The fire was indeed so intense and devouring that it consumed the very stones and burnt flourishing orchards to the ground, destroying animals of all kinds; and which was even more deplorable, it burnt very many human beings of different ages and both sexes. I myself saw birds flying about half burnt, in their attempt to escape.[1]

Edward's intervention in Scottish affairs predictably led to hostilities. In March 1296, the Earl of Buchan attacked Carlisle. The inhabitants successfully defended the city, but about half of it was once more reduced to ashes when a Scottish prisoner broke free and started a fire in the prison. Edward responded by leading his army into Scotland and compelling Balliol to abdicate. In an escalation of the conflict William Wallace, a Scottish knight, defeated an English army at Stirling, then harried Cumberland and demanded the surrender of Carlisle. The Scots were repulsed, but during their retreat they sacked Lanercost Priory. In 1298 Edward defeated Wallace at Falkirk, and returned with his army to Carlisle. From Stanwix he summoned the county nobility and sheriffs to meet on 5 September 1298 'to punish the malice and rebellion of the Scots and to place his followers in possession of the land he had granted to them in Scotland'.[2] This military council has been referred to as the first Carlisle parliament. In 1300 Edward convened another parliament in the city, when he sought the financial aid to force a lasting and total Scottish submission. It was a far grander event. The king and queen travelled to Carlisle, and were guests at the abbeys of Holm Cultram and Lanercost, and at the episcopal palace at Rose. Preparations had been made by John Halton for the parliament to be held in the great hall of the castle. Richard Slater and Robert Wittering represented the county of Cumberland, and Henry

3. This king's head in Carlisle Cathedral may well represent Edward I, and is perhaps contemporary with Edward's stay in the city when the cathedral was being rebuilt, after the fire of 1292.

Spencer and Andrew Serjeant represented Carlisle in this parliament that gave Edward the backing he required for an invasion of Scotland.

A contemporary narrative describes the brilliant pageantry as the army left Carlisle, prepared to attack Caerlaverock Castle.

> They were habited not in coats and surcoats, but were mounted on powerful and costly chargers and, that they might not be taken by surprise, they were well and securely armed. There were many rich caparisons embroidered on silks and satins; many a beautiful pennon fixed to a lance; and many a banner displayed. And afar off there was heard the neighing of horses; hills and vallies were every where covered with Sumpter horses and Waggons with provisions and sacks of tents and pavilions, and the days were long and fine; they proceeded by easy journies, arranged in four squadrons.[3]

As the army advanced, stores and 'engines of war' were transported by sea to the Scottish coast. The chief port of embarkation was Skinburness, a chartered market town under the lordship of the abbot of Holm Cultram. Between 1301 and 1303 the town was literally washed away by the sea, indeed a dramatic change of fortune.[4] Caerlaverock capitulated in July 1301, and in September and October Edward stayed chiefly at Holm Cultram, Rose, Lanercost and Carlisle before leaving in mid-November for the south. It was at Holm Cultram that the bishop of Glasgow, a prisoner, swore allegiance with great solemnity. The victory, however, did little for the border region. In 1301 John Halton pleaded for an indulgence in the payment of a royal tenth. He pointed 'to the miserable state of the diocese for the past four years and more owing to the depredations of the treacherous Scots'. Monasteries were destroyed, several churches were reduced to ashes and the clergy could no longer live on their benefices, but were forced to beg alms.

Scottish affairs continued in a state of great turmoil, with Wallace waging a guerrilla war until he was captured and hanged in 1305. In 1306 Robert Bruce stabbed John Comyn, of the house of Balliol, in the church of the Grey Friars at Dumfries. His rival thus removed, he was crowned king of Scotland at Scone and, in contravention of his solemn oath of fealty given to Edward in Carlisle Cathedral in 1297, he took up arms against his English overlord. At the request of Edward, Pope Clement V gave a commission to the archbishop of York and the bishop of Carlisle to excommunicate Bruce. Cardinal Petras Hispanus, the papal legate, preached in Carlisle Cathedral, and 'revested himselfe and the other bishops which were present and then, with candels light and causing the bels to be roong they accaused, in terrible wise, Robert Bruce, the usurper of the Crowne of Scotland, with all partakers, aides and mainteiners'.[5]

Edward again summoned his army to assemble in Carlisle in the summer of 1306, and while his son ruthlessly wasted Scottish lands, Edward, now aged and in poor health, followed slowly. He arrived at Lanercost with his queen in September, and stayed there for six months, apart from a short visit to Carlisle and Bishop Halton at Linstock. From Lanercost the king summoned a Parliament to meet at Carlisle on 20 January 1307. Writs were addressed to the Prince of Wales, the archbishop of York, 19 bishops, three times as many abbots, seven earls, 63 barons, two knights from 37 counties, and one or two burgesses from 165 boroughs together with the great officers of state. The members for Cumberland were John de Denton and William de Langrigg, and Andrew Serjeant and Richard Habrickly represented Carlisle. The writs to the barons specified that the business of the parliament, held in the Great Hall of the castle, was to include the Scots war and the treason of Bruce. The Great Hall may have been a large wooden building in the outer bailey, or the present hall, adjacent to the king's palace in the inner bailey, may have been used.

The splendour of the occasion provided the greatest pageantry in Carlisle's history, but the accommodation of so many distinguished visitors must have presented difficulties. Meanwhile the army, gathered for the invasion of Scotland, was encamped nearby; the whole district between Lanercost, Holm Cultram and the Solway was thronged with soldiers, traders, and wagons laden with stores.

The 1307 parliament was a landmark in the struggle between emergent nationalism, represented by the king, and the attempt by papal power to suppress this tendency in favour of internationalism. In more mundane terms this asked the question whether the international Church should draw revenue from monastic lands in Britain. A long petition was read in Norman French, in the presence of the king and the cardinal legate, complaining of the heavy financial demands upon the revenues of monasteries by the papal collector William Testa, and of the papal granting of Provisions. These were appointments to benefices, often of non-resident Italians or other foreigners, in derogation of the rights of their patrons. The legislation that arose from this petition was embodied in the Statute of Carlisle, which forebade the carrying abroad of money raised by taxation of Church property in England. This bold declaration was followed, however, by a deeply humiliating volte-face. Edward issued letters to all concerned postponing the statute's operation and giving permission to William Testa and his colleagues to continue their financial activities and to take the money abroad. This decision was taken undoubtedly because Edward was a sick man, unwilling to imperil his recently-acquired good relationship with the Pope when the most important issue was a successful war with Scotland.

During the summer, Edward made a solemn offering of the horse-litter in which he had travelled to the north, and the horses belonging to it, in a ceremony at Carlisle Cathedral. On 3 July he mounted his charger and set off towards Scotland. Four days later Edward I died, on Burgh Marsh, bringing to a close what was arguably the most brilliant, but most unsettled, period of Carlisle's history.

At the eastern end of the cathedral's south aisle is the carved head of a king: it may well represent Edward I. A sculptor could conceivably have seen the king close enough to have produced a stylised carving of him. Edward's long face and strong features are clearly reproduced, but the extent of the beard and absence of his well-known drooping eyelid (a feature shared by his father) make it impossible to claim with absolute certainty that the sculpture represents him.[6] Certainly Carlisle had reason to be grateful to him for the funds that he brought to the city, which permitted an immediate start to the rebuilding of the cathedral after the fire of 1292.

Edwardian blight

Edward's Scottish conquest remained unfinished at the time of his death, but his policy had awakened a deep antagonism and aggressive nationalism in Scotland. As the Scots fought for their independence the border region was torn apart by continuous internecine warfare, which culminated in the raids of 1312-22. The diocese of Carlisle was continually overrun and wasted, and large sums of money were wrung out of it for appeasement. In 1312 Robert Bruce raided Lanercost for three days, 'doing an infinity of damage'.[7] He was paid by the people of Cumberland, Westmorland and Northumberland during the following year in order to buy off a threatened invasion, but the policy of appeasement provided no solution. On 16 April 1314

> Edward de Brus, Robert's brother, invaded England by way of Carlisle with an army contrary to agreement and remained there three days at the Bishop's manor house, to wit, at Rose and sent a strong detachment of his army to burn the southern and western districts during those three days. They burnt many towns and two churches, taking men and women prisoners, and collected a great

number of Cattle in Inglewood Forest and elsewhere driving them off with them on the Friday [i.e. 19 April]; they killed few men except those who made determined resistance; but they made an attack upon the city of Carlisle because of the Knights and country people who were assembled there. Now the Scots did all these wrongs at that time because the men of that March had not paid the tribute which they had pledged themselves to pay certain days.[8]

The city, commanded by Bishop Halton, was too strong for Bruce to take, but nothing could be done to protect the surrounding district. In July 1314, following the disastrous English defeat at Bannockburn, Sir Andrew de Harcla was charged with the custody of the city and castle. Under Sir Andrew's command were four knights, 50 men at arms, 15 esquires, 30 hobelars, 110 archers and 40 Irish archers. In addition, 60 archers held the Caldew gate, 56 held Bokard's gate and 60 held Richard's gate.[9] Even this force was inadequate to intervene outside the city either at the time of Bannockburn or during the later raids on the city. Cumberland had little option but to pay off the Scots once again, the county's appeasement probably amounting to 600 marks in total.

In 1315, Bruce mustered all his forces, and besieged Carlisle for 10 days:

On every day of the siege they assaulted one of the three gates of the city, sometimes all three at once; but never without loss, because there were discharged upon them from the walls such dense volleys of darts and arrows, likewise stones, that they asked one another whether stones bred and multiplied within the walls. Now on the fifth day of the siege they set up a machine for casting stones next the church of Holy Trinity,[10] where their King stationed himself, and they cast great stones continually against the wall, but they did little or no injury to those within, except that they killed one man. But there were seven or eight similar machines within the city, besides other engines of war which are called Springalds[11] for discharging long darts, and staves with sockets for casting stones, which caused great fear and damage to those outside. Meanwhile, however, the Scots set up a certain great berefrai like a great tower, which was considerably higher than the city walls. On perceiving this, the carpenters of the city erected upon a tower of the wall against which that engine must come if it had ever reached the wall, a wooden tower loftier than the other; but neither that engine nor any other ever did reach the wall, because, when it was being drawn on wheels over the wet and swampy ground, having stuck there through its overweight, it could neither be taken any further nor do any harm. Moreover the Scots had many long ladders, which they brought with them for scaling the wall in different places simultaneously; also a sow for mining the town wall, had they been able; but neither sow nor ladders availed them aught. Also they made great numbers of fascines of corn and herbage to fill the moat outside the wall on the east side, so they might pass over dry shod. Also they made long bridges of logs running upon wheels, such as being strongly and swiftly drawn with rope might reach across the width of the moat. But during all the time the Scots were on the ground neither fascines sufficed to fill the moat, nor those wooden bridges to cross the ditch, but sank to the depths by their own weight.[12]

On the ninth day a general assault was made upon all the city gates and upon the whole circuit of the walls, which the citizens valiantly repulsed. On the eleventh day the Scots retreated in despair to their own country leaving behind them all their engines of war. Carlisle Castle was never captured during the period of English weakness, but the defence-less suburbs were devastated repeatedly. The leper hospital of St Nicholas was razed to the ground in 1296 and several times thereafter. The *Chronicle of Lanercost* reports on the havoc caused in Cumberland: 'These raids provide very monotonous reading; but nothing short of constant repetition could give any adequate notion of the horror and cruelty of this kind of warfare, or of the utterly defenceless conditions into which the lamentable rule of Edward II allowed the northern counties to fall'.[13]

Harcla now became the mainstay of the realm against Bruce. He was appointed warden of Carlisle in 1317, and chief commissioner of the army in Westmorland in 1318. In 1319 he was made warden of the west marches of Cumberland and Westmorland, and on 15 May 1321 Harcla was summoned as a baron to the parliament at Westminster. When the king's council urged him to assemble all men between the ages of 16 and 60 to repulse the Scots, however, the borderers pleaded that the warden was unable to protect them: 'nothing but the Kings presence with the whole power of England will abate them [the Scots] or they must leave the country'.[14]

Although inadequate for fighting the Scots, Harcla's forces were able to defeat the Earl of Lancaster, the king's cousin, at Boroughbridge, when he revolted against Edward and attempted to join up with the Scottish forces. For this victory Edward conferred the earldom of Carlisle on Harcla in July 1322. This was a unique honour for a commoner without influence, who raised himself to eminence by his own efforts in the field. Harcla's resources, though, were severely stretched by mid-1322. On 17 June, Bruce advanced into England via Carlisle, and burnt the bishop's palace at Rose. After this he 'plundered the monastery of Holm Cultram notwithstanding that his father's body was buried there' and then proceeded to plunder as far as Furness. On returning to Carlisle, the Scots 'lay in their tents around the town for five days trampling and destroying as much of the crops as they could by themselves and their beasts'. On 30 September they invaded England again. They crossed the Solway and 'lay for five days at Beaumond [Beaumont] about three miles from Carlisle, and laid waste the country all around'.[15]

As Edward was still reluctant to engage the Scots in battle, Harcla made a hazardous, and treasonable, decision that usurped the monarch's power. He made a peace treaty between England and Scotland, in which he and the Scottish king would be the arbiters

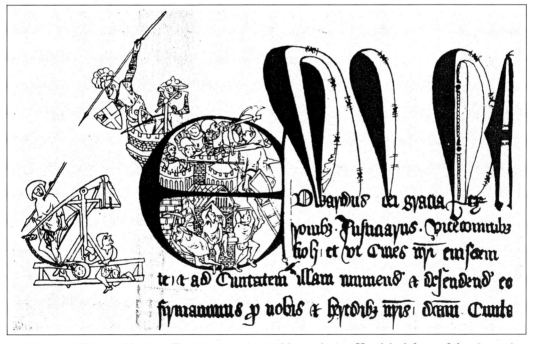

4.   Charter of Edward II, 1316. The illuminated initial letter depicts Harcla's defence of the city against Robert Bruce in 1315. Note the siege weapons, and the chain armour worn by the knight.

for its enforcement. The *Chronicle of Lanercost* puts Harcla's actions in the most favourable light:

> Wherefore, when the said earl of Carlisle perceived that the King of England neither knew how to rule his realm nor was able to defend it against the Scots, who year by year laid it more and more waste, he feared lest at last he [the King] should lose his entire Kingdom; so he chose the less of two evils, and considered how much better it would be for the community of each realm if each King should possess his own kingdom freely and peacefully without any homage, instead of so many homicides and arsons, captivities, plunderings and raidings taking place every year. Therefore on 3 January [1323] the said earl of Carlisle went secretly to Robert the Bruce at Lochmaben and, after holding long conference and protracted discussion with him, at length, to his own perdition, came to agreement with him.[16]

Events moved fast. Harcla concluded his unauthorised treaty with Bruce on 3 January; on 8 January he was summoned to report to the king, but declined to attend. Sir Antony de Lacy, sent by the king to take Harcla by craft, entered Carlisle Castle on 1 February with an armed band on the pretext of consulting upon some household matter, and arrested the unprepared earl. On 2 March, Sir Galfrid de Scope, the king's justiciar, arrived in Carlisle. After a perfunctory trial, sentence was passed. The justiciar

> pronounced sentence upon the earl as if from the mouth and in the words of the King condemning him first to be degraded and deprived of the sword given him by the King, and in like manner of knightly rank by striking off from his heels the gilded spurs, and thereafter to be drawn by horses from the castle through the town to the gallows of Harraby [a distance of about one-and-a-half miles] and there to be hanged and afterwards beheaded; to be disembowelled and his entrails burnt; his head to be taken and suspended on the Tower of London; his body to be divided into four parts, one part to be suspended on the tower of Carlisle, another at Newcastle-on-Tyne, a third at Bristol and the fourth at Dover.[17]

Such brutality was characteristic of the age, but that the punishment should be presented as a public spectacle reflects unfavourably on the populace and judiciary alike. The *Chronicle* paints an heroic picture of the earl's last moments. When his sentence was pronounced, he answered: 'Ye have divided my carcase according to your pleasure, and I commend my soul to God'. And so:

> with most steadfast countenance and bold spirit, as it seemed to the bystanders, he went to suffer all these pains, and, while being drawn through the town, he gazed upon the heavens, with hands clasped and held aloft and likewise his eyes directed on high. Then under the gallows, whole in body, strong and fiery in spirit and powerful in speech, he explained to all men the purpose he had in making the aforesaid convention with the Scots, and so yield himself to undergo the aforesaid punishment.[18]

The irony of Harcla's final disgrace is that Edward had, for some three years, been trying to negotiate peace with Bruce, and had used Harcla and the bishop of Carlisle as his intermediaries. Three months after the earl's death, indeed, the king concluded a 13-year peace with Bruce.

The decay of the borders during the reign of Edward II is indicated by the region's economic and military state. In the economic sphere Church income based upon glebe lands and tithes fell severely. For the diocese of Carlisle, the values of both temporalities (revenue from lands and tithes) and spiritualities (revenue received for spiritual services) in 1291 were £3,171; in 1318 this had fallen to £481. The bishop claimed, successfully, for a reduction in papal taxation, asserting that the Scots had slain men and women . . . burnt nearly all the churches, houses and buildings, driven off their cattle, carried away their treasures, ornaments, and every movable of value, and destroyed the whole county, so that the lands of the bishopric lay uncultivated, the sources of his revenues wasted, and he himself reduced to a state of indigence and want . . .[19]

In the military sphere, gentry who could afford it sought to protect themselves and their property. A start had already been made at the end of Edward I's reign, when fortified or at least defensible stone towers were added to the churches of Newton Arlosh, Burgh-by-Sands and Great Salkeld to give some security to parishioners against Scottish raiders. Following Edward's death, licences to crenellate and enclose houses with a stone wall were granted to landowners at Scaleby, Drumburgh and Dunmalloght.[20] The bishops of Carlisle were not immune from attack; on the contrary, they were a particular target for punitive Scottish raids. John de Kirkby obtained a licence from Edward III to crenellate his palace at Rose in 1335, and this was repeated by his successor Gilbert Welton in 1355.[21] Many other licences are recorded in the patent rolls, and it has been claimed that almost every substantial old house in Cumberland has one of these pele towers, but they are often only apparent because of the thickness of the walls. In many places they stand alone by farm houses, once the seats of country squires. Most of the peles, however, date from the 15th or 16th century. Regional defence and personal security were also provided by castles. Some of these are enumerated in a document that records the change of guardianship of the march, in February 1323: Carlisle, Naworth, Cockermouth, Egremont and Highhead in Cumberland, and Appleby, Brougham and Mallerstang in Westmorland.

Wars and Plague, 1327-1485
The disastrous reign of Edward II came to an end in 1326 when he was forced to abdicate, and was succeeded by Edward III, a boy of fourteen. By then Scotland had gained complete independence under Robert Bruce, but Bruce was dying. The *Chronicle of Lanercost*, reporting on an abortive raid on England in 1327, commented that 'my lord Robert de Brus, who had become leprous, did not invade England on this occasion'.[22] Nevertheless he was crowned king of Scotland in 1328, but died in the following year and was succeeded by his son David, aged five. Edward took this opportunity to intervene, supporting the claim of Edward Balliol to the Scottish throne. Balliol was crowned, but lost his credibility when he ceded the Scottish lowlands to England.

Relief was at hand for Scotland, though, when Edward's ambitions were diverted towards France. The French Wars, from 1337-1453, had the unfortunate but foreseeable result that Scotland entered an alliance with France. The policy of mutual support that ensued affected the security of Carlisle and the border country, as did English raids into Scotland. In 1338, the Earl of Warwick and his noblemen, including John Kirkby, Bishop of Carlisle, led an army into Scotland through Berwick, while Lord Lucy's forces ravaged Galloway. Inevitably, the people of Cumberland and Carlisle suffered reprisals. The Scots entered Cumberland in the middle of October, and rallied for three days on the east side of the city. The besieged citizens sent out archers to harass the Scots, but the city was surrounded, and much of the surrounding countryside was burnt, including the hospital of St Nicholas and Rose.

In 1345 the Scots, with Sir William Douglas, governor of Lochmaben, at their head besieged Carlisle, but were repulsed. Bishop Kirkby distinguished himself in the encounter, fighting with great bravery, and spurring on the English to victory. Kirkby was a redoubtable character. It is said that his 'tenure of the see was the stormiest on record. When he was not fighting with the Scots in the open field, he was engaged in feuds with the Pope, the chapter of York, or his own archdeacon, but he appeared to care as little for the threats of excommunication from Rome as the actualities of invasion from Scotland'.[23]

For over half a century Carlisle had been the scene of constant warfare. The border counties had been devastated and the war seemed never-ending. Another enemy, more deadly and against which there was no defence, struck England in 1349. This was the Black Death – a lethal combination of bubonic and pneumonic plague. It began in eastern Asia, but spread rapidly over mainland Europe, England, Scotland and Ireland. Plagues were not unknown before the Black Death, and the *Chronicle of Lanercost* recorded the plague and murrain (a plague that affected both oxen and cattle) that visited the north in 1319: 'Few beasts . . . were left, and so for that year men had to plough with horses . . . and at the same time too, the fish of the sea were found dead on the shore in great numbers'.[24] Carlisle was ill-prepared for the Black Death, as the most elementary hygienic measures had been neglected. The squalid state of the city streets was spelled out in the king's order of 25 April 1345:

> Commission to J. bishop of Carlisle, and Thomas de Lucy setting forth that the King understanding that in the city of Carlisle the air is so corrupted and tainted by dung and manure heaps and much other filth put in the street and lanes that the men dwelling there and coming to the city for its defence are stricken with a dreadful horror, the benefit of purer air is prevented, the state of the men is grievously injured and many dangers result from the corruption . . .[25]

The Black Death caused profound demographic change in medieval society where, it is generally thought, a third of the population died. In 1363 Bishop Appleby of Carlisle complained to the Pope that the plague had dramatically affected the number of priests in his diocese. Henry Knighton, a canon of Leicester Abbey and a contemporary observer, wrote that:

> After the pestilence many buildings both great and small in all cities, towns and boroughs fell into total ruin for lack of inhabitants; similarly many small villages and hamlets became desolate and no houses were left in them, for all those who had dwelt in them were dead, and it seems likely that many such little villages would never again be inhabited.[26]

The desolation of Carlisle was recognised in a charter of Edward III, dated 1352. Economic privileges were granted, because

> the said city is situated on the border of Scotland for the protection and refuge of the adjacent parts against the hostile incursions of the Scots our enemies, and is devastated already as well by a mortal pestilence lately raging in those parts as by the frequent invasions of our said enemies in those parts and on account of other misfortunes, and is more than usually cast down.[27]

In 1356 the accounts of Richard de Denton, a vice-sheriff of the county, testify to the sad state of the countryside:

> by reason of the mortal pestilence lately raging in those parts the greater part of the manor lands attached to the King's castle at Carlisle were still lying uncultivated. For eighteen months after the end of the plague, indeed, the entire estate had been let go to waste for lack of labourers and divers tenants, mills, fishing, pastures and meadow lands could not be let during that time for want of tenants willing to take the farms of those who died in the said plague.[28]

While one might suspect an overstatement of the manor's impoverishment from one who was responsible for the collection of revenues, it has to be noted that further outbreaks of plague took place in 1361, 1362, 1369 and subsequent years. There were 12 national outbreaks between 1361 and 1485, with further attacks in the succeeding two centuries.

Opportunistic border raids did not stop because of the plagues. William Lord of Douglas complained to Edward in 1357 that a great force from Cumberland and Westmorland had plundered his lands, holding his people to ransom and stealing cattle, sheep and horses. In 1380 the Scots set fire to one of Carlisle's streets by shooting burning arrows over the walls. One of the more serious raids of 1383 ended in disaster for the Scots. There is a colourful 18th-century account of this in Nicolson and Burn's *History:*

> ... the Scots entered with fire and sword into Cumberland and Westmorland and the forest of Englewood, and came to Penrith fair where they rifled booths and houses, spoilt and seized upon all the goods they found there, killing and taking many, and bringing away the rest, and so returned with great joy into Scotland: But they had small cause to joy in their booty; for with such cloth and other commodities as they took away with them, they carried into their own country such a violent pestilence, that a third part of all the people where the infection came died thereof.

The English, during their retaliatory action, fared little better:

> The English, to revenge the damage done by the earl of Douglas at the fair aforesaid, raised a power and went therewith over the water of Solway, and invaded the Scottish borders on that side with fire and sword, and took a great booty of cattle and other goods: But in the meantime the Scots hearing thereof, gathered together to the number of 500 men and lurked prively in ambush at a strait, till such time as the Englishmen came to pass by them, and then with so large a noise and clamour they set upon them, that in their retreat there were 400 of English slain, and a great number of the residue for haste were drowned in the water of Solway and hereby the booty of cattle and goods, which they had taken, was recovered again by the Scots.[29]

There was now good cause for alarm on the borders, as Carlisle's defences were ruinous, and the county gentry no longer looked on the city as a safe refuge. The mayor and citizens petitioned the king *c.*1380:

> Their walls are in part fallen, the greater part on the point of falling from weakness ... the gates cannot be shut without difficulty ... The inhabitants are now so few they cannot resist the Scottish attacks. The seigniors of the county around, who used to repair to the city in war time, have raised castles of their own on account of its weakness, and many knights, esquires, and others no longer come to the city for same reasons, and the castle which is the K's, is open on the side next the city and utterly destroyed ... Wherefore they beg the K. and Council to take order for remedy of these defects which have been laid before every Parliament these 10 years and nothing done.[30]

The plea was accepted and remedial action was taken in county and city alike. The gentry were instructed to remain in their border homes and look after their own defences. In addition, nobles were ordered to fortify and repair all castles within three or four leagues of the frontier, and were given the responsibility of keeping them manned. All substantial laymen, those who had land valued at 100 marks or more, were ordered to remain upon their estates. In Carlisle itself, the defences of the castle were strengthened. Two 'great gunnes' were placed on the keep, and a lesser one in an angle of the outer bailey. The introduction of cannon did not, however, displace the 50 men-at-arms and 100 mounted archers of the Carlisle garrison.[31]

After the battle of Otterburn in 1388, a peace treaty was signed, which helped to release tension on the borders. Secondary to this was the introduction of licensed jousting to settle disputes, which reduced the number of punitive raids. It was tragic that at this time an unrelated calamity should have befallen Carlisle. On Ascension Day, 1391, about three-quarters of the city was destroyed by an accidental fire. Houses and other buildings were damaged in the market-place and the main streets. St Cuthbert's church was also burnt. The Crown remitted the farms of Ellerton in Inglewood to the citizens for four years, to help them recover from this disaster, and also from the destruction by the Scots and French.

The year 1399 witnessed a dynastic revolution. Richard II was tried and imprisoned, having been deposed by Henry of Bolingbroke. Thomas Merks, Bishop of Carlisle, defended Richard before his captors in Westminster Hall with outstanding courage, attempting to uphold the established order against anarchy.[32] Lucky to escape with his life, Merks was demoted to a suffragan in the diocese of Salisbury.

The disastrous Hundred Years War ended in 1453, when the forces of Henry VI were finally driven out of France. Within two years, however, England was plunged into a civil war that resulted from the inflated ambitions of the nobility. The onset of the Wars of the Roses in 1455 affected border security as the Scots were drawn into the conflict. After the Lancastrian defeat at Towton, Queen Margaret and her supporters, in alliance with the Scots, crossed the border and attacked Carlisle. The city did not fall despite the burning of the suburbs and mill, and compensation was paid by order of the Yorkist king, Edward IV. It was only the accession of Henry VII in 1485 which brought a prospect of peace and stability on the borders.

Carlisle's economy

The economic and judicial powers of Carlisle were strengthened by a charter of Edward III, dated 1352.[33] The city was granted complete independence of the county, the right to have its own bailiff, sheriff, coroner and court, and to keep profits from the chattels of felons. Self-government was ensured by free election of mayor and bailiffs, and the free guild was confirmed. The economic substructure of Carlisle was strengthened by the right to hold markets twice a week and an annual fair lasting 15 days. Burgesses were granted the right of inheritance of their tenements, whether on the lord's manor or in the city. This privilege and the right to their own courts effectively brought feudalism within Carlisle to an end.

The city's economy was underpinned by a stable demand for provisions and labour from the cathedral establishment and the king's fortress. In comparison with the dioceses of York and Durham, Carlisle was impoverished; indeed the canons were probably less wealthy than the Cistercian monks at Holm Cultram. Income must have been generated for the city, however, for at the time of the Dissolution 44 people were attached to the cathedral, of whom 20 were canons. It is unlikely that revenue from urban property amounted to even 10 per cent of their expenditure in the city, which must have been a very favourable balance of payments for the citizens. The military presence in Carlisle undoubtedly brought money into the city. The amount was dependent on Anglo-Scottish relations, and it peaked when Edward I established his headquarters and, later, parliament in Carlisle. The king's presence brought physical benefits too. In 1300, Master Walter of Hereford was paid for work, probably in the Great Hall of the castle, later to be used by parliament. Edward II initiated extensive works in the inner ward which housed the royal palace, records referring to a new stone tower for the king's chamber with two portcullises and double vaults. Maintenance and modernisation of Carlisle's defences included an outlay of £500 on the wall, gate and bridge in 1344, while in 1378 John Lewyn, the leading military engineer in the north, was brought in to build the castle's new outer gatehouse. Richard, Duke of Gloucester, later to be Richard III, was appointed warden of the western marches and frequently stayed in the castle. At this time the Tile Tower was built, in

5.   Miserere seat in the cathedral, dating from the 15th century. Is it a product of the carver's uninhibited fantasy, or does it reflect the citizens' animosity to the Scots?

brick, a recent innovation in military architecture. It bears Richard's emblem, and has gun ports, a reminder that artillery now played a vital rôle in warfare.

The increased activity of city guilds indicates that Carlisle was beginning to thrive economically. Of most importance was the free merchant guild, or guild mercatory. This was an association of leading traders who united for mutual protection and to formulate trading laws. The eight trade guilds were formed later (the exact date is not known) and had a lower status than the merchant guild. They were for merchants (who were not in the merchant guild), weavers, smiths, tailors, tanners, cordwainers (shoemakers), glovers (including skinners) and butchers. These were all connected with the rural economy, with the exception of goldsmiths and silversmiths. Redness Hall, a fine jettied and timber-framed building (built 1377-99 as a residence for Richard of Redness) became the meeting-place of the trade guilds after Richard left it to the city in his will. The ruling oligarchy of the merchant guild was to develop into the mayor, aldermen and citizens of the town council.

The Church in Carlisle

Carlisle Cathedral was rebuilt in the 14th century. It not only exhibits our rich cultural heritage but also symbolises the devotion and determination of the men who built it. The fire in 1292 destroyed the Early English choir and apse which had just been completed, and had replaced the Norman east end. It is possible that the canons had intended to rebuild the whole church in this style, complete with new transepts and probably a nave and tower. The second rebuilding began almost immediately, and indulgences were granted for contributions in Lincoln (1295) and York (1290 and 1307). When Edward visited the city in 1306-7 the work, this time in the Decorated style, was under way. In the choir, the fire-damaged piers were replaced and the clerestory and roof were reconstructed, while the Early English arcading in the north and south choir aisles was retained. The supreme achievement of the restored cathedral was the magnificent east window, with its flowing stone tracery and stained glass. It seems likely that building work continued throughout the 14th century, as Bishop Welton appealed for funds to restore the choir during his episcopate (1353-62), and the Pope granted an indulgence (remission of temporal punishment for sins) in 1363 'to penitents who visited the Cathedral, which had been burnt, on the five feasts of the Blessed Virgin, or who would lend a helping hand to the fabric'.[34] A bequest in the will of John de Salkeld of Maughanby, dating from 1359, possibly refers to the east window. It has been suggested that the choir was not completed until c.1390, and the stained glass was installed c.1390-1400.[35] Given that it is inconceivable that building work continued during the Scottish invasions of Edward II's reign (1307-27), during the Black Death (1348-9) or subsequent outbreaks of plague, the restoration was a remarkable feat that testifies to the spirit and determination of those who undertook it.

Church administration in Carlisle was less admirable than the cathedral restoration. The hospital of St Nicholas, reportedly decayed by 1340,[36] received a serious stricture from the clerical commission in 1393, which reported neglect, corruption and overstaffing:

> . . . by the carelessness and negligence of the masters and ministers notorious defects exist, both in the buildings, books, vestments and other ornaments, and in the diminished number of chaplains, brethren and sisters, to correct and reform the same, take order for the application of the profits and emoluments to the repair of the buildings and support the master, brethren and sisters dwelling in them, remove useless officers, ministers and servants and substitute others, and punish delinquents certifying what alienations of lands, tenements and goods bestowed on the hospital have been made and by whom, whether the number of chaplains ordained at its first foundation has been reduced, and all their proceedings herein.[37]

There is no reference to its primary use as a leper hospital: leprosy appears to have disappeared from Europe by this time.

The Carlisle clergy had also neglected seemliness and decorum in their churches. In 1379 Bishop Appleby lamented that fairs and markets were being held on Sundays and festival days in churches and churchyards throughout his diocese, so that worship was impossible.[38] The material resources of the Church, however, received a boost when Richard III came to the throne. In 1484 he replaced many of the cathedral's possessions which had been destroyed by the Scots, granted the prior and canons tithes of the king's mill in the city, and gave them two tuns of red wine from Gascony, to be used in the cathedral.

The topography of late medieval Carlisle

After the fire in 1292, a major change in the street pattern took place.[39] The old Roman road from the market-place to the west gate fell out of use, while Fisher Street (*Vicus Piscatorum*) led to the original castle entrance at the eastern corner of the inner ward. The entrance was moved to its present position on the outer bailey in 1168, and Castle Street (*Vicus Castri*) gave access to it. Southgate (*Porta Botchardi*) was some distance to the north of the citadel, and the Blackfriars held land outside the original city wall.

It can be inferred from an Elizabethan map that the cathedral and monastery buildings were enclosed by a wall. The cathedral's nave, of which much has now been lost, served as one of the parish churches. An early church on the site of St Cuthbert's, at right angles to the Roman Blackfriars Street, has been mentioned before, while St Alban's church (or chapel), adjacent to Fisher Street and St Alban's Row, is first referred to in 1201. Holy Trinity church, located outside the walls in the 12th century and not to be confused with the 19th-century church in Caldewgate, presumably was destroyed by the Scots in their raids of the 14th century, and not rebuilt.

During the 12th and 13th centuries there was much housing development in the city, especially along English and Scotch Streets. Much of this was destroyed in the fire of 1292, in which the densely-packed wooden and thatched buildings must have burnt rapidly. As country people moved into Carlisle in the face of Scottish raids in the early 14th century, all possible building plots were sought. The Inquisition of 1344 reported the ruinous state of the city defences, and put part of the blame on citizens who dug too near the wall and undermined its foundations. In 1345 Peter Tylliol, and the mayor and bailiffs came into conflict with the king's and bishop's men, when they attempted to appropriate as waste ground a 'certain long street in the King's highway and to build on the fosse of the castle'.[40] The result of this intensive building was overcrowding and squalor. A period of prolonged development after the fire is suggested by the claim of 1,500 damaged houses in 1391.[41] The Black Death in 1349 reduced the population drastically, though, and in 1380 the mayor declared that the inhabitants were so few that they could not resist Scottish attacks. The city's population may be estimated from the poll tax return of 1377, which includes all men and women over 18, excepting clergy and anyone who avoided registration. The assessment was 287 households, or 678 taxpayers. Allowing for children, possibly half as many again in a society with low life expectancy, the total population probably numbered about a thousand. Thus the claim of 1,500 damaged houses seems exaggerated, perhaps deliberately in order to gain more assistance, but this must be weighed against the fact that Carlisle was granted 500 oaks from Inglewood by the king in response to its plea.

Carlisle did not recover from the series of plagues and fires for two to three centuries. Chancellor Hugh Todd, writing *c.*1690, commented on the state of the city: 'the scarrs of these dreadful wounds are yet apparent for the town is so thin and empty of inhabitants that it looks like a country village well walled about rather than a citty [*sic*]'.[42] Nevertheless some fine houses were being erected in the mid-14th century, of timber-framed or cruck construction, with a central hall open to the roof, and a screen passage at one end giving access to a buttery and pantry. Jones describes one example which no longer exists, but Redness Hall is still standing.[43]

The fine new houses were inhabited by the well-to-do clergy and emergent middle classes. The 'Episcopal Register of the See of Carlisle' (*Testamenta Karleolensis*) of 1353-86 includes 157 wills and grants of probate.[44] These indicate widening horizons in the late 14th century, with the acquisition of household goods and even items of ostentatious display. Some clergy farmed on a substantial scale and lived in well-furnished residences where they were waited upon by numerous servants. They left bequests of clothes, beds, hangings and brewing utensils, and the fabric of churches across the diocese benefited from their endowments. The wealthier citizens left land as well as jewels, arms and armour. Large fees were taken by ecclesiastical landlords when a tenant died, for example heriot (his best beast), and money was frequently given so that masses would be said for the dead man's soul.

At the beginning of the Tudor period, therefore, the city's fabric was comparatively recent, having been considerably rebuilt after the fire of 1391, and the population density was far lower than at its highest point in the medieval period. The 16th-century town map, the earliest of Carlisle still extant, shows the medieval street pattern but not the congestion of the early 14th century. One gains the impression of a spacious and orderly city, with large gardens and orchards behind the street frontages, but also the beginning of the Lanes development.

6. Shoemakers' Guild regalia. A symbol of the dignity and self-esteem of the city guilds.

7. The fine Guildhall, timber-framed and jettied. The fine building on the right no longer exists.

Chapter Five

Tudor Carlisle

The accession of the Tudor dynasty to the throne in 1485 marked the beginning of fundamental change in English society. National policy, though, had to face the reality of civil anarchy and warfare, and the threat of the Catholic Stuarts, in the north.

Henry VII and Henry VIII

The sharply contrasting characters and policies of the first two Tudor monarchs had a profound effect on the borders. Henry VII's policy of maintaining good relations with James III of Scotland and with the French king neutralised the destabilising effect of the 'auld alliance' between France and Scotland, which had been signed by every Scottish king since John Balliol, and by James III as recently as 1484. The peace treaty which was signed in 1502 followed truces in 1486-91, 1491-4 and 1494-1501. When Henry VIII came to the throne in 1509, however, foreign policy was reversed, with dire consequences on the border. Henry's grand designs on the continent brought him into conflict with Louis XII; a revival of the 'auld alliance' had disastrous effects on border peace; and his sister Margaret's marriage to James IV of Scotland had repercussions when their granddaughter, Mary Queen of Scots, laid claim to both the Scottish and the English throne.

When Henry clashed with Louis, James of Scotland was drawn into the struggle but suffered a disastrous defeat at Flodden, in 1513. Retribution against Scottish borderers by Lord Dacre only exacerbated the disorder. The cessation of Anglo-Scottish warfare did not bring peace and stability to the marches because lawlessness and violence had become endemic. It was a problem that both governments had to face. A notorious example is that of the Armstrong clan, who were credited with the ability to muster 3,000 horse.[1] With their powerful allies they were a formidable enemy for Scottish or English peacetime forces. A Scottish attempt to quash them in 1528 was a fiasco because of the collusion of border clans, and an English foray into the so-called Debatable Lands failed because the Armstrongs had been made privy to the raid by Ritchie Graham, a member of a powerful family on the English side of the border which was united briefly with the Armstrongs. The episode shows the anarchic state of the borders, with the border clans answerable to neither nation, either feuding with each other or acting together to defeat authority.

Despite the political upheaval, ecclesiastical and cultural development continued apace. The Renaissance was succeeded by the Reformation, and in a mere 50 years the medieval outlook was overtaken by a more humanistic world view. This is made evident in the decoration and furnishings of Carlisle Cathedral. The paintings on the back of the choir stalls and the decorative screens that enclose St Catherine's chapel contrast with the naturalistic painted ceiling in Prior Senhouse's room in the deanery tower, and with the Salkeld screen, which has confident and realistic portraits and the Tudor rose.

At the beginning of Henry VIII's reign, the corruption and laxity of many monasteries was becoming increasingly apparent, but it was revolution rather than reform that was to dominate Henry's relationship with the Church. In 1532 he renounced papal authority in order to secure a divorce from Catherine of Aragon. In the diocese of Carlisle, Bishop Kite recognised royal supremacy over the Church in 1534, parish clergy followed their bishop's lead and none of the monastic clergy are known to have dissented. Henry, though, soon used his newly-acquired powers to plunder the Church. Two inquests in 1535, into monastic

8.   Medieval paintings on the back of the choir stalls, north aisle, dating from the late 15th century.

9.   Renaissance screen in the cathedral, erected by Lancelot Salkeld, the last prior and first dean, *c.*1541.

morals and ecclesiastical revenues, provided the pretext and incentive he wanted. Scurrilous and barely credible charges were laid against the monks in the 10 monastic houses of Cumberland, including Christopher Slee and his successor Lancelot Salkeld, the last two priors of Carlisle. These inquests were followed by the passing of a statute in 1536, which dissolved the smaller monasteries of England, those with a revenue of less than £200 a year. The larger monasteries were 'persuaded' to surrender over the next four years. Under the 1536 Act, eight of Cumberland's monasteries and the friaries of Carlisle, Penrith and Appleby were dissolved, leaving only Holm Cultram and the priory of Carlisle. Lancelot Salkeld gave up the latter in January 1540, and two years later Henry founded in its place 'The Dean and Chapter of the Holy and Undivided Trinity of Carlisle', appointing Salkeld as dean. The new establishment was made up of the dean, four canons, eight minor canons and three other clergy, a choir of 10 men and boys, a schoolmaster, seven lay helpers and six poor almsmen.

Robert Aske, a lawyer, and a number of northern clerics and gentry, linked the destruction of the monasteries and the intrusion of the Crown upon local communities with economic grievances, namely the enclosure of common land and the frequent imposition of entry fees on impoverished small tenants. These complaints were transformed into a movement with an emotive title – the Pilgrimage of Grace. This began in Lincolnshire in 1536, ostensibly to halt the campaign against the monasteries. After its first outbreak in Westmorland, the insurrection spread to Penrith and then to Cockermouth. At a meeting on Moota Hill, the abbot of Holm Cultram swore allegiance to the cause, but the active support of the citizens of Carlisle, desperately needed by the rebels, was not forthcoming although they paid lip-service to the movement. By 3 November 1536, 15,000 rebels had assembled at Burford Oke, some seven miles from Carlisle, and negotiations began between Sir Christopher Dacre (the mayor), Sir Thomas Clifford (captain of the castle, and son of the unpopular warden of the west marches) and the insurgents. The rebellion came to an ignominious end when the rebels dispersed to their homes, on the understanding 'that the soldiers should not ride on the commons'.[2] Clifford's insensitive treatment of the situation, and his use of borderers to pursue the insurgents itself stoked up the fires of rebellion again. Four to five thousand men marched on Penrith, and then to Carlisle, to threaten the city, but were defeated by a force commanded by Sir Charles Dacre, who took between seven and eight hundred prisoners. About six thousand prisoners were taken in Cumberland and Westmorland, from whom 74 were named as principal offenders, and were put to death where they dwelt, according to martial law. Twelve of the prisoners taken during the assault on Carlisle were hanged in chains, the rest with ropes as 'iron is marvelous scarce'.[3] It was forbidden to take the bodies down, and there are many cases on record of wives and daughters removing the bodies at night for burial, in the churchyard if the priest could be persuaded to help, or in ditches if all else failed. By March 1357 the rebellion was over, the ringleaders had been executed and their goods, valued at 300 marks in Westmorland and about a third of that in Cumberland, had been forfeited. The commander of the government forces, the Duke of Norfolk, acknowledged that the uprising had been primarily a protest against tithes, inflated rents, enclosure of the land and exploitation of 'poor caitiffs'.[4] Most churchmen did not involve themselves with the rebels, a notable exception being the abbot of Holm Cultram, and neither did the higher nobility of the northern counties, for example the Cliffords, Percys, Dacres, or Nevilles support rebellion.

The border may well have been quiet by 1537, but Henry was sufficiently alarmed to reorganise the Council of the North, giving it wider jurisdiction and a permanent base at York. It had begun as a personal council for the future Richard III, had lapsed under Henry VII, but was restored by Henry VIII in 1525. In addition the defences at Berwick and Carlisle were strengthened. At Carlisle, Stefan von Haschenperg, a Hungarian surveyor

10. The twin-towered citadel, built by Henry VIII in 1537.

11. Half-moon battery, Carlisle Castle, *c*.1540. (M.E. Nutter.)

and military engineer, redesigned the defences in accordance with new continental practices. Emphasis was placed on heavy ordnance, and the structure of the keep was reinforced to bear the weight of heavy guns which were set at roof level, two on each face. The wall of the inner ward was also greatly strengthened, not only to repel gunfire, but also to provide a broad platform for more guns. Perhaps the most striking features were the half moon battery which was constructed at the entrance to the inner ward, and the breastwork, long since disappeared, which gave protected access to inner and outer gateways. The main addition to the city defences was the massive twin-towered citadel which replaced the former southern gate. This survives in outline as the towers of the county court.

Soon after this reconstruction, further hostilities broke out. An English invasion of Scotland across the eastern marches, in the autumn of 1542, was answered by a Scottish attack across the western marches. While James remained at his castle at Lochmaben, the Scots crossed the River Esk to burn and spoil the Grahams' English territory. Sir Thomas Wharton, captain of Carlisle Castle, was forewarned by spies and his prekers (lightly-armed horsemen, who acted as scouts) and raised a force from the local gentry. Under the leadership of Dacre, they advanced from Carlisle and crossed the River Line to intercept the enemy. The Scots had little stomach for a fight, apart from the valiant Lord Maxwell who resisted strongly before being taken prisoner. Abandoning arms and provisions, they retreated across the Esk pursued by English horsemen, and were driven westwards across the treacherous terrain of Solway Moss, between the rivers Esk and Sark. The 5,000 Scottish horsemen, unable to traverse the bog, fled on foot through Liddesdale. Here they were attacked by borderers who had no ties of loyalty to either kingdom and had no scruples against plundering the defeated rabble: 'because they shuld the more spedily flye, they take also their botes from theym'.[5]

In 1547 the turbulent Henrician period terminated in spectacular fashion, when the gunpowder store in the castle keep exploded, leaving the keep 'marvellously cracked'.

Edward VI and Mary Tudor

When Edward VI succeeded his father in 1547, more moderate policies began to be adopted, and action was taken to reinvigorate the 'laws of the marches'. The first initiative was taken in 1549, jointly by Edward VI, King Henry of France and the Regent, on behalf of Mary Stuart, Queen of Scots.[6] The treaty dealt with the perennial problem of the Debatable Lands by forbidding nationals of either country to settle there, but in 1552 division of the land was finally settled by the English and Scottish commissioners, with the French ambassador as arbiter. The earthen boundary (the Scotsdike) still runs east to west between the rivers Sark and Esk. The ordinance, that officers, captains and gentlemen should 'dwell upon their own offices and at their own house', also ensuring that their tenants were well horsed, undoubtedly concentrated noblemen's minds on border defence, and had the economic advantage that more revenue from borderlands would be spent locally.[7]

The accession of the zealous Catholic Mary Tudor to the throne in 1553 was welcomed by a large part of the clergy and by the powerful magnates in northern England. In 1558, Mary Stuart married Francis, the Dauphin of France, and French troops were brought in to support the Scottish regent against her own people. Thus England was a Catholic country allied with Spain, through Mary's marriage to Philip, and Scotland was a Catholic country allied to France. Within two years, however, a political reversal had taken place, as Mary Tudor died and was succeeded in November 1558 by Elizabeth, and in Scotland the arrival of the Calvinist John Knox from Geneva in 1559 led to a rebellion motivated by religious and patriotic fervour. The people, aided by the Protestant nobles and the English fleet, compelled the French troops to leave Scotland.

Elizabeth I

In the first year of her reign, Elizabeth restored royal supremacy over the Church. The re-established Anglican Church compromised between Catholic and Protestant doctrine, while the Edwardian prayer-book was restored, giving the Church of England its first creed. All the bishops except one refused to take the oath of supremacy (to the Sovereign), and were deprived of their sees. Owen Oglethorpe, Bishop of Carlisle (1557-60), is remembered primarily for his willingness to crown Elizabeth, although he then sided with the Catholics and was deposed. In the north west there was a good deal of recusancy, and a number of Catholic priests were still serving in the 1560s under the protection of the Dacres. Secular officeholders too were often Catholic, for example seven of the twelve J.P.s in Cumberland and six of the nine in Westmorland. Church life was at a low ebb in the diocese of Carlisle. The cathedral was in a state of decay, and Bishop Best lamented that of his canons 'three . . . are unlearned and the fourth unzealous. Briefly the city is decayed by them and God's truth slandered', while the Cumberland clergy were dismissed as 'wicked imps of Antichrist and for the most part very ignorant and stubborn'.[8]

The intractable problem of border lawlessness continued, as the initiatives of 1549 and 1552 had proved ineffective. In September 1563 commissioners met at Carlisle to tackle the problem of cross-border justice, so that it could be administered regardless of where crimes were committed. All the mechanisms that were negotiated foundered on suspicion and lack of co-operation. Border tranquillity was also threatened by those who wished to replace Elizabeth with Mary Stuart, whom they saw as the rightful heir. The situation was inflamed because the more Catholic and feudal part of England was adjacent to Scotland. Mary, however, was forced by her Protestant lords to abdicate in 1567, in favour of her infant son (later James VI of Scotland and James I of England), and a regent. After defeat in battle, Mary fled across the Solway to Workington, and appealed to Elizabeth for protection. Her claim to the English throne made her too dangerous to be allowed freedom, and she was taken to Carlisle Castle. Richard Lowther, who conducted Mary to Carlisle on Elizabeth's orders, commented on her pitiable condition, the 'meanness of her attire', and her tears on hearing of the regent's intention to execute some of her followers.[9]

Mary immediately became a focus of political intrigue. The Earl of Northumberland, an ardent supporter, attempted to obtain custody of her, either with or without Elizabeth's permission. On 22 May 1568, an alarmed Lowther warned Sir William Cecil 'of great anger and threats of the Earl of Northumberland against him in consequence of his refusal to deliver the Queen of Scots into his custody'.[10] Elizabeth's advisors soon became aware of the potential problem of Mary being held so close to the Scottish border, especially as she was now 'mended in body and countenance' and 'had hope of relief from France'.[11]

Opinion in Carlisle was favourable to the vivacious and attractive Queen of Scots. She was considered to be 'wise, eloquent, and according to her power liberal, which, with her behaviour, wins the affections of many, especially the simple'.[12] It is not difficult to appreciate the spell that Mary cast upon her followers and on the ingenuous citizens of Carlisle, or the anxiety that this caused to those charged with her custody. In his report to Cecil, Knollys spoke of her spirited behaviour: 'This ladie and prynces is a notable woman: she semethe to regard no ceremonius honor besyde the acknolegynge of hyr estate regalle: she shoethe a disposition to speake motche, to be bold, to be plesant, and to be very famylyare'.[13] Although Mary was a captive, she was allowed some freedom of movement under close supervision, as Knollys records:

> Yesterday she went out at a postern to walk on a playing green towards Scotland – waited on by Scrope and himself, with 24 of Read's halberdiers, and some of her own gentlemen etc: where 20 of her retinue played at football before her for 2 hours very strongly, nimbly and skilfully, without

foul play – the 'smalnes of theyr balle occasyonyng theyr fayrer playe', and twice since coming, she did the like in the same place, and once rode out hare hunting, galloping so fast, and her retinue so well horsed, that they feared a rescue by her friends in Scotland, and mean not to permit this in future.[14]

12.   Lady's Walk in the 1560s. (M.E. Nutter.)

Meanwhile, Mary's supporters attempted to establish a court party at Carlisle. Lord Herries requested leave for himself and a hundred other nobles to come and go from Scotland 'while our sovereign abides here' and that Lord Fleming should have 'licence to pass to France for her money and other affairs'.[15] The English authorities became increasingly alarmed at this activity, and on 13 July 1568 Mary was moved, against her wishes, to Henry Le Scrope's castle at Bolton in Wensleydale. (Scrope was governor of Carlisle Castle, and warden of the western marches.) Fears that Mary might raise the north in her cause were justifiable, and disorder was reported on the border in August 1568. In September there was an unexplained affray in the graveyard of Carlisle Cathedral, after which members of prominent Cumberland families, Musgraves, Dacres, Curwens and Salkelds, were questioned about 'a conference with a Scotsman', which apparently took place.[16]

It appears that Mary was unable or unwilling to pay the expenses incurred while keeping her court in Carlisle. On 13 March 1569, the mayor and council of the city petitioned the Earl of Shrewsbury, asking him to intercede with Mary for payment of a bill for £286 1s.4d., due to several poor men of Carlisle.[17]

Much evidence of this episode in Carlisle's history was lost during the 19th century. The royal apartments, in Queen Mary's Tower, were almost completely destroyed in 1834, and only remnants survive today. The Lady's Walk, outside the south curtain wall, was made considerably narrower when the castle ditch was remodelled, and it is now difficult to visualise it as an agreeable promenade. Fortunately, Nutter's early 19th-century print of the walk gives an idea of how it looked in Mary's time.

Within a few months of Mary's departure from Carlisle, rebellion flared up in the northern counties, but whereas the Pilgrimage of Grace was supported by minor gentry and commoners, this rebellion was provoked by the northern earls. Of the four great northern lords, Sir Thomas Percy, Seventh Earl of Northumberland and Charles Neville,

Sixth Earl of Westmorland, took action to uphold their feudal status and the Catholic religion. Henry Clifford, Second Earl of Cumberland, was an old man and lacked conviction at the crucial moment, while Leonard Dacre was in London fighting a lawsuit.[18]

At first the rebellion prospered, and the rebels laid siege to Barnard Castle, which was held by Sir George Bowes. By 13 December, Bowes' position was desperate, and Scrope marched to Westmorland against the rebel earls, leaving Bishop Best in charge of Carlisle Castle. The bishop found himself threatened, and warned, also on 13 December, that 'last night there were 40 or 50 of the Hetherington's lodged in Carlisle who were not my friends and above 60 Scotch and other soldiers, for what purpose I could not tell', and that he had been told privately of a plot to kill him and take the castle.[19] The warning was timely:

> the same night Dacre [Francis, youngest brother of Lord Dacre] conveyed 200 soldiers in small numbers into Carlisle, beside those that came into the town next morning under cover of mustering them for the Queen; and when they perceived the castle furnished with men and strongly warded he departed, and the soldiers went home.[20]

Sir George Bowes, with his garrison in mutiny, abandoned Barnard Castle ignominiously on 14 December, but soon the crisis had passed and the badly-led rebellion was disintegrating. The rebels retreated to Hexham, and then into Liddesdale, having been refused access to Naworth by Leonard Dacre. Northumberland was taken prisoner, and was beheaded two years later. Westmorland escaped to the Netherlands, where he lived as a pensioner of Spain.

Leonard Dacre, nicknamed Crookback, was the head of a powerful family who had, with some justification, been suspected of secret association with the rebel earls and of treasonable activity with the Duke of Norfolk. He now sought to strengthen his northern fortress at Naworth, and gathered together about three thousand of his loyal supporters with the pretext of resisting the rebels. Lord Scrope was instructed, by the earl of Sussex for the queen, to apprehend Dacre, but could not field a Cumbrian force for service against him. He told Lord Hunsdon and Sir John Forster, wardens of the east and middle marches, that

> no force in this country is to be credited against him; the gentry and others are for the most part freeholders and tenants either to Lord Dacre, which title he usurps, to his sister, the Countess of Cumberland, or to the Earl of Northumberland, and would in this case rather take part against us rather than for us; so that although in any other service I can levy a good number, yet the force of credit to this purpose must be brought with you.[21]

Lord Hunsdon, the northern commander, decided to avoid a battle and to link up with Scrope at Carlisle. Hunsdon's report to William Cecil relates the dramatic sequence of events preceding the battle at the River Gelt, which is between Carlisle and Naworth Castle:

> Leonard Dacre, having more courage than the rebel Earls, and having above 3,000 men English and Scots, whereof 1,000 were horsemen, and not meaning to suffer me, being three or four miles on this side of his house, to pass to Carlisle, set upon me with his whole force, and his foot being for the most part archers gave the lustiest charge upon my shot that ever I saw; whereupon, leaving Sir John Forster with 400 or 500 horse for my relief, I charged his foot and overthrew them; Dacre with his horsemen fled, being chased for three miles; Dacre was overtaken, but rescued again by certain Scots. There are 300 or 400 slain, and 100 taken. We were not 1,500, whereof 500 were foot, but God will not suffer rebellion to prosper.[22]

Dacre's response to events had been disastrously ill-judged and ill-timed. His association with Norfolk, who was paradoxically his rival to the patrimony of the Dacre estate; his failure to support the northern earls during the rebellion, but his provocative show of strength when they had been vanquished; and his precipitous attack of Hunsdon when Scottish forces were advancing to his aid were rewarded by the loss of his estate and title, and enforced exile.

It was a tragedy for the northern counties that, after the crushing of the rebellion, reconciliation between Scotland and England, based upon a common interest in border peace, did not last. Endemic raiding and lawlessness persisted, and the frontier remained so insecure that even Carlisle Castle was not immune to raids. The problems were compounded by the enmity of noble border families to the English warden, the mutual distrust of wardens, and government unwillingness to punish transgressors amongst their own subjects. The notorious Kinmount Willie episode encapsulates many of the border problems.

William Armstrong of Kinmount ('Kinmount Willie') was leader of a powerful clan on the Scottish side of the border and a notorious reiver (border robber). When returning from a routine meeting of the deputy wardens of the English west march and the deputy keeper of Liddlesdale, Scott of Buccleuch, he was seized, and incarcerated in Carlisle Castle. This was in breach of border law, according to the Scots, as he was seized on a truce-day. Protests from Buccleuch to Scrope failed, in the face of the deep animosity between the two men, and diplomatic moves also failed to obtain Armstrong's release. As a last resort, he was rescued on a stormy night with the help of English sympathisers in the castle. Prominent English border families, the Grahams and the Carletons, were implicated in the operation, as was Buccleuch. The affair became notorious, a romantic glow being cast on what was essentially an anarchic incident, of which less dramatic examples were commonplace. They indicate the complicity of border gentry and lack of backing for the warden from government on both sides of the border, as offenders were not punished. Border lawlessness affected all classes of society. John Meye, Bishop of Carlisle (1577-98), warned that the number of raids from both countries was increasing dramatically at the end of the 16th century:

Most of the gentry dwelling within 20 miles of Carlisle are put in fear of their lives, houses and goods so that not only they, but the Justices of the Peace and others are forced to keep cattle in their houses nightly and dare not suffer them to feed and depasture upon the ground.[23]

Meye depicted the plight of Cumbrians 'who are daily threatened both by letters and messages, to be robbed and spoiled, and to have their houses burnt, unless they will bestow upon the Borderers such money and other things as they may require'.[24] In this context of mutually destructive border crime, Elizabeth and James VI decided that new action must be taken. Commissioners appointed by both nations met in Carlisle and agreed on measures such as the reinvigoration of the Church, a curb on the unilateral actions of the wardens and a promise of direct action against wrongdoers regardless of their nationality. These were codified in the Treaty of Carlisle in May 1597, promising much but achieving little. In the period of unease that followed, the borderers were threatened by famine and plague, both related to the 16th-century population explosion.

It is estimated that the population of Cumberland and Westmorland grew by 43 per cent between 1563 and 1603.[25] The muster returns of 1534 give a range of 1,250-1,870. The ecclesiastical returns of 1563 give a lower figure of 1,160-1,550, but a considerable increase is shown in the 1597 corporation census, where the range is 1,780-1,980.[26] By the end of the century the population increase had outstripped food production, so even one bad harvest had a disastrous effect. In 1587-8 there was a period of famine, followed by plague, which resulted in very high mortality. A series of failed harvests, from 1594-7, and the consequent rise in food prices caused widespread starvation. In various parishes in 1595-6, the number of burials recorded was two, three, or even four times the normal figure.[27] A poorly-nourished and weakened population was ill-prepared for the great pestilences at the end of the century.

In 1592 a great plague broke out in London. By 1593 it had spread to Newcastle and by the autumn of 1597 was at its height. In September the plague erupted in Penrith and Carlisle. The death toll was horrific: on the Penrith parish register 583 deaths are recorded between September and December in the following year. Of the 323 households in Carlisle 242 were affected, but the number of deaths was not recorded. Life in the city was totally disrupted, many families, surnames and trades completely disappearing. The dean of Durham lamented the decay of agriculture and the depopulation of villages in the northern counties. He declared that 'people go sixty miles from Carlisle to Durham to buy bread'.[28] Carlisle council took emergency steps to limit the spread of pestilence, removing filth from streets, preventing swine wandering in the city, and enforcing the ban on the sale of corrupt fish and meat. New measures were made mandatory: affected houses were marked with a red cross and sealed off, while part of the churchyard was set aside for plague victims. Isolation hospitals for the sufferers were built outside the walls, at Gosling Syke, Stanwix and the Bitts, each one being provided with a nurse, who was paid 2s.6d. a week. A complete census of the town was ordered to ascertain the number of households and the number of inhabitants. Daily visits were made to discover new cases, and a weekly collection was taken in each street for the relief of the poor. Admission to the city of anyone who was infected, or suspected of infection was prevented, and even people from the suburbs of Rickergate, Caldewgate and Botchergate were refused entry unless they obtained a permit.

*　*　*　*　*

The Elizabethan map of Carlisle shows a walled and spacious city, but not a homogeneous one. The castle, cathedral close and city stand apart from each other, separating the military, ecclesiastical and civil elements. Houses were poor quality, with timber, clay and thatch being the main building materials. In 1577, 12 inns, 60 alehouses and three taverns were recorded, no less than one household in six, but they were usually run as a part-time occupation.[29] The Church suffered further change in the early years of Edward VI's reign, c.1547, when St Alban's, along with other chantries, was suppressed.

A struggle for the government of Carlisle took place in the early years of Elizabeth's reign. The Dormont Book of 1561 had defined the constitution and powers of the city council, but the conflict concerned mayoral elections. In the mid-16th century the mayor was elected by a majority of all freemen, but they had become subordinate to the corporation aldermen, an élite body made up of six members of the merchant guild and a number of local gentry. In 1561 Robert Dalton, leader of the popular party, was elected mayor. Three years later he stood for the mayoralty again and, expecting trouble, the Council of the North appointed Scrope, the bishop and two deputy wardens of the west march to act as commissioners to oversee 'ye quyet election of a new maire'. According to Dalton's opponents, however, his supporters assembled in the market-place and defied the sheriff, who ordered them to disperse. The door of the moothall was burst open, to the consternation of the commissioners and aldermen, and the sheriff was 'well nigh strangled with his own chain'. The commission finally rejected Dalton's election, but in spite of this he was elected mayor again in 1565, and claimed to be elected in 1566, with a majority of 380 to 44 votes. The state intervened once more in 1567, with a charter:

13. The *Dormont Book* (1561) redefined the constitution and power of the city council.

the government of the city should be by the mayor with eleven worshipful persons of the city; that the mayor should not do any act without the assent of the majority of the eleven. Also that the mayor and eleven should choose to them 24 able persons, and that the 36 should choose the mayor. That on the death of any of the 36 they should fill up that number.[30]

Dalton was then ordered by the commissioners to resign the mayoralty and surrender his freedom of Carlisle. Despite this he was to serve again in 1568-9. The charges and counter-charges of corruption and the claim that consecutive periods of office were illegal do not mask the significance of the change from a democratic to an oligarchical system of local government. Power was vested in the élite of the merchant guild and the local gentry, but a degree of compromise was apparent in the junior council of 24, which expanded, and began to take four members from each of the eight guilds. This remained the case until the Governing Charter of July 1637, when the council reverted to 24 members.

Carlisle was not economically reliant on its agricultural hinterland. Border anarchy was not conducive to prosperous agriculture, and much farming took place in a common field system, which was inherently unproductive and did not allow progressive farmers to make improvements. Many of the landholdings were smaller than the four acres considered by the Elizabethan government to be the minimum to support a labourer and his family. That farming was predominantly small-scale is evident from the fact that in the manor of Carlisle, which extended four to five miles from the city, between 60 and 70 per cent of landholders in the early 17th century held five acres or less. No farmer was able to let land lie fallow, so soil exhaustion was a problem.[31]

The economic assets that made Carlisle more than a market town were the garrison and the Church. Although its strength varied according to the political climate, the garrison was normally sufficient to make an appreciable economic impact. In 1563, 29 soldiers and 22 gunners were stationed at the castle, and in 1596 there were 65 gunners and officers, whose pay amounted to £949, of which £400 was for the warden. The strengthening of defences also brought money into the city. For example, £823 was spent in 1555, £575 in 1577, £243 in 1578 and £220 in 1584. The cathedral also brought money into Carlisle, despite being relatively poorly endowed. Its community numbered 44 clergy and officers, including five lawyers, thus accounting for about seven per cent of the city's households. The Church was the largest employer in Carlisle, and also the owner of the most property. By 1650, the first date at which property assets were quantified by the Church, the dean and chapter owned 50 properties outside the cathedral close, including shops, and held a substantial amount of farmland around the city.

The garrison was dismantled after 1603, and contemporary accounts of the city are depressing. In 1606 Charles Hales wrote that 'the city is become poore and daily is like to grow greater poverty, not having in ye same any such trades which may suffice to sett their poore on work'.[32] This comment is rather defeatist, and other sources, although geared towards the wealthier tradesmen, suggest that there were many trades in Carlisle at the end of the 16th century. The freemen's register and probate records cover the period up to 1620, and show that there were eight trade guilds in the Elizabethan city, surviving from the medieval period. Stedman draws attention to the striking preponderance of leather trades. Leather workers accounted for 43 per cent of the 112 admissions to the freedom of Carlisle between 1612 and 1620.[33] The probate records of 1564-1620 show that 23 per cent of the total population was connected with the leather trade, while no less than 70 per cent of the citizens farmed to supplement their income. The occupational structure of Carlisle appears to have been relatively varied and unspecialised at this time.

At the turn of the century, Elizabeth was approaching the end of her long life. Her successor was to rule both England and Scotland. Would unification bring peace to Carlisle?

Chapter Six

Carlisle in the Stuart era

James I

In March 1603 Queen Elizabeth died, and was succeeded by James VI of Scotland (James I of England). As James entered his new kingdom, at Berwick, intelligence reached him of the pillaging of the western marches. A band of two to three hundred men, mostly from the notorious area between the Leven and Sark, had penetrated as far as Penrith. These marauders were mostly members of the predominant Graham clan, who had doubled in numbers in the previous half-century, and were capable of deploying a formidable mounted force. When faced by a disciplined army of 200 foot and 50 horse from the Berwick garrison and loyal borderers, however, they fled in disarray, leaving their houses to be burnt or blown up.

After dealing with this initial disloyalty, James made plans to prevent any future rebellion. In April 1605 a royal commission met at Carlisle, and was instructed to ensure that all persons within its jurisdiction, except noblemen, gentlemen and their household servants, were forbidden the use of armour and weapons, and of horses, 'savinge meane naggs for their tillage'.[1] Incorrigible troublemakers were to be dealt with more drastically: 'All in whom there can be expected no hope of amendment may be removed to some other place "where the change of aire will make in them an exchange of manners" '.[2] This measure was immediately acted upon, and 150 members of the Graham clan were transported to serve in the 'garrisons and cautionary towns of Flushing and Brill'.[3] The enforcement of this banishment was singularly inept, and within three weeks many of the expatriated Grahams began to reappear in their former haunts. The Privy Council initiated a more radical solution, transporting the Grahams to Ireland, where they were settled on the land and given stock. On 15 September 1606 the commissioners reported to the council:

> There are not now left between Leven and Sarke more than three Grahams of ability, of whom two are now more than 80 years of age. All the notorious offenders whose manner terrified all peaceable men are gone away. Some of their wives who cannot go now will follow in the Spring.[4]

A reminder was given that the problem was not solved: 'Although Esk, Sark and Leven are purged of evil men, there remain others fit to follow in Bewcastle and Gillesland'.[5]

A dominant rôle in border peace-keeping was played by Lord William Howard, the third son of the Duke of Norfolk. He had married (as a child, in an arranged alliance) Elizabeth Dacre, one of the three co-heiresses of the Dacre estates.[6] Through his wife, William acquired Naworth Castle, which had been in a ruinous state since Leonard Dacre had fled the country.[7] As he was a Catholic, William and his family had suffered grievously during Elizabeth's reign, and it was some time before he could take possession of his inheritance. His position was still delicate when James came to the throne, but the king realised that William was too useful to be disturbed. Lord William took up residence at Naworth in 1603, and began to transform the castle into a family home. He was a man of considerable mettle, who relished the challenge of border lawbreakers. In a letter he wrote:

> I was away 'fishing', and I took as many as I could get. I was in hopes to have taken Antons Edward himself but, for want of a better, was glad to take his son Thomas Gifford and Jock

Stowlugs, the last but not the least in villany. I desire to keep him for a jewel of high price. Pray cause the records to be searched, if you find matter sufficient to hang the other two 'hould up your finger' and they shall be delivered. I confess myself a Southern novice.[8]

Lord William was prepared to pursue rigorously the policy of exile. He advocated that wives and children should be sent out too, under threat of death if they were to return. Protestants among the northern gentry both hated and feared him because of his influence at court. It was said that 'all men in these countries for their own safetie must and will yield unto him, for some simple men in their countrie neglecting God for him and given this for a reason – there is mercie with God but no mercie with my Lord William'.[9] Relentless law enforcement suppressed disorder in the countryside to some extent, but left untouched the underlying malaise of extreme poverty, the pernicious consequences of which were crime, violence and corruption.

At this inopportune time of disorder and poverty, the king sought to regain land around Carlisle, which the Crown contended was in its demesne and had been 'lost' during the Tudor period through administrative incompetence. The king was the major landowner in the vicinity of Carlisle, his manor containing 1,300 acres of arable fields and pasture in the fields of Stanwix, Castlefield and Upperby. From 1603 the remainder of the city, the castle, citadel and city walls, together with 59 acres of demesne land in Broadmeadows, the Swifts and Sanceries, were held by Lord Clifford. As a royal servant and captain of the castle he was a surrogate for the Crown. Approximately half of the manorial land was claimed by the inhabitants as freehold, or by the dean and chapter, who held 159 acres. The freeholders and 148 customary tenants were mainly traders, craftsmen and husbandmen of the city, its extra-mural suburbs of Rickergate and Botchergate, and the settlements of Upperby and Stanwix. These freeholders included local gentry, some of whom had been elected to the guilds, and the families of the Earl of Northumberland, Lord William Howard and Sir Edward Musgrave. After investigation 148 acres of the manor were identified as royal demesne, instead of freeholds. In July 1611 Clifford was granted a 60-year lease of the castle, its demesne and the manor, at a total rent of £50 per annum. Thus he gained rents and services due from tenants, and perquisites of the manorial court. Clifford became the *de facto* proprietor of the manor and, after two decades of litigation, he restored nearly 400 acres to the Crown. Tenants paid higher rents to absent landlords, but gained security and peace.

Despite this increased security, Carlisle itself was not prospering. In 1617, during the only royal visit to the city in the early modern period, Bishop Snowden gave a loyal address to the king. He lamented that:

The Citie of Carlisle is in great ruine, and extreme poverty, partly because the Lieutenant is not there resident, and partly for that the inhabitants exercise themselves in no Arts or trades, neither have they other meanes of livelyhood besides fishing. In the country at large many of the meaner sort, live dispersedly in cottages, or little farmes, scarcely sufficient for their necessary maintenance, whereby idleness, thefts and robberies are occasioned.[10]

The city's misfortune was compounded by the famine that raged across Cumberland and Westmorland from late 1623 to early 1624, in which many children died. The merchant guild attempted to attract more money to the city, and even sought the king's help. Four schemes were advocated, which came to nothing. These were to have a nobleman, such as the warden had been, permanently resident in the castle; to transfer one of the three court sittings of the Council of the North from York to Carlisle; to create a university in the city; and the granting of a licence allowing townsmen to export sheepskins. On a more positive

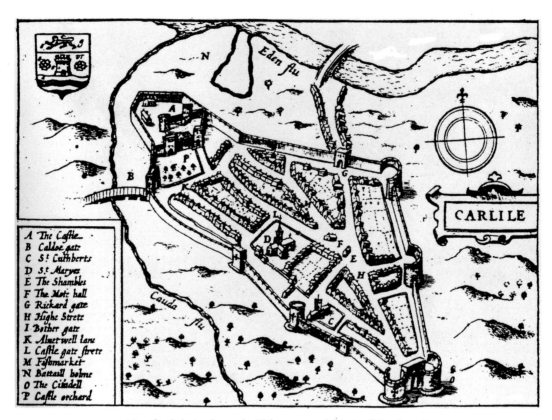

A The Castle
B Calloe gate
C S.t Cuthberts
D S.t Maryes
E The Shambles
F The Moit hall
G Richard gate
H Highe Strete
I Bother gate
K Almet well lane
L Castle gate strete
M Fishmarket
N Battaill holme
O The Citadell
P Castle orchard

14. Carlisle in the early 17th century. Map by John Speed.

note, farming still supplemented the town's income, and there were signs of the emergence of more specialised urban activities.

The Church also had difficulties at this time. The bishop complained that it was 'served by poor vicars and multitudes of base hirelings, and some leaning to the puritans, while elsewhere in the diocese recusants are at large'.[11] The cathedral was in decline too, both physically and spiritually. Three travellers reported in 1634 that it was 'nothing soe fayre and stately as those we had seen, but more like a great wild country church; as it appeared outwardly, so it was inwardly, never beautified, nor adorned one whit . . . the Communion also was administered and received in a wild and unreverent manner'.[12] Five years later, King Charles I complained to the dean: 'Our Cathedral church at Carlisle is fallin exceedingly into decay and indeed so far that if thereby be not present care taken for the repair thereof it cannot be long upheld'. The dean and chapter were admonished for their 'long continued absence' which together with 'some negligence of your predecessors' had hastened the decay of the fabric.[13]

Charles I
James I died in 1625 and was succeeded by Charles I. Charles sought to impose the English forms of worship on the Scottish kirk, and provoked rebellion. The Scottish Assembly refused to acquiesce to its own dissolution, declared the episcopacy abolished and restored

the full presbyterian government of the Church. So started the Bishops' War, so named because of the English bishops' attempt to reimpose the episcopal Church in Scotland. In December 1639 the king sought to raise a mighty army to reduce Scotland to obedience but, reaping the penalty of ruling without a parliament, was frustrated in his attempt to raise sufficient funds. The Scots gained the initiative, and seized Northumberland and the bishopric of Durham. In the autumn of 1640, after taking Newcastle, they prepared to invade Cumberland.

In anticipation of this, Carlisle's garrison had been increased to 500 men in 1639, and now the power to declare martial law was given to the governor. Orders were issued by the deputy lieutenant and the justices of the peace for a general muster of one out of five able men in the county: 'upon the firing of the beacons all the men chosen should repair to Carlisle with seven days' provisions, upon pain of death'.[14] Those that remained were to provide arms and allowances. Following the defeat of their army, however, the English had little choice but to agree, at the Treaty of Ripon, to 'the cessation of arms and the payment of a competency towards the maintenance of the Scottish army'.[15] Carlisle escaped invasion, but had to pay compensation to the Scottish army and have its garrison disbanded.

The Bishops' War was followed by the devastating Civil War. This broke out in August 1642, between the irreconcilable factions of king and parliament, and most affected Carlisle when Scotland intervened. In 1643 an abortive attempt was made to seize Carlisle for parliament by Sir Wilfrid Lawson, with Scottish backing. David Leslie, the Scottish leader, marched into the county from Newcastle with 800 horse, but was prepared to retreat when, opposed by county forces, he was faced with the fording of the Eden at Salkeld. Barwise of Ilekirk, M.P. for Carlisle, boldly rode into the river, however; the Scots followed, and the county forces retreated with all haste to Carlisle. When the city appeared doomed to fall, however, Leslie returned to Newcastle. It has been suggested that he wished to give the royalists time to re-provision, so that his men could draw pay for longer from the English parliament. For whatever motive Leslie withdrew, his action gave the citizens time to purchase vast quantities of food, which was stored in the citadels and fratry.

After the combined Scottish and Cromwellian victory at Marston Moor in 1644, northern England became subject to parliamentary power, with the exception of Carlisle which remained courageously and defiantly loyal to the king. David Leslie was instructed to return to the city, and take it. He established his headquarters at Dalston Hall and sealed off Carlisle with troops at Stanwix, Harraby, Botcherby and Newtown – which commanded respectively the routes to the north, south, east and west. Thus started the 1644 siege of Carlisle, of which we have a detailed account. This is the diary kept by Isaac Tullie, aged 18, who was inside the besieged city.[16]

The word siege conjures up a picture of bloody assaults on city walls and the destructive pounding of defences with artillery. The siege of Carlisle, lasting from October 1644 to 25 June 1645 was not like that. A policy of containment and attrition was followed by the besieging forces, but during the first five months they carried this out with astonishing laxity. The small-scale fighting was confined almost entirely to predatory raids by the garrison into the surrounding countryside to take cattle and provisions, and counter-raids by the Scots to seize the citizens' cattle. There was a massive disparity in numbers between the opposing forces. Leslie commanded 4,000 horse and foot, while Sir Thomas Glenham's garrison and the citizens of Carlisle only numbered 700. The county gentry were able to supply money but were not prepared to risk open intervention. To deny the enemy cover for an attack, the command was given 'to fire and pull down all the suburbs', but little fighting occurred in the first six weeks apart from skirmishing outside the walls.

By Christmas the siege was beginning to affect the citizens more seriously. All cattle and corn was taken from them, carried to a central store and distributed according to necessity.

Money for soldiers' pay was also becoming scarce, and plate was collected from which 'Carlisle Coins' were struck.[17] Money was confiscated during house searches, which were mounted under the pretence of searching for plate. By March the city was still contributing £60 each month to soldiers' pay. As Tullie records, though, all was not doom and gloom:

> The pleasantnesse of the day invited Sir Thomas Glenham, with many other Gent, and Gentlewomen, to take the aire neere Botcherby; against whom the enemie drawing out all their horse, stood to see them course a Haire and take it, under their noses; some week opposition they made, but Capt. Dixon having run one of them up to the hilt, they fairely drew homewards.[18]

By 3 April the provisions for horses were exhausted in the town, and thatch from the houses was given as a feed. Occasionally the horses were still taken, under close guard, to pasture outside the city. The Scots now chose to tighten their hold on the city, and erected defences at Calcoats Bank, Fusehill and Etterby, and later at Murrell Hill, the Swifts and adjacent to the Sally Port (an entrance through the wall, still so-named). By June the citizens were in dire straits, 'and no wonder [considering] their small quantity of hors flesh without bread or salt. Hempseed, dogs and rats were eaten . . .' but Tullie also reports that the citizens retained their sense of humour:

> Now were gentlemen and others so shrunk that they could not chuse but laugh at one another to see their close [clothes] hang as upon men on gibbets; for one might have put their head and fists between the doublet and the shirts of many of them.[19]

By mid June it was clear that the position was hopeless, and foot soldiers were beginning to steal away from the city. The discipline of the garrison had deteriorated, and was made manifest when the soldiers seized the common bakehouse, and 'took away all the hors flesh from the poor people, who were as neere starving as themselves'. The townsmen petitioned Sir Thomas Glenham, telling him that they could not endure the famine any more, but had neither answer nor redress. Four days later

> a few women of the scolds and scum of the citty, mett at the Cross brayling against Sir Henry Stradling there present; who first threatened to fire upon them, and when they replied they [would] take it as a favour, he left them with tears in his eyes, but could not mend their commons.[20]

On 24 June 1645 the king was defeated at Naseby, and final defeat of the Cavaliers was inevitable. Carlisle had given its all to the Royalist cause in vain, and on 25 June the articles of surrender were agreed, with terms honourable to Glenham's garrison.

The surrender of the city was followed by a recurrence of the plague, and the parliamentary commissioners reported that Carlisle was 'the model of misery and desolation'.[21] The newly-appointed governor found that 'upon his entrie the cittie had no money in Common chist nor plaite or other things necessary to be used in the cittie'.[22] Many gentry and some citizens suffered after the war for having borne arms against parliament. Sir Patrick Curwen was fined £2,000, and Charles Howard of Naworth (Lord William's grandson) was fined £4,000. Sir Timothy Fetherstonehaugh had his estate confiscated, was brought to trial as an example to others, and was sentenced to death. His last testimony ends on a melancholy note: 'I have few friends, legacies I have none, God knows I have nothing'. Sir Timothy's poignant farewell to his family was written while he awaited execution: 'I hope I shall die a good Christian. I desire my children to serve God diligently and never to meddle with any great matters of state'.[23]

One of the most devastating consequences of Carlisle's surrender was the wholesale destruction of the cathedral. Hugh Todd, writing in 1697, attributed this to the Scottish and parliamentary forces.[24] The demolition of the cloisters, part of the deanery, chapter house and prebendary houses, and of most of the cathedral nave could be attributed to premeditated vandalism, but the fabric of the buildings had been neglected for a long time. The destruction could be due to the primacy of current needs over cultural heritage.[25] Stone from the cathedral buildings was used to build the guard houses on each of the city gates and in the market-place.

The Restoration

After the death of Oliver Cromwell in 1658 and the short rule of his son Richard, the Cromwellian Protectorate was overthrown by dissatisfied military chiefs. In the Declaration of Breda, Charles II granted a free and general pardon, leaving parliament to decide if there were to be any exceptions to it, and an amnesty for all political offences committed during the Civil War. The comparative liberalism of the political settlement was compromised, however, by the efforts of the court party to gain control of the borough corporations. The charter of 1664 reinforced that of 1637, but required city officials to take an oath of obedience and supremacy, and ruled that the recorder and town clerk should be approved of by the Crown. Accordingly, when the town clerk, John Pattinson, died in 1666, the corporation humbly conformed and asked the king's approval for the proposed successor. More serious trouble arose in 1680-1 when a restive city dismissed Sir Philip Howard, one of its Tory M.P.s, in favour of the Whig Lord Morpeth. Retribution followed when Chief Justice Jeffreys arrived on the northern circuit, and the jury decided that the charter had been infringed and forfeited. The charter was surrendered by a servile council, and was carried off by the chief justice. Another charter was passed in 1684, which gave the Crown power to remove arbitrarily any of the corporation's officers.

James II and the Glorious Revolution

After Charles' death in 1685 his successor, James II, a Catholic, attempted to pack parliament with his supporters, which would give a semblance of constitutional authority to his actions. In Cumberland and Westmorland, the deputy lieutenants and justices of the peace presented a united front of opposition to the introduction of Catholics into the house. The king's response to the rebuffs he received was the autocratic annulment of many corporations' charters, the exclusion of deputy lieutenants and magistrates who had adhered to the penal and test statutes, and their replacement with Catholics and Dissenters. In Cumberland all the justices, except eight who had declared in favour of the king's plans, were dismissed. Carlisle's corporation abjectly surrendered, as in 1684, the rights and privileges that had been gained over centuries, when James packed his nominees onto the council. The humble address of the mayor and corporation to the king shows the city's grovelling submission:

> Being now at liberty by the late regulations made here, to address ourselves unto your majesty we beg leave to return our late but unfeigned thanks for your majesty's most gracious declaration of indulgence which we will endeavour to maintain and support against all opposers. We likewise thank your majesty for the royal army, which really is both the honour and safety of the nation . . . And when your majesty in your great wisdom shall think fit to call a parliament, we shall choose such member as shall certainly concur with your majesty in repealing and taking off the penal laws and tests, and not hazard the election of any person who hath anyways declared in favour of those Cannibal laws. Surely they do not consider what a sovereign prince by his royal power may do, that oppose your majesty in so gracious and glorious a work; a work which heaven shines upon, and with no less blessing (we hope) than a prince of Wales; that there may never want of your

issue to sway the sceptre, so long as the sun and moon endure. That your majesty's reign may be long and prosperous, and blessed with victories over all your enemies .[26]

The corporation had become a mere board of court nominees. In March 1687 the Catholic Sir Francis Salkeld was made a freeman and an alderman, and nine commissioned officers of the garrison, all Irish Catholics, were all admitted to the freedom of the city. On 10 June 1688 James II became the father of a son, and this news was greeted with great jubilation by the officers of the garrison. In a drunken debauch they threw their clothes onto a huge bonfire in the market-place, and 'then ran about naked like madmen'.[27]

In general, though, the country reacted against the Catholic dynasty. The Whigs and Tories made a secret alliance, and sent an invitation to Prince William of Orange in June 1688, offering him the throne of England. Prince William accepted the offer, and landed at Torbay on 5 November. Meanwhile, alarm was spreading in Cumberland as reports were received that Irish troops had been summoned to England by James in the early autumn. Substance was given to these fears by rumours that Irish and Scottish troops were operating in Lancashire, and that Carlisle had been seized by Catholics, and the citizens disarmed. On 10 December Sir John Lowther ordered the chief constable of Westmorland to summon the militia to Penrith, while on 16 December Carlisle surrendered to Sir Christopher Musgrave. The late governor and popish officers retired to Corby, and by the end of the year the city and county were held for William. James II left England during the week before Christmas, and on 16 February 1689 William and Mary were declared joint monarchs.

During the Stuart period, the endemic problem of border lawlessness continued to impoverish the countryside and debilitate the economy of Carlisle. In 1662, the 'Act for the preventing Theft and Rapine upon the Northern Borders of England' was passed, which gave the responsibility of border law enforcement to the people:

> a great number of lewd, disorderly and lawless persons, being thieves and robbers, who are commonly called Moss-Troopers who resided in Northumberland and Cumberland and the adjoining parts of Scotland, and who had taken advantage of the large wastes and intricate pathways in those parts, were committing notorious crimes and then escaping from one Kingdom to another to avoid justice.[28]

Before the Act was passed, borderers maintained armed horsemen themselves if affected by raiders, so inhabitants of more remote and sheltered areas contributed nothing. The Act ordained that £200 per year should be collected from all the people of Cumberland to employ a force of 12 men. Further legislation introduced transportation to 'His Majesty's Dominions in America' for raiders, and also introduced a form of insurance. A book was kept in each market town, in which theft and damage were recorded. Compensation was paid by the county keeper, who had a maximum allowance of £200 each year. These measures seem to have been effective, and from this time the border became a safer place.

A memorable picture of the conditions in Cumberland and Northumberland is to be found in Roger North's account of the journey of Chief Justice Sir Francis North through the border counties c.1676. Roads were dangerous and Sir Francis was given an armed guard. The route from Newcastle to Carlisle was 'impassable for coach – his lordship was forced to take horse'. The inhabitants were parochial, uncooperative, but not unfriendly:

> Here his lordship saw the true image of a Border country. The tenants of the several manors are bound to guard the judges through their precinct; and out of it they would not go, no not an inch, to save the Souls of them. They were comical sort of people riding upon negs, as they called their small horses, with long beards, cloaks, and long broadswords with basket hilts, hanging in broad

belts, that their legs and swords almost touched the ground. And every one in his turn, with his short cloak and other equipage, came up cheek by jowl and talked with my lord judge. His lordship was very well pleased with their discourse, for they were great antiquarians in their own bounds . . .[29]

It is surprising that in a century of warfare and lawlessness the northern borders should have been opened up significantly to the Scottish cattle trade by mid-century. The Borough of Carlisle had the right to collect toll on all cattle passing into and out of Cumberland, although at the beginning of the century this amounted to no more than £5 per annum. In 1624 the citizens were still complaining that cross-border trade was failing to develop, but by 1639-40 the annual revenue from cattle tolls amounted to £110. In 1662, toll was paid at Carlisle for 18,574 cattle, for which the corporation received £85.[30] It is probable that the same number of animals avoided the tollgates. It has been said that by mid-century Scotland was little more than pasture for England. Cattle were driven along the droving routes from Scotland, across fords on the rivers Esk and Eden, through Carlisle and along the Eden valley to Brough in Westmorland, and to Bowes, before arriving at the markets of southern and eastern counties.

The economy of Carlisle was controlled and structured in the late 17th century by the eight craft guilds, but their influence on the city's government had declined since the early decades of the century. This was partly due to the charter of 1637, which reduced the membership of the common council from 32 (four from each guild) to 24, not necessarily chosen from the guilds. A list of guildsmen in 1684 has survived, and is summarised below:

Guildsmen	Number	Percentage of total
Butchers	60	15
Glovers	80	20
Merchants	46	11.5
Shoemakers	48	12
Smiths	28	7
Tailors	26	6.5
Tanners	53	13.25
Weavers	59	14.75
Total	400	100[31]

The 400 guildsmen of 1684 represented approximately 20 per cent of the total population of the city. Stedman has suggested that there was a guild member in two out of every five households. Some guilds allowed outsiders to buy their way into the community and exercise trading rights within the city; in 1684, 26 guildsmen are known to have lived outside the city. There were also honorary members, not actually working in the craft themselves. For example, in the late 17th century, the Tanners Guild had high social cachet and admitted professional people and gentry, such as lawyers, doctors, surgeons and Church dignitaries, including the dean and the Earl of Carlisle. The merchant guild admitted county gentry and lawyers.

Statistical analysis of probate records to examine the occupational structure of Carlisle is unavoidably biased towards the better-off. From 1621-1700 the largest occupational groups were:

	percentage of total
Leather trades	15.6
Distribution trades	12.2
Professional classes (incl. clergy)	6.7
Textile workers	2.2

In 1564-1620 nearly 70 per cent of the 215 people who left probate records had a subsidiary income from agriculture. This dropped to 50 per cent for 1621-1700, suggesting, as we have seen before, movement towards a more urban, specialised, economy.[32] Despite these signs of change, Carlisle's economy may best be described as stagnant at the end of the 17th century. Trade with the rest of the county, as measured by the toll paid on animals and goods passing through the city, was sluggish and much affected by local and national difficulties. For example, the total revenue was halved in 1598, a plague year, and the Civil War cut trade to about a third of its previous value. Not until 1686 was the pre-war total exceeded.

Probate records also show us something of the lifestyle of Carlisle's more prosperous citizens. Thomas Syde, a butcher of Rickergate (d.1613), left two houses with appurtenances (the rights belonging to property) in the city, two tenements in Scotby, a shop under the Moothall, a stall in the shambles and two-and-a-half acres of land near the city. He also left money for his son's education. Thomas Pattinson, a merchant in Botchergate, lived in comfort and style, his house's furnishings including eight feather beds, and silver plate and spoons. The possession of more than one house was not infrequent. For example, Thomas Thompson, tanner, left 'all my houses in Castlegate' when he died in 1611. One wonders whether he was a craftsman or an honorary member of the guild. In a lower stratum of society, some testators owned a few sheep, a pig or a cow, but others had nothing except the tools of their trade and clothing. Richard Durrance, a miller of Richardgaite (sic) only left five sheep and clothes.[33]

At the end of the century, contemporary accounts of the appearance of Carlisle are available. Todd wrote in 1697 that

> . . . the walls of the city are in the same condition which William Rufus left them . . . There are in the town and suburbs about four hundred houses, which may contain two thousand inhabitants who live in a middle and somewhat poor condition having no manufactory or stable commodity to enrich themselves by.[34]

Celia Fiennes visited the city in 1698, and her observations are particularly valuable for the information they give about the buildings in Carlisle:

> . . . the cathedrall all built of stone which looked stately but nothing curious; there was some few houses as the Deans and Treasurer and some of the Doctors houses walled in with little gardens their fronts looked gracefully else I saw no houses except the present Majors (sic) house of brick and stone, and one house which was the Chancellors built of stone very lofty 5 good sarshe [sash] windows in the front, and this within a stone wall'd garden well kept and iron gates to discover it to view with stone pillars.[35]

The 'Chancellors' house referred to was Tullie House. Celia Fiennes comments that 'the walls of the town and battlements and tower are in very goode repair and looks well', but that the castle defences were more ruinous: 'there remains only some of the walls and ruines of the Castle which does shew it to have been a very strong town formerly; the walls are of prodigious thickness and vast great stones, its moated round and with draw bridges'.

She also observes that 'The streets are very broad and handsome well pitch'd . . . there is a large market place with a good Cross and Hall and is well supply'd as I am inform'd with provisions at essye rates'. Perhaps the most vivid impression of the late 17th-century city may be found in a 19th-century photograph of the west side of English Street. This shows, sandwiched between Victorian shops, a range of 17th-century buildings with clay walls and a stone-tiled roof, which were probably the sort of buildings that lined the main streets of 17th-century Carlisle.[36] The nearby Main Guard, built in 1645 and shown in Nutter's painting, is atypical as it was a military building. A parliamentary survey of the property belonging to the dean and chapter, c.1650, and prepared before the sale of 37 houses, describes a 10 per cent sample of the houses within the city walls. Three were single-storey, one having a hall, parlour and stable; 25 had a ground floor with one or more lofts; and nine had two storeys. Many retained the medieval feature of a hall open to the roof (between 25 and 40 per cent of the sample).[37] The 1673 hearth tax returns show that there were few multi-hearth dwellings and a low average of hearths per household in comparison with other towns. Houses were built from clay and timber, except for a few stone buildings, and bricks were not used extensively before the late 17th century, if one excepts the Tile Tower built in the 15th century. There are documentary references to Carlisle's brickmakers and bricklayers, and also a brick kiln at Murrell Hill in the 1670s and 1680s, but the contract for rebuilding the timber-framed Moot Hall in 1669 was drawn up between a stonemason, a carpenter and the corporation. Stone was also used to face and roof Tullie House when it was built in 1689. Few examples of early brick buildings survive, but the best examples are in the cathedral close. Brick began to be used widely only in the 18th century.

Chapter Seven

Eighteenth-Century Carlisle

The political scene

The predominant feature of local politics in Carlisle during the 18th century was the struggle among the great landowners for control of the parliamentary seats, in which they resorted to bribery and outrageous manipulation of the electorate.

After the revolution of 1688 the Musgrave interest in Carlisle was pre-eminent. Christopher Musgrave occupied one of the parliamentary seats, while a Lowther held the other. Musgrave's downfall was sparked off by an incident in 1692, in which he had an acrimonious dispute with John How, an alderman and future mayor, in the castle precincts. A meeting of aldermen that evening disfranchised Musgrave, but the country party in parliament rallied in defence of one of its members. As a consequence of this, John How and six members of the corporation were summoned to the bar of the House, on a charge of breach of privilege. On arrival they were put into custody, and before release were ordered to restore Musgrave to the freedom of Carlisle. Musgrave's cause suffered nonetheless, and in the 1695 election he was rejected by the electorate 'amid scenes of barbarous riots'.[1] James Lowther and William Howard were returned as members for Carlisle.

Although elections were regularly manipulated by the wealthy during the 18th century, deference to the candidate could not be taken for granted in the city. Both the Howards and Lowthers employed professional agents to canvass and persuade. A spoils (patronage) system affected a few but the main instrument of persuasion was 'treating', the distribution of food and drink to the electorate. In 1695, the Howard election expenses totalled £1,130. After a parliamentary bill to restrict the amount of treating, expenses dropped to £200 in the 1698 election, which was known as the 'dry' election.[2] Physical persuasion was used too. When Captain Stanwix declared his candidature in 1701, the garrison's soldiers set out to influence the freemen by solicitation and threats. It was said to be unsafe for anyone who did not support Stanwix to go out into the streets, but this coercion did not have the desired effect.[3] Neither could deference to the lord be relied upon. Spedding, the Lowthers' agent in 1721, reported to his employer that the voters would give him 'no answer than they would be glad to drink any of the candidates health', but judged that whoever offered most in the way of inducement would get the votes.[4] The voters may have been guilty of venality, but they retained a measure of independence.

For the last four decades of the century, Sir James Lowther, Earl of Lonsdale, made persistent attempts to make Carlisle one of his pocket boroughs.[5] In 1759 he became an alderman, and gained a hold over the corporation which he later used to control the electorate. His two candidates were defeated in the 1768 general election, but after the Whig and Tory parties agreed to share the two seats a temporary end was put to local rivalries. This came to an end in 1784, because of political differences on national issues. It was now that Lowther brought into play his influence over the corporation. During the night of 13-14 January 1785, 1,447 freemen (nicknamed 'mushrooms') were admitted. They were recruited from Lowther's Westmorland estates and Whitehaven collieries, and some were appointed aldermen and councillors. The other freemen sought legal redress for this, but in the two by-elections of 1786 the Tory candidate was elected on the strength of the mushroom voters, despite consolidated support for the Whig candidate from the original freemen. In each case, the result was overturned by a parliamentary select committee. The

15.   Lord Lonsdale's 'Mushrooms'. Manipulation of the Carlisle electorate at the 1786 by-election.

third mushroom election in 1790 provoked violent scenes, when the Whig supporters partially demolished Lonsdale's house, 'Mushroom Hall', in Fisher Street. Again, the select committee ruled in favour of the Whig (Blue) candidate.

In 1796, Lonsdale tried a different approach. He attempted to force the election of 'mushrooms' to the guilds, but was not successful. Lonsdale's death in 1802 brought the disreputable affair to a close, but his own cause had been damaged. Tory support among traditional freemen was now less than half its 1768 level. The Earl of Lonsdale's successor was Sir William Lowther, who agreed a compromise for control of one of the seats. Carlisle then began a decade of political tranquillity.

The Jacobite Invasions
The 1707 Act of Union was unpopular in Scotland, where some looked forward to a Jacobite restoration, which would lead to a revival of Scottish independence. The accession of the first Hanoverian, George I, to the Anglo-Scottish throne in 1714 further aggravated Jacobite sympathisers and aroused latent Scottish nationalism. This caused concern in the border counties, and Lord Lonsdale ordered the ill-trained and poorly-armed militia 'to throw away their pikes and get firelocks in their place'.[6] On 30 October 1715 a rebel force numbering 1,000 to 1,200 foot and 600 horse reached Longtown and, avoiding Carlisle, advanced to Brampton, where 'James III' was proclaimed. The next day they moved towards Penrith, but were confronted by 14,000 men who had been assembled by Lord

Lonsdale and the Bishop of Carlisle.[7] As the rebels advanced, the militia fled in confusion, every man for himself. Lord Lonsdale retired to Appleby Castle, and the bishop to his seat at Rose Castle. The Pretender was then able to enter Penrith in triumph, where he was proclaimed once more. In this debacle, both the disorganised militia and an apathetic government, which expected a mob armed with guns, scythes and pitchforks to defeat an organised body of highlanders and professional soldiers, must be blamed for the transitory success of the rebel forces. The rebels did not prosper, however, and were compelled to surrender soon after reaching Preston, as nobody of consequence took up their cause.

Between 1715 and 1745 the country was lulled into a false sense of security, as the standard of living rose and religious fanaticism dwindled. In Cumberland and Westmorland subsequent events suggest an indifference to both the Stuart and Hanoverian houses. Certainly the people were not willing to risk their lives or possessions for either side. In August 1745 Prince Charles, son of the 'Old Pretender', landed in the Western Highlands and raised clans of Catholic sympathisers in his cause. Despite receiving little support from the Presbyterian lowlands he defeated the Government forces at Prestonpans (near Edinburgh), and advanced into England with only about five thousand men. Few measures had been taken in Cumberland to meet this threat, as such a venture had seemed impossible but, after Prestonpans, Colonel Durand was sent to command the defences of Carlisle. He arrived on 10 October to find the defences neglected and the garrison more feeble than its numbers had suggested. The Cumberland and Westmorland militia were mustered by Lonsdale and brought into the city, but it was still more of a rabble than a fighting force. William Gilpin wrote that 'Every soldier pretended to be as wise as his officer; and in fact he was as wise, for in the two regiments of Cumberland and Westmorland there was not an officer who knew how to draw up a platoon'.[8] As their statutory month of service expired a few days after arrival, the militia was only persuaded to stay with the promise of advance pay. While one would suppose that they would have had a common interest with the citizens, their relationship was tarnished by greed. The militia was compelled to pay exorbitant prices for provisions, and even straw for beds was not available. Captain Wilson, son of one of the parliamentary members for Westmorland paid 30s. so that he could rest in a cobbler's stall.[9]

On 11 November Prince Charles, who was quartered at Blackhall, received intelligence that Marshal Wade was marching from Newcastle to relieve Carlisle, and decided to withdraw to Brampton. Thomas Pattinson, the city's deputy mayor, sent a jubilant but somewhat premature dispatch to the Government, claiming that the city had routed the enemy. He added that 'I think the town of Carlisle has done his majesty more service than the great city of Edinburgh, or than all Scotland together'.[10] Unfortunately for Pattinson, the deplorable state of the Newcastle-Carlisle road prevented the arrival of reinforcements, and on the next day the rebels returned. They placed women and children from the countryside in front of their army in wagons, and forced countrymen to fix scaling ladders to the city walls. The 'great Mr. Pattinson instantly surrendered the town and agreed to pay 2,000 pounds to save it from pillage', and the militia threw down their arms and deserted their posts.[11]

Carlisle surrendered on 15 November, and the keys of the city were taken by the mayor to Brampton, and handed to Prince Charles. The statement by Colonel Durand, Captain Gilpin and officers of the garrison, addressed to the Council of War on the day of surrender, is a melancholy document:

The Militia of the Countys of Cumberland and Westmorland, as also the Militia of the town of Carlisle, having absolutely to a man refused to defend the castle, and the Garrison, consisting only of two companies of invalids amounting to about 80 men, many of whom are extremely infirm, and

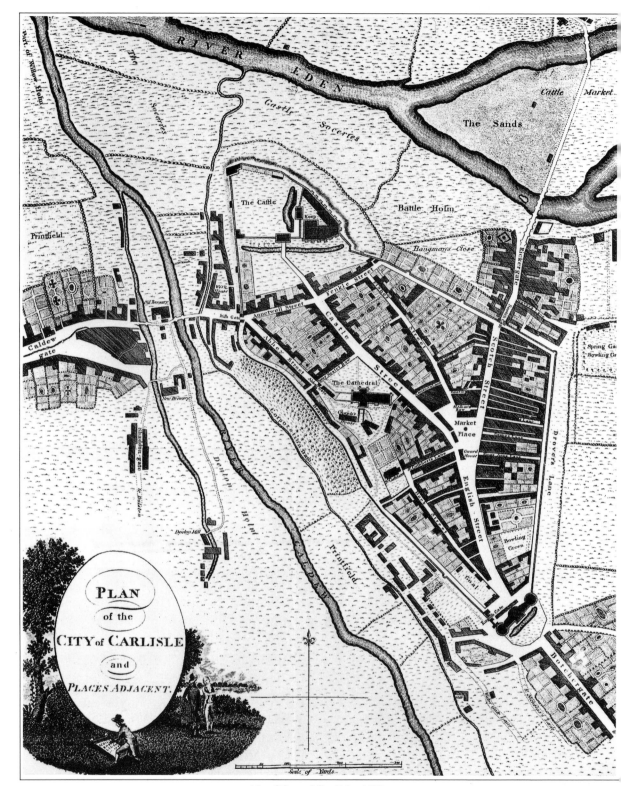

16. Map of Carlisle, 1790.

the castle very large, so that there are neither men to manage the guns nor man the walls, and the Mayor and inhabitants of the town together with the officers of the militia having sent to treat with the Rebels against the opinion and protest of Colonel Durand, Captain Gilpin, and the rest of the officers of the Garrison, and being refused any terms, and threatening to destroy both town and militia with fire and sword unless the castle be surrendered, it is our opinion that the castle being not tenable, it is for his Majesty's service that it be abandoned, as it will be absolutely necessary for the preservation of the lives of his Majesty's subjects, who would otherwise be exposed to inevitable ruin.[12]

After the rebellion had been quashed, Colonel Durand was tried by court martial, and acquitted. The mayor and town clerk of Carlisle were put in custody but the militia officers were treated with contempt, and no notice was taken of their conduct.

In Carlisle the rebels were not received as friends, and as the main body of Jacobite forces advanced southwards there were frequent skirmishes between the invaders' garrison and the citizens. This caused the governor to 'seize the parents of opponents as if the punishment of fathers would deter sons'.[13] Prince Charles gained little support, and on reaching Derby and being faced by a disciplined English army, his forces retreated to the border to escape annihilation. They reached Carlisle on 19 December, and left a garrison of 400 to cover their retreat when they heard that the Duke of Cumberland was pursuing them, and had reached Penrith. The duke reached Carlisle on 21 December, and took up quarters at Blackhall. By the next day Carlisle was fully invested. On 27 December, six 18-pounder guns arrived from Whitehaven, the walls were breached and the rebel governor surrendered after a 10-day siege, on condition that the rebels would not be put to the sword. The duke took up residence at Highmore House, where the prince had lodged, and the garrison was imprisoned in the cathedral. The clergy protested at the desecration of their church, and their outrage was voiced by James Ray of Whitehaven:

After the capitulation was agreed upon . . . the officers yielded themselves prisoners immediately and the men laid down their arms in the market place and retired into the Cathedral; so that they defiled the Temple, which used to be a House of Prayer, but has now become a Den of Thieves, where there was a Guard set over them, till his Royal Highness could otherwise dispose of them.[14]

On 10 January 1746 the prisoners were sent to Lancaster and Chester, but the problem of the desecrated cathedral remained. On 23 January Thomas Jackson complained to the chancellor, John Waugh, that 'the Rebels made a most nasty church', and the prebendary, named Wilson (later the dean), declared that 'cleaning and washing . . . proves of little use for the flags being old, spongy, and ill laid, the earth under them is corrupt and till that is removed the Cathedral church will not be sweet, nor will it be safe to have service in it'.[15] Sulphur and tar were burnt in the church before it was pronounced fit for worship again.

After the decisive English victory at Culloden on 16 April, Carlisle was one of the places selected for the trial, in August, of Scottish prisoners. There were 370 prisoners, and 'lots were cast when 19 will be ordered for transportation and every 20th man will be tried'.[16] Thomas Cappock, who had been installed as bishop by the Young Pretender was sentenced to death together with other prisoners. It is said that Cappock told his fellow captives to be of good courage for 'they should not be tried by a Cumberland jury in the next world'.[17]

1745 was a turning-point in the history of Carlisle. The crushing of the Jacobite rebellion signalled the end of Anglo-Scottish warfare: Carlisle was the last English city to be besieged and Cumberland was the last county to be invaded. By the early 18th century, the small-scale border warfare of bands of marauding reivers and moss troopers had been stamped out. The surviving border castles and pele towers are physical reminders of the period.

The state of Carlisle

Travellers and early historians draw a depressing picture of Carlisle in the mid-18th century. Defoe visited the city in 1724: 'The City is strong, but small, the buildings old, but the streets fair, the great church is a venerable old pile . . . there is not a great deal of trade here either by sea or land, it being a meer frontier'.[18] A merchant from Bristol, John Crofts, wrote in 1759 that 'Carlisle is a small deserted dirty city, poorly built and poorly inhabited . . . [the cathedral] is miserably ragged and dirty inside and out'.[19] Hutchinson provides a comprehensive description of the 18th-century city:

> Carlisle at the beginning of the present century exhibited no marks of modern convenience and elegance. The buildings mostly of wood, clay and laths bespoke the poverty and bad taste of the inhabitants . . . the streets, though spacious were paved with large stones and the centre part, or causeway, rose to a considerable height. The fronts from the houses were paved in the same manner, the consequences of which were that the kennels or gutters were deep trenches, and stone bridges were placed in many different parts, for the convenience of passing from one side of the street to the other. These gullies were the reservoir of all kinds of filth where, when a sudden heavy rain happened, by stopping the conduit of the bridges, inundated the streets so as to render them impassable on foot . . . the houses did not exceed the height of one storey and were chiefly covered with thatch.[20]

Hutchinson in 1794 also commented on trade:

> . . . little more than half a century ago . . . their trade consisted in that of a good weekly market, two annual fairs, and two extraordinary well attended statutes for hiring servants . . . the business for the whole year was settled at these meetings, as in many places the intercourse between town and town, or man and man, was not yet carried on by way of post carriers and other public conveyancies . . . the necessaries of life were uncommon cheap and the chief part of their wearing apparel was of their own spinning . . . pride and luxury in eating, drinking, furniture and dress had not yet made their entrance within the city walls.[21]

This somewhat medieval city began to change during the early 18th century, but its development was constrained by three major factors: the warfare and anarchy which ended *c.*1745, the poverty of Carlisle's hinterland which limited its development as a market town, and the city's isolation and the difficulty of long-distance transport. The latter two factors must be discussed, as the effect of war has been seen already.

The countryside in the vicinity of Carlisle was in the same state as the city at the beginning of the 18th century. Celia Fiennes described the poverty: 'its reckon'd but 16 miles from Peroth [Penrith] to Carlisle but they are pretty long . . . you pass by the little hutts and hovels the poor live in like barnes some have them daub'd with mud-wall others drye walls'.[22] Agriculture was backward too, and the enclosure movement had barely begun. On his journeys from Carlisle to Penrith, Sir John Clerk observed that

> . . . the ground to the west was a fine country all enclosed after the English way . . . these inclosures tho' they are not perfectly fencible, yet they beautify the country and keep the ground warm and distinguished in their marches . . . To the east . . . for the most part there are only wild moor and commons.[23]

A recent study has argued that the predominantly subsistence agriculture of Cumberland was enforced by the small size of the farms: by the end of the century, farms with a rent of more than £100 a year were still rare. Changes were only possible if farm sizes were increased, and apart from a limited amount of engrossing by major landowners, such as

17. Carlisle – a walled
city, *c.*1770.

18. Carlisle from the west
in the 18th century. (M.E.
Nutter.) The approach
road from the west over
Caldew, Little Caldew and
Mill Dam is shown.

19. Carlisle from the
north in 1795. (Robert
Carlyle.) The east wall of
the city is decaying. Stone
bridges span the old and
new channels of the Eden,
the Priest Beck bridge
being some sixty yards
upstream from the present
bridge.

the lords of Carlisle and Lonsdale, this was not taking place. It was only in the latter part of the century that efficient estate management and husbandry began to improve matters, but even by the end of the century one third of the county remained uncultivated.[24] Between 1780 and 1820, however, the rate of change increased, and thousands of acres were converted from waste into arable and pasture, while land ownership was concentrated in a few hands and customary tenures were replaced by leases.

Transport developments

By the early 19th century, Carlisle had been transformed into one of the four great textile manufacturing centres in Britain.[25] This was largely due to the improvements in transport during the second half of the 18th century. The first notable attempt to improve communications to Carlisle was the restoration of an earlier limited trade by sea from collieries in the Maryport area via the Solway and the River Eden, and overland to Carlisle. The initiative came from three Carlisle citizens, Thomas Pattinson, John Hicks and Henry Orme, who were empowered by an act of parliament to waive coastal duties between Ellen Foot (later Maryport) and Bank End on the Eden, to build wharfs, cranes and warehouses, and to dredge the Eden as necessary. The preamble to the act referred to the shallowness of the river, which had prevented the carriage of manure and lime to improve the large tracts of land which were lying waste, coal to burn the lime, and the export of agricultural produce.[26] This brave entrepreneurial venture was severely limited in scope, though. The 'boats, lighters and barges' that could navigate the river were restricted to a maximum of 40 tons, and were dependent on the state of tide and wind. Land transport was required for the five miles from Bank End to Carlisle, and transhipment was required at Maryport, to open up distant markets.

It was the radical transformation of road transport that was of most importance to Carlisle in the 18th century. The first turnpike act was passed in 1662, but carrier services were limited almost entirely to the south of England: in 1715 only one per cent had reached the area north of Lancashire and Yorkshire.[27] The second period of road transport development was initiated by the formation of turnpike trusts in the 1750s, promoted by landowners in order to permit the commercial exploitation of their estates.[28]

Long-distance travel was inordinately slow in the early 18th century. Lord Harley, for example, travelled from Hexham to Carlisle in May 1725: 'From Hexham to the Long Byers are computed 17 miles and we are coming it eight hours twenty minutes, a way which no coaches hardly ever know to pass but those of the Judges who are necessitated to go through it once a year'. He made better time on his subsequent journey from Carlisle to Penrith: 'This is computed 16 miles and we came it in 5 hours and twenty five minutes'.[29] In 1734 there is a reference to a coach service from Carlisle to London, which took nine days.[30] This was considerably quicker than the packhorse trains, which completed the journey in anything between 12 and 18 days.[31] It has already been mentioned that General Wade failed to relieve Carlisle in 1745, because the road from Newcastle was so bad. He reached Hexham in three days, and could proceed no further. After this experience it is hardly surprising that the first turnpike road to be constructed from Carlisle was primarily for military rather than commercial use. The 1751 turnpike act was 'for laying out, making and keeping in repair, a road proper for the passage of troops and carriages from the City of Carlisle to the Town of Newcastle upon Tyne'. Public money was to be used for the construction of the road, but tolls and duties were to keep it in repair. By 1758, when the road was completed, £16,500 and £7,500 had been spent on the Northumberland and Cumberland sections respectively.[32] Before Telford and McAdam introduced more advanced techniques early in the next century, turnpikes were built very badly. The

20. Regulator stage coach notice, 1819.

Carlisle, 26th April, **1819.**

THE Public are respectfully informed THE OLD-ESTABLISHED

REGULATOR

LIGHT POST COACH is *REMOVED* from the Coffee-House and Bush Inns, to Mr. SNOWDEN's, the Blue Bell Inn, SCOTCH-STREET.

It will start every Evening at 11 o'clock, and run through Kendal, Lancaster, and Preston, to the Angel Inn, Liverpool, and the Swan Inn, Market-street-lane, Manchester, in 19 Hours; from whence Coaches proceed to Derby, Nottingham, Leicester, Coventry, Birmingham, and LONDON, at Reduced Prices, in 55 Hours, including a Night's Rest in Manchester; and Passengers may secure their Places through.

Luggage and Packages 1d. per lb. to Lancaster; 2d. per lb. to Liverpool and Manchester; 3d. to Derby, Nottingham, Coventry, and Birmingham; and 4d. to London. And small Parcels 1s. to Lancaster, 2s. to Liverpool and Manchester; 3s. to Derby, &c and 4s. to London.—Insurance 2s. for every £5 for 50 Miles, and 2d. per £1 for every 20 Miles additional.

The Proprietors commenced this Coach in hopes of accomplishing a direct Connection from the South by Way of Manchester and Liverpool into Scotland; but from the great objections made by Messrs. Wilson and Fairbairn to start it on the arrival of the Wellington from Glasgow, they have been obliged to remove it from them, being determined to offer every Accommodation in their power that can promote a direct and satisfactory Conveyance for Passengers, without any delay in Carlisle; and sincerely hope by this exertion very soon to establish Coaches daily to Glasgow and Edinburgh.

PERFORMED BY

TAYLOR, SIMPSON, WEBSTER, & Co. Carlisle and Kendal;
COOPER, GARTH, & Co. Preston;
R. CHAMBERS & Co. Liverpool;
WEATHERALL, COOKSON, RICHARDSON, & Co. Manchester;
And WM. WATERHOUSE & SON, Lad-lane, London.

Who will not be accountable for any Loss or Damage whatever, unless properly Entered and Secured.

Military Road soon deteriorated, in parts being little better than a cart-track, and in the 19th century it was described as 'the worst engineered road in the country'.[33]

The turnpike acts that were passed after 1755 opened up Carlisle to London, Lancashire, Yorkshire and West Cumberland. They were built on a commercial basis, with little hope of early return on capital investment. Landowners were not aiming to be entrepreneurs, but subscribed to the trusts in order to benefit their own estates. Not everybody supported the improvements, though. Mannix and Whellan wrote in 1847 that 'When local acts were obtained for their improvement the exaction of tolls gave rise to much popular fury, the people then not clearly seeing that the advantages obtained by good roads greatly counterbalanced the amount of tolls levied for their formation and repair'.[34]

The introduction of turnpikes soon brought great changes in road traffic. Packhorses gave way to carts, post-chaises were introduced in 1754, and carrier wagons in 1757.[35] In 1762 a stage-coach was running over Shap for the first time, but the journey was still difficult and the road over Stainmore was still the main route from Cumberland to London. Coaches, mail and carrier services began to proliferate. For example, a 'Carlisle and London new Post Coach on steel springs' was inaugurated on 1 January 1775, taking three days via Ripon and Sheffield.[36] Comfort was increasing, but fares were not cheap. Passengers inside the coach paid £3 10s., while sitting outside was half-price.[37] Even at this early date the service was part of a co-ordinated system, with connections at Sheffield for Birmingham, Bristol and Plymouth. The main termini in Carlisle were the 'Coffee House' (now the *Crown and Mitre*) and the *Bush Hotel* in English Street. In 1785 a mail service from Carlisle to Manchester was introduced, which superseded the postboys – a euphemism for old men on horseback. The first mail coach in England had been established between London and Bristol in August 1784 by John Palmer, a Bristol businessman. National development of a co-ordinated service followed Palmer's appointment as Comptroller General in 1785. Posting stages were established on all routes, so that horses could be changed every 14 miles, and crews after 70 miles. Eighty coach horses were stabled at Carlisle. Services speeded up as turnpikes and coach construction improved, and in the 1830s, the journey-time from London to Carlisle fell to two days, and later to 32 hours.[38] Cost of postage dropped too. In 1823 a letter from Carlisle to London cost the recipient 13d., to Manchester 10d., and to Newcastle 7d. In 1840 the penny post was introduced by Rowland Hill, greatly to the benefit of commerce and the individual in remote areas of England.

A parallel development of carrier services took place. Messrs. Handley advertised 'expeditious waggons in 7 days from Carlisle to London, twice a week, by way of York'.[39] This was again an integrated service, with connections from Leeds to the south. From Carlisle there were two wagons a week to London, six to Newcastle, two to Kendal, five carts to Edinburgh, four to Glasgow and four to Whitehaven.[40] This dramatic increase in the volume of road transport gave rise to considerable material and social change. Bailey and Culley wrote in 1794 that 'the turnpike roads have brought the manners of the capital to the extremity of the Kingdom. The simplicity of ancient times has gone. Finer clothes, better dwellings and more expensive viands are now sought by all'.[41] In 1777 Nicolson and Burn noted '. . . that few people now make their own clothes. In the articles of clothes they have departed of late years from their ancient simplicity'.[42]

The topography of the city

Little change since 1700 is revealed by the 1746 map of Carlisle (see front endpaper). The city was still a military centre, with a garrisoned castle and sentries posted at the gates. The map shows minor development outside Ricard Gate, Botcher Gate, Cauda Gate and Shaddon Gate: while the street pattern was almost identical to today, crofts occupying the area behind the street frontages. A closer-knit development was starting to appear in the Lanes area, between Scotch Street and the east curtain wall. Direct entrance to the city from the south was blocked by the citadel, and English Street was approached from Caldew Brow. The Eden was in two branches with the Priest Beck Bridge joined to Eden Bridge by a causeway across the sands. Drove Road, today's Lowther Street, skirted the city outside the east wall. The River Caldew had a millrace on each side with two corn mills on the older race, the Corporation Dam. It is recalled by names such as English Damside and Irish Damside.

In the more prestigious areas of Carlisle, medieval disorder was cleared away as classical values in architecture, such as symmetry, proportion, elegance and order were adopted. This was limited in extent and took place later than in southern England. Tullie House was built in 1689 and the Town Hall was rebuilt in 1717. The handsome Georgian houses

21.   The Priest Beck bridge, approach by Eden Terrace. (John Landseer.)

22.   Drove Lane, on the line of Lowther Street, and the ruinous eastern wall of the city. The lane was used by drovers to avoid tolls.

in the cathedral precinct date from the early years of the century, and St Cuthbert's church was rebuilt in 1778. The corporation failed to introduce much space and elegance into the urban landscape until c.1790, when the first tentative steps were taken. Carlisle's main thoroughfare was opened up by the demolition of the Shambles, which was 'formed of wood, covered with different kinds of slates, which gave them a grotesque and antique appearance'.[43] It was replaced by a row of butchers' shops, which extended from Scotch Street to Fisher Street. They still stand there today but are enclosed in the covered market. Carnaby's Folly, built on pillars over a well at the north end of the Shambles, was also demolished. The act for 'Lighting, Paving and improving the Streets' was the next significant sign of urban renewal. It was passed in 1804, and made the corporation responsible for the condition of city streets. A comprehensive scheme of urban planning was still not undertaken by the corporation, however. The Guard house was replaced by the fish market between 1829 and 1842, but the market-place had still not been cleared by 1847, when Mannix and Whellan hoped 'that the old buildings adjoining the market house will soon be swept away, as their renewal would much improve the general appearance of the market place'.[44] A further sign of change was the construction of Georgian terraced houses in Abbey Street and Castle Street in the early 19th century, their uniform and elegant style contrasting with the jumble around them.

Carlisle society

The comparison between Hutchinson's description of the self-sufficient and unsophisticated life of the citizen at the beginning of the 18th century contrasts strongly with the evidence from a trade directory in 1790. A great proliferation of service trades supplemented the core of professional people serving the diocese and the city courts. The *Universal British Directory* lists 18 clergy and 19 lawyers, 35 innkeepers, 50 people selling shoes and clothing, 73 in food shops and 13 selling wines and spirits. Other trades were connected with the well-to-do: three watchmakers, three hairdressers, one perfumier, two jewellers and three people engaged in printing, stationery and bookselling. This indicates that there was a growing number of citizens who had a disposable income. The professional class was increasing too. The directory lists 15 doctors, surgeons and druggists, while 88 are classified as gentry.

An early sign of leisure and literacy was the establishment of the *Carlisle Journal* in November 1798, the *Carlisle Patriot* in January 1813, and a spate of short-lived journals between 1807 and 1827. Chapbooks also proliferated in the late 18th and early 19th centuries. These were little books or pamphlets, often illustrated with crude woodblock prints, and sold by chapmen or hawkers. They dealt with a wide variety of topics ranging from religious homilies to humorous, romantic or supernatural subjects and the popular ballads of the day. Ferguson lists 180 chapbooks in the 'Bibliotheca Jacksoniana' library at Tullie House, of which 14 were printed in Carlisle, 17 in Whitehaven and 60 in Penrith. He also recollected 'Pinners-up' and 'Long-Song-Sellers' at Carlisle fairs in the days of his youth.[45]

Theatre, music, literature and assemblies are four aspects of leisure and culture that are hardly documented in 18th-century Carlisle. The city's first theatre opened in 1813, built by William Macready in Blackfriars Street. Its façade can still be seen, opposite St Cuthbert's church. A subscription library was opened in Devonshire Street in 1768 and remained there until 1896, when it was superseded by Tullie House. Better documented than cultural activities is sport. From Elizabethan times, and possibly before, horse-racing was held on Kingmoor. It moved later to the Swifts, and then to Blackwell, its present home. Two silver racing bells, reputedly the earliest surviving prizes for horse-racing in the country, are displayed in Carlisle Museum. There are also many records of prizes in

23.   The Town Hall in 1780. Note the single stairway.

24.   Carlisle Cathedral *c*.1800.

corporation and guild accounts of the 17th century. Another 'sport' was catered for by a cock-pit that was erected in 1785 by the Duke of Norfolk and Sir James Lowther, on the west side of Lowther Street. In 1835 cock-fighting was made illegal, and the pit became a smithy. It was demolished in 1876. The bowling-green at Spring Gardens, shown on the map of 1746, is evidence of rather more refined tastes.

Religion

At the end of the 18th century the Anglican Church was in decline. Neglect and poverty were evident throughout the diocese, with pluralism and absenteeism widespread. Catholicism was debilitated too, and only recovered in the following century with the influx of the Irish. This was provoked by the evictions of c.1816 and the failure of the potato crop in 1846. In the late 18th and early 19th centuries, the Methodists became the main dissenting group. Their evangelism led them to welcome warmly all those without traditional allegiance, and the group grew rapidly. John Wesley first preached in Carlisle in 1770, when there were only 15 members. He visited again in 1780-1, and in 1785-6 the Methodists built their first chapel, in Fisher Street, where they joined two other dissenting groups. The Quakers were a smaller group, but were prominent in industry and trade. They met in Carlisle from the early 18th century, and opened the Friends' Meeting House in Fisher Street in 1776. The Scottish Presbyterians opened their chapel there in 1731. In 1783 the Methodists broke from the Church of England, as the Anglicans disliked 'enthusiasm' and the bishops refused to ordain Methodist ministers. The chapel was enlarged considerably in 1795, and when the Carlisle circuit was formed, in 1801, there were 290 members. In 1805, Carlisle displaced Whitehaven as the chief circuit of Cumberland, and in 1817 a second chapel, to seat 1,100 people, was built on the site of the present Methodist Central Hall, in Fisher Street.

*   *   *   *   *

Carlisle was not unchallenged as the predominant town in Cumberland throughout its history. At the end of the 17th century Whitehaven, created by the Lowther family, experienced a phenomenal but short-lived period of growth. In 1775 its population was 10,000, and it was the third largest port in Britain. As late as 1816 Whitehaven was recognised as one of the largest towns in the north of England.[46]

Chapter Eight

The Industrial Revolution in Carlisle

The industrial revolution of the late 18th and the first half of the 19th centuries was arguably the most significant period in Carlisle's history. Two facets, of overriding importance, will receive primary attention: the dynamic growth of the textile industry, and the efforts to create a transport system necessary to support large-scale industry.

Early industry and the growth of the factory system

Carlisle's textile industry began to develop in the 18th century. The first factory to which there is reference is a woollen manufactory, which was set up in December 1724 when the Guliker brothers leased the abbey mill from the corporation. The firm produced broad and plain cloths, but went bankrupt in 1740.[1] A short-lived woollen manufactory was started by George Blamire and Richard Ferguson in 1746 at premises below the Town Hall. Wool was not suitable initially for large-scale mechanisation and was not competitive when America's plantations started to pour out cheap cotton. It did not reappear until the cotton industry was in trouble 100 years later. In 1750 R. and W. Hodgson started to manufacture a coarse linen cloth called Osnaburghs, a coloured stripe and check fabric which was exported to the southern part of North America for the clothing of slaves. Some years later, fustian (a mixture of linen and cotton yarns) was made in Caldewgate, and there was a large weekly market for wool.[2] The initial impetus for the growth of large-scale industry was provided by improved roads. For example, the Newcastle firm of Scot Lamb set up a calico printing business in Carlisle in 1761, the Newcastle to Carlisle turnpike having opened in 1758. They were soon to employ hundreds of men, women and children, as the soft waters of the Caldew were suitable for bleaching. This prepared cloth for printing, and was a lengthy process, often taking six to eight months. Cloth was exposed to sun and rain, and steeped in alkaline solutions. Much land was occupied around the city by printfields, in which the cloth was laid out. In 1794 there were four of them, that provided employment for about a thousand people.[3] It was the development of bleaching powder *c.*1800 that made the printfields obsolete, and on Jollie's map of 1811 there are no references to them.

From 1758 Carlisle received a boost in money supply, which led to the expectation of a more expensive lifestyle. Several hundred French prisoners taken in the Seven Years War were sent to the city, where the officers were hardly restricted. They each received an allowance of 7s. per week, generous compared with contemporary labourers' wages of 8-10d. per day. Money circulation was also increased by the stationing of the Westmorland militia in Carlisle. The influx of wealth and development of industry, including, for example, breweries and an iron foundry as well as the burgeoning textile industry, affected society as a whole. Banking services for the increasingly capitalist economy were also established, rapidly becoming specialised businesses in their own right rather than appendages of industrial firms. A study of the handloom weavers in the city exemplifies the rapid growth, technical innovation and eventual human cost of the industrial revolution.

Handloom Weavers

In the early decades of the 19th century there was an explosive growth in the population of Carlisle. Massive immigration of poverty-stricken Irish and Scots led inevitably to the erosion of wage rates and the lowering of living standards, as an over-abundant labour supply made the weavers vulnerable to exploitation. The greatest growth in population took place in the new industrial areas outside the city walls, principally to the west and south, on the low-lying area by the Caldew and the corporation dam. The following table illustrates the population growth from 1788-1851, dividing Carlisle into two areas: the extramural (Rickergate, Caldewgate and Botchergate) and intramural (English, Scotch, Fisher, Castle and Abbey Streets).

	Intramural		Extramural	
	Population	% growth	Population	% growth
1788	4,761		2,555	
1801	5,745	20	3,882	51
1811	6,145	7	5,467	40
1821	7,199	17	7,362	34
1831	8,356	16	10,713	45
1841	8,456	2	13,227	23
1851	8,307	−2	18,039	36[4]

The number of handloom weavers in the city can be calculated from the Muggeridge report of 1840. Of a total population of 21,200 there were 2,439 adults and children employed in weaving, with 18 per cent of the total population dependent directly upon the weavers' earnings.[5] It appears that the number of looms in use peaked c.1840, rising from 1,200 in 1816 to 1,963. By 1846 there had been a substantial decline to 1,600 looms.[6] Even in the 1860s many weavers were still eking out a living on their antiquated machines.[7]

In 1770, a weaver's output had been limited by the supply of yarn.[8] Hargreaves' spinning jenny, patented in 1770, revolutionised this, and when Arkwright's water frame took the production of yarn from cottage to factory, in the 1780s, possible output increased enormously. Kay's flying shuttle, on the weavers' looms, introduced in the 1750s and 1760s, had been limited at first by the bottleneck in yarn production, but at the turn of the century, when the mule (a cross between water frame and spinning jenny) appeared, all brakes on the weavers' output were removed. These innovations help to explain why wages increased so dramatically for weavers, between 1770 and the boom years at the beginning of the 19th century. In 1770, 8s. to 10s.6d. per week could be earned by a head of household, while Eden records an increase in income in the 1790s: 'A good weaver, with constant work, can earn 12s. to 15s. a week, but in general 8s. or 9s. a week seem to be the usual earnings'.[9] When the mule was introduced at the end of the century the weavers reached the zenith of their prosperity.

Wages during this period, and their subsequent decline, are related to the price of food and rent in Table 1.[10] After the boom year of 1805 until the end of the Napoleonic Wars, in 1815, earnings were reduced but still remained high. It was hoped that the considerable wartime market would be replaced by the opening-up to trade of the continent and America, but it was not the weavers who benefited from this. The export of great quantities of yarn enabled foreign weavers to expand their cloth production, and supply their own markets. This not only reduced the demand for English cloth, but also weakened the weavers' bargaining position with their employers. Absence of effective regulation of the labour force by unions or guild, the continued influx of immigrants and the laissez-faire attitude of the government caused a devastating fall in income after the war. As the secretary to the committee of weavers stated in his evidence to the Muggeridge report: 'It is in the power of the masters to reduce wages arbitrarily in weaving. The weavers are too poor to support

25.   The cottage-based textile industry. a. spinning wheel.
b. hand loom. c. spinning jenny.

Table 1
Average wage (shillings and pence) for hand loom weavers

Year	Weekly wage	7 year period	Average wage	Average over 7 years Food in lbs	Rent Index
1797	29s.				
1798	30s.				
1799–1801	25s.	1797–1804	28s. 8d.	281	6
1802	29s.				
1803–4	24s.				
1805	25s.				
1806	22s.				
1807	18s.	1804–1811	20s.	238	9
1808	15s.				
1809	16s.				
1810	19s. 6d.				
1811–12	14s.				
1813	15s.				
1814	24s.				
1815	14s.	1811–1818	14s. 7d.	131	12⅓
1816	12s.				
1817–18	9s.				
1819–20	9s. 6d.	1818–1825	8s. 9d.	108	16
1821–25	8s. 6d.				
1826	7s.				
1827	6s. 6d.	1825–1832	6s. 4d.	83	22
1828	6s.				
1829–36	5s. 6d.	1832–1834	5s. 6d.	83	25
1837	4s. 6d.				
1838	5s. 6d.				

The table should be interpreted thus: from 1797 to 1804 a weaver could earn 26s. 8d. per week which would buy him 100 lbs of flour, or 142 lb of oatmeal, or 826 lbs of potatoes, or 55 lbs of butchers meat. This would give a general average of relative proportions of these articles of 281 lbs. The rent index shows the relative amount of work that a weaver would have to perform to meet his rent. Thus six pieces of woven cloth would be required in the period 1797-1804, but for the last period (1832-1834) he would need to weave 25 pieces.

a strike and too numerous and too much scattered over the country to support a union'.[11] In the post-war years, wages fell to below subsistence level, partly because they were subsidised by the poor rate. In the first twenty years of the century, even before the widespread introduction of the power loom, poverty was rife. The *Carlisle Journal* reported in 1812 that 1,081 families, 39 per cent of the population, were receiving poor relief, the majority being weavers.[12] In 1819, the *Journal* asserted that:

> An eighth of the population consists of paupers living on the contribution of the rest.
> Three eighths have low wages and live on a pittance.
> A quarter with difficulty support their families.
> An eighth – the middle class – struggle to maintain their place in society.
> An eighth are exempt from this disorganised state of existence.[13]

About half of the population of Carlisle lived in dire poverty, while another quarter only survived with a struggle.

Two other influences on wage rates must be considered. In 1834 the Poor Law Amendment Act was passed. Although supposed to end the Speenhamland system, thus reducing the poor rate and permitting wages to rise to their true market level, its operation was tempered by economic expediency rather than compassion.[14] This is illustrated by the case of a Carlisle weaver which was cited in the commissioners' report :

A weaver, who had four children under ten, and whose wife had been sick for eight months presented a bill for the quarter's house rent, 13s.6d.; he had 4s. weekly as a regular allowance, on account of sickness in his family; strong objections were made by two of the members [of the Management Board] against paying his rent. The allowance system they urged was only an inducement to the master weavers to lower wages; many had lately increased the length of the cut, without proportionately increasing the price, which however they termed raising the wages. It was admitted that the weavers, in order to complete the cut by Saturday morning, often worked the whole of Friday night, and every day 12 or 14 hours. The applicant offered to put his children, except the eldest who assisted him in weaving, into the [work] house; his demand [for rent relief] was ultimately granted, as having the children in the [work] house would entail a greater expense. The above weaver stated his claims to be 6s. weekly.[15]

The act did not terminate outdoor relief; nor did it persuade employers to increase wages: Table 1 shows that by 1837 the average wage had fallen to 4s.6d. per week. The second influence was the introduction of the power loom. Cartwright's loom was invented in 1785, but its development was initially unsuccessful, and it was not until 1803-13 that patents were taken out for improved machines. Carlisle was to the fore in pioneering the new invention, and Jollie wrote in 1811 that 'Messrs. Holme have their manufactory for weaving, which is performed by the cast iron looms, that go by steam, and which they have the credit of introducing into this part'. Early power looms were constructed in Carlisle as well, and Jollie mentions 'the workshop of Mr. Marsden'.[16] Despite the sixfold increase in productivity and corresponding financial advantage, notwithstanding the lower rate for each piece of cloth, the widespread adoption of the power loom was surprisingly late in Carlisle. In 1829 only 89 were used, out of a total of 55,000 in Britain, but in the next 10 years Carlisle followed the national trend. The drop in wages from 1825 can be related to the increased use of power looms, but by 1829 the wage rate had stabilised and was not influenced by further mechanisation. Wages were below subsistence by this time, and could not well be reduced without an outcry from the ratepayers.

In 1841 the city council appointed a mendicity society to enquire into the state of the poor, and to devise methods for their temporary relief. A summary of their findings is given in Table 2, which shows that 309 families (1,146 individuals) were destitute and entirely reliant on public charity. In total, 1,351 families (5,561 people), a quarter of Carlisle's population, were living on 3s. or less per week, with the greatest concentration of poor in the Caldewgate and Botchergate districts. The deprivation of the handloom weaver has been depicted mainly in statistical terms, but in 1846 Jerrold described the living conditions of the city's weavers:

On what do these people live? Oatmeal gruel forms their breakfast; potatoes with dripping or the liquid fat from a little morsel of bacon, their dinner; and either a drink of beer (so small that it is sold at a penny a gallon!) or a mere drink called 'tea' is taken with bread as the evening meal. Butcher's meat, many of these men and their families do not taste often for six, nine, or twelve months together. As to clothing, a hand-loom weaver, after marriage, scarcely expects to purchase a new coat; he may be able to obtain a second hand one from a pawn shop, stores are usually to be had that have remained past the legal time of redemption, but a patched up covering he has had for years is usually all his change for a Sunday . . . he saunters in the lanes or into the fields, rather than show his tatters and threadbare habit in church or chapel. The loom shops, which usually hold 4 looms, and less frequently, but two, are wretched places. For avoiding dryness that would injure their work, they are sunk below the level of the street, and are unpaved either with brick or stone. I shall never forget my visit to one of these squalid cells where the family lived. A

26. The factory-based textile industry. a. spinning mule. b. water frame. c. power loom.

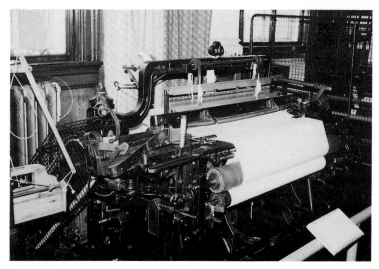

Table 2

The State of the Poor in Carlisle: 1841 (Carlisle Journal 1 January 1842)

DISTRICT	CALDEWGATE	ST CUTHBERT'S	ST MARY'S	BOTCHERGATE	RICKERGATE	TOTAL
No settled income						
Families	88	25	5	133	58	309
Persons	326	98	10	506	206	1,146
Less than 1s. per week						
Families	108	40	20	120	46	334
Persons	497	194	60	570	162	1,465
Less than 1s. 6d. per head per week						
Families	226	45	27	61	52	411
Persons	914	228	65	242	174	1,625
Less than 2s. per head per week						
Families	34	56	5	36	26	157
Persons	141	274	20	127	130	692
Less than 3s. per head per week						
Families	56	58	6	20	—	140
Persons	314	223	25	73	—	635
Total Number						
Families	512	224	63	370	182	1,351
Persons	2,174	1,017	180	1,518	672	5,561

The total population of Carlisle in 1842 was approximately 22,000 father with his daughter and 2 boys were working in it – but this man has taken a room overhead, as a sleeping place for the whole family. His daughter's average earnings were 4s. weekly, the elder boy's 2s. and the younger boy's 1s.6d.; for having to attend to his children's work, he could not earn more than 6s. himself. Thus a man, his wife, his daughter, 2 boys and an infant had thus to be supported on 13s.6d. a week. The weaver's house – or rather room – for he has often but one for himself and family has to be rented.[17]

The handloom weavers were of course an integral part of the factory system, which eventually replaced them. The development of two of Carlisle's largest firms illustrates the growth and mechanisation of the industry which was at first so beneficial and later so devastating for the weavers.

The Great Carlisle Textile Firms
The Fergusons of Holme Head: As mentioned above, Richard Ferguson started a linen business in 1746. His sons, John, Richard and George, leased a six-acre site at Warwick Bridge in 1790, and built a mill there, together with dyehouses and warehouses. A water-wheel was erected, and a 700-yard mill-race harnessed the Cairn Beck. When a fire destroyed the mill in August 1793, the *Cumberland Pacquet* reported that the main building had been gutted, part of the water-powered carding engine had been damaged and also cotton twist, produced on water frames. This implies that factory-based cotton-spinning was established by this date, although mechanisation of weaving had to wait to the next century. The mill was rebuilt on a massive scale, by the standards of the day, and the Fergusons carried on the business until 1809, when they leased the mill to their brother-in-law, Peter Dixon, and his sons. The subsequent history of Dixon's is reviewed below. In 1824, Joseph Ferguson, of the third generation, began to dye and finish cotton goods at

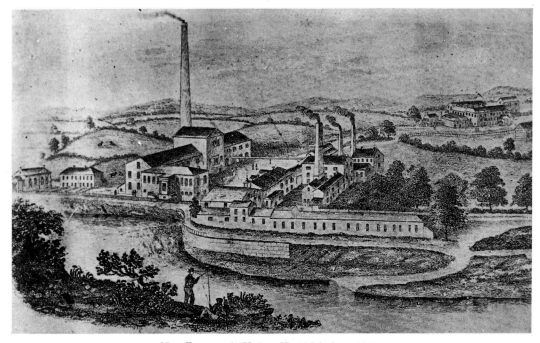

27.   Ferguson's Holme Head Works, *c.*1854.

the Friggate Works – on the old millrace about five hundred yards north of the present Holme Head Works. He introduced 'beetling' of the cotton cloth (pounding it, to produce a silken finish), similar to the treatment of linen. The product, named 'Silesias' by Ferguson, was an immediate success in the United States. In 1828 he opened another mill at Holme Head, previously occupied by Carrick and Johnston, the cotton spinners. The firm continued to prosper and a new works for dyeing and finishing was built in 1837. Joseph Ferguson took a paternal interest in his employees, providing cottages and allotments for them, and also a school for their children. In 1852 Ferguson completed the purchase of the Holme Head estate, but was still in business only as a finisher. It was in 1865, two years after Ferguson's death, that the firm erected a spinning mill and weaving shed, thus becoming an integrated manufacturer. In the second half of the century, the firm installed new plant and pioneered new systems of dyeing and finishing, and early in the 20th century large extensions were made to the spinning and weaving machinery, the printing, dyeing and bleach works and the finishing plant, so that by the time of its centenary in 1924, Ferguson's was a major cotton manufacturer of international repute.

Peter Dixon

When Peter Dixon and his sons took over Langthwaite Mill from the Fergusons in 1809, the original three-storey mill was extended with a new wing of four storeys and an attic, and a new reservoir was built to increase the water supply. This extension was financed by a £6,694 loan to the Dixons from their uncle, George Ferguson. In 1832 a steam engine was installed (coal being supplied by the canal) to supplement the power supply and make it secure at times of low water. When James Losh visited in 1826 he reported that the works operated 24 hours a day: 'The day labourer working from 6 a.m. to 7.30 p.m. and the night labourer 7.30 p.m. to 6 a.m.', made possible by the installation of gas lighting.[18]

When the Dixons erected Shaddon Mills in Carlisle in 1836 they made an abortive attempt to sell Langthwaite Mill. A sale notice refers to the imminent opening of the Newcastle-Carlisle railway, an adjacent coal depot, dye-houses big enough for 130 vats, a bleach-house, 34 cottages, a gas-house and accommodation for a steam engine.[19] Clearly the factory was keeping abreast of new technology, and it continued to prosper. Additional machinery was installed, and by 1847 the firm employed 320 people. Shaddon Mills was a magnificent building of seven storeys, with ground plan dimensions of 224 by 58 ft., and a chimney that was 305 ft. high. A factory of this size could not have operated with the available water power, and steam power was used from the beginning: the factory had a large engine-house and a boiler-house with seven boilers. Coal was imported from West Cumberland by canal, and from 1838 by the Carlisle and Newcastle railway. Peter Dixon and Sons was to become a major industrial enterprise, and it was claimed that the factory '. . . alone gives employment in the various departments of their cotton works to about 8,000 hands'.[20] Of course Dixon's had their considerable factory at Warwick Bridge too, and they used handloom weavers, employed in their own cottages, within a 20-mile radius. This system was supplemented in the 1840s, when they erected a building that housed several hundred power looms.

In the 1860s the supply of American raw cotton was cut off by the civil war (1861-65), and the freeing of American slaves also affected Carlisle:

The golden age of the cotton trade in Carlisle fell with the abolition of slavery in America. Formerly every great slave plantation took a large quantity of ginghams for its negroes, and always adhered to the same pattern . . . but the free negro demands a gaudier article; he is capricious, and must be tickled and attracted by new patterns. This altered state of things the Carlisle spinners have, from various causes, been unable to adapt themselves to, and it seems probable that the trade will shortly leave Carlisle.[21]

28. Langthwaite Mill at Warwick Bridge, taken over from the Ferguson brothers by Peter Dixon in 1809.

29. Shaddon Mills, erected in 1836.

Peter James Dixon, John Dixon and Joseph Forster were declared bankrupt on their own petition in 1872, as a direct result of these problems. A new joint stock company, Peter Dixon and Sons Ltd., was formed in January 1873, acquiring Langthwaite Mill and the Carlisle factories, but it ceased to trade in 1883. The greatest of the Carlisle cotton firms had ceased to adapt to the changing conditions of trade, or to diversify into new products with new technology.

These firms and others like them could not have developed so much or so fast without the support of a transport system which allowed large-scale trade and the carriage of raw materials. This was provided by the canal, which played a vital rôle in the history of Carlisle.

The Carlisle Canal

At the end of the 18th century Carlisle was expanding rapidly, the population having increased from 4,000 to 9,600 between 1756 and 1790. The directories of 1790 and 1811 indicate the increasing specialisation of trades and professions, but industry was still small-scale and dependent on road transport. This dependence imposed a limit on industrial expansion, so the bulk transport system had to be developed, as was recognised at the time:

> The increase of population is owing to the advance in trade and manufacturers, at present flourishing and progressive. Carlisle, from its central situation, is well adjusted for the extension of trade, and may by the exertion of a liberal and public spirit, vie with the first manufacturing towns in the Kingdom. A canal from the Western sea to Carlisle would facilitate the progress of trade, increase the wealth of the rich, and make living more comfortable to the poor.[22]

Three of the remarkable polymaths of the late 18th and early 19th century, who played an important rôle in the development of industrial Britain, independently put forward plans for the construction of such a canal. These men were William Chapman, Thomas Harrison and Thomas Telford.[23] Their proposals were all radically different, as no firm criteria were specified. In 1795 the first scheme was submitted by Chapman, for 'a canal across the narrow waist of Britain between Newcastle and Carlisle and Maryport.[24] This was supported more enthusiastically in Newcastle than in Carlisle, however, and the plan was dropped. A committee was formed in 1807 to promote a canal to the sea, so that the city's coal supply could be improved. Chapman was asked to report, and gave his preference for a terminus as Maryport, with its existing harbour and coal supplies. If his estimated cost of £90,000-£100,000 was too great, he also suggested a terminus east of Bowness. A canal to take 45-ton craft, which would be capable of the short coastal voyage to Maryport, would cost about £40,000. If this could be enlarged to take 90-ton vessels, at an extra cost of £55,000-£60,000, they would be able to trade throughout the Irish Sea and through the Forth-Clyde canal to North Sea ports. Such a canal, Chapman envisaged, could be a step towards a sea-to-sea waterway.[25]

The next scheme was submitted in the following year, by Thomas Harrison. This was a grandiose scheme which envisaged Carlisle as the 'Emporium of North West England', to rival the ports of Liverpool and Glasgow. His suggestion was a canal capable of taking ships of 4-500 tons, so that direct trading with America and the West Indies would be possible without transhipment at the canal entrance.[26] Later in 1808 the committee consulted Thomas Telford. He agreed with the use of Bowness as a port, and also envisaged an eventual link to Newcastle.[27] The committee deferred their decision for a decade, and in 1818 Chapman submitted another report. This recommended a route from Fisher's Cross to Carlisle at an estimated cost of £73,382, with a later extension to Newcastle. The canal was to take small vessels which would be capable of the short and sheltered coastal journey from Fisher's Cross to Maryport, where cargoes would be transferred to ocean-going ships.[28] The report was accepted, and it is significant that the subscriptions to it from Carlisle industrialists matched those from the great landowners.[29] This indicates not only a substantial cotton industry before the canal, but also recognition that bulk transport by waterways was required if the industry was to grow and prosper. Chapman's estimate of total annual tonnage emphasises the importance of low-weight but high-value goods such as cotton, yarn and manufactured goods for export, even though heavy materials such as fuel, lime and stone formed most of the cargo.[30]

   The canal was opened in 1823. It was 11¾ miles long, 54 ft. wide and 8 ft. 6 in. deep. The locks were 78 ft. long and 18 ft. 3 in. wide. A wooden jetty was built into the Solway at Fisher's Cross (re-named Port Carlisle), and the basin was approached through an entrance lock. In all there were eight additional locks before reaching the Carlisle basin, which measured 450 ft. by 120 ft. The total rise from the sea was 70 ft. The route was favourable, no bridges being necessary, and the canal was used by coastal craft of less than 100 tons. At the Carlisle basin a three-storey brick warehouse and a building for coal and lime storage was built. The canal was supplied with water from the Eden and Caldew, and from a reservoir to its south in the parishes of Grinsdale and Kirkandrews-upon-Eden.

30.   Carlisle Canal share certificate.

31.   The canal basin in 1835. (J.W. Carmichael.)

The opening ceremony took place on 12 March, and 18-20,000 people lined the banks.[31] The *Carlisle Journal* reported the proceedings:

> About nine o'clock the Committee of the Canal Company proceeded in coaches to Burgh, where the vessels (fourteen in number) were waiting orders to advance; and having taken their place on board the 'Robert Burns', the whole moved forward in two divisions elegantly decorated with a profusion of handsome flags and streamers, and some of them were provided with small cannon which were frequently fired during their progress. At 15 minutes before three o'clock the 'Robert Burns', Captain Geddes, with a general cargo from Liverpool, preceded by an excellent band of music in a boat, entered the Basin amidst loud continued cheering, and at the moment of her entry a salute of 21 guns was fired from two 6-pound field pieces which had been procured from the Castle and placed at the entrance of the canal, and the signal was promptly answered by 21 guns from the batteries of the Castle.[32]

In theory, Carlisle was now integrated into the national economic system, and the committee attempted to build up a commercial trade. The treasury waived coastal duties on coal, stone and slate carried between Whitehaven and Carlisle, but private enterprise was slow in initiating a coal trade. The committee itself had to ship the first cargo from West Cumberland and sell it in Carlisle. In the following year it took the initiative again, and imported two boat-loads of brick for public sale. A timber-yard had also been built by the committee.

The newly-formed Carlisle and Liverpool Steam Navigation Company was granted an exclusive berth at Port Carlisle in 1825. This was to be built by the canal company and paid for over 10 years. The Steam Navigation Company then bought a second-hand packet-boat, the *Bailie Nicol Jarvis*, and offered it for lease. The combination of steam-boat in the

32.   Ships berthed in the canal basin. This picture shows the type of boats that used the canal.

Solway and packet-boat on the canal enabled passengers to leave Carlisle in the morning and arrive at Liverpool during the evening. The passenger trade grew, and the *Solway Hotel* was built at Port Carlisle.[33] A second steam navigation company, the Carlisle, Annan and Liverpool, started operation in 1833.

Chapter Nine

The Social Consequences of the Industrial Revolution

Unregulated economic growth affected Carlisle dramatically. The fabric of the city was radically changed, and while industrial development benefited some of the citizens it had a devastating effect on others. A sharp increase in the number of inhabitants led to overcrowding, and the related problems of poor sanitation and disease.[1]

Insanitary housing conditions

The pressure on housing in the city was caused predominantly by the great influx of immigrants in the early 19th century. Rawlinson reported in 1850 that

> A great portion of the present crowded state of the buildings is comparatively modern. Most of the confined lanes, yards, courts and alleys were, in the first instance, gardens attached to houses, fronting the main streets. These houses have gradually been changed from private dwellings into shops, hotels, taverns, stables, workshops, offices and outhouses, until every available open space has now been built upon.[2]

Conditions in the city were grossly overcrowded and insanitary:

> The working classes of Carlisle live almost entirely in lanes, between the principal and secondary streets . . . it is asserted that from 9 to 10 thousand persons reside in these lanes, courts and alleys . . . Many of these lanes are entered by a covered passage and some are closed at one end. They are in general only a few yards in width. In some the doors are opposite each other and not more than 3 yards apart . . . in many instances there is only one privy to a whole lane and these ruinous and filthy. In some lanes privies and middens are crowded among the houses and not infrequently under the same roof. They are in contact with a dwelling house on each side and have living and sleeping rooms above them. The infiltration from the middens and liquid refuse in contact with the wall, in some instances passes through, to the great inconvenience of the adjoining occupants. Some of the cottages are built back to back when in a single row they have all the faults of a double structure in not having windows, or ventilation openings, in the back or side walls. The houses are let off in tenancies having one common stair to several tenancies.[3]

Two particular locations can be studied in detail from plans included in the 1845 Reid report (Ills. 33 and 34). The first covers a congested housing block bounded by Fisher Street, St Alban's Row, Scotch Street and Rosemary Lane. It was an area of narrow courts and lanes, with access by covered passages, and houses and shops were adjacent to privies, ash-pits, pigsties and stables with no sewers or drains. (The proposed sewers shown on the plan had not been installed by 1850.) Ash-pits and privies were situated below bedrooms and adjacent to kitchens. One cellar kitchen shared a building with a stable, alongside an ash-pit marked 'very foul'. The second plan shows the 'Lanes' area, which was also described by Rawlinson:

> This block of property consists of lanes, courts, out-yards, banks, shops, hotels, stables and cow sheds, schools and dwelling houses, amongst which are crowded and confined yards, privies and cess pools, middens and other nuisances. Many of the privies and cess pools are in immediate contact with the dwelling houses. Some are within them, the cesspools and middens extending beneath the living or sleeping-room floor. Drainage is either absent or most imperfect, surface

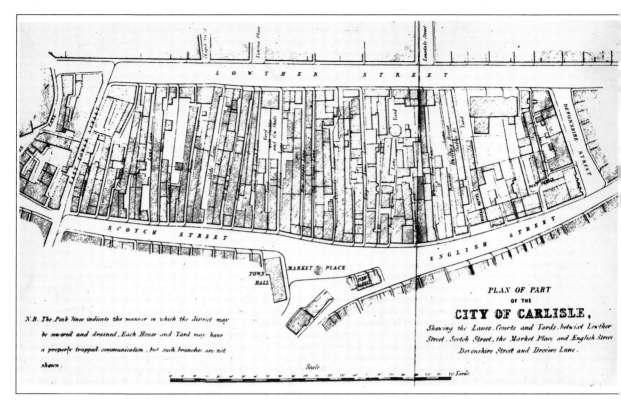

33.   Plan of part of the city of Carlisle, 1845.

34.   Plan of a portion of the city of Carlisle, 1845.

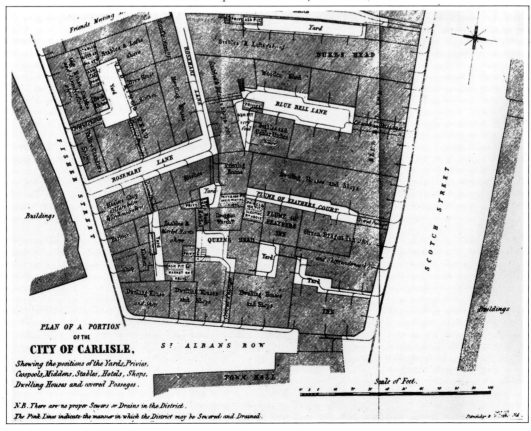

channels alone having been provided, not however with any view to refuse drainage for this purpose they ought not to be used, but merely to carry away rainfall.[4]

Rawlinson deplored this state of affairs. The absence of street ventilation was a problem that

> most intimately concerns rate-payers and inhabitants generally. It is of serious importance to the wealthy, as also to every class who own house-property; but, connected with house ventilation, it is health or disease, life or death, to the working man and his family. No fact is more firmly established than the one which places foul air, and excess of epidemic, endemic, and contagious diseases, as cause and effect.[5]

The dangers of such conditions to public health remain unchallenged, but the belief that foul air caused illness was superseded in medical circles by the theory of germs in the latter part of the century.

The squalor of the inner city was, on the evidence of the Rawlinson report, exceeded only by the low-lying industrial areas outside the city gates. In Moffat's Yard, adjacent to West Tower Street, for example, 'there is only one privy for 28 families, other properties being without conveniences at all, and in some of the lodging houses more than 20 people are living in one room, and that adjacent to the filthiest privies and dunghills'.[6]

It is evident from contemporary records that there were degrees of extreme poverty in an impoverished community. Two groups will be singled out: the handloom weavers and the lowest class of all, the tramps and vagrants who lived in lodging houses. Reid draws attention to the crowded living conditions of the handloom weavers, aggravated in many cases by the necessity of erecting the loom in the main room. He describes Brown's Row:

> ... about 40 dwellings and 281 inhabitants, and is almost entirely occupied by weavers ... One side of the street consists of dwellings almost peculiar to it, being 5 or 6 cottages of one storey, and in many cases containing the loom in the dwelling room; the floor is below the level of the street, and the ceiling is very low. Another description of rooms met with in this place (and common to several other places, viz. Broadguards, Duke-street, Water-street, etc.) is very small bed-rooms, partitioned from the general apartments only sufficiently large to take two beds, with a small space of from one foot and a half to two feet between them; when the door is closed, and these beds occupied by 5 or 6 individuals, the atmosphere must be almost suffocating.[7]

Undoubtedly the worst housing conditions were to be found in the common lodging houses, lived in by craftsmen in search of work and beggars, who were always moving from place to place. There were 72 lodging houses in Carlisle: 17 in Botchergate, 14 in East Tower Street, 13 in Caldewgate, 12 in both Scotch Street and Rickergate, and four in English Street. There were '360 men, women and children sleeping habitually within the city, without any means of observing the rules of decency ... they constitute one large forcing bed for the generation of vice'.[8]

In the absence of a sewage system, refuse and sewage built up in the streets, to the detriment of the city's water supply:

> Very few houses have proper necessaries, none are arranged to empty into drains; a few empty into cess-pools, but the greater proportion are connected into ash pits. The contents are taken out in barrows (during the night) and carted away to farmers in the neighbourhood to whom they are sold ... many of the inferior houses have no privies. There are no public necessaries.[9]

The water supply was a major health hazard. Water was obtained either from the river, or from shallow wells, which were liable to be impregnated with the contents of cesspools, sewers and graveyards. 'The common well water used in Carlisle was scarcely fit to be used by the lowest class of animals, and the pumped water supply only marginally better.'[10] In general water for household use was sold from carts. At 1d. for eight gallons it was a scarce commodity for a poor household. As Reid commented, 'Many of the poor are in the habit of getting water from tradespeople. Great complaints have been made, both as to the mode of supply of water, the quantity to be obtained, the quality, and the price'.[11] In a few of the main streets there was under-drainage, but 'it is wholly defective . . . In consequence of the defective state of the sewers the corporation now refused to grant leave for opening communications with water closets'.[12] One of the most offensive features of the drainage system was the open sewer that surrounded the city and emptied into the rivers. In addition to all these problems, there were 18 slaughterhouses in Carlisle, chiefly situated in the courts and lanes, and without proper drainage.

The apathy of the corporation, that permitted unregulated building and insanitary conditions, was not shared by all citizens. In 1831 a voluntary body, the Carlisle Sanitary Association, was formed. It sought to galvanise all sections of society into remedial action. Property owners had it in their power 'to remedy many of the evils loudly complained of

35.   Slum property. a. Union Court in the Lanes, photographed in 1981. b. Bay Horse Lane, Rickergate, in 1937.

by the poorer classes, who live in immediate contact with, and grievously suffer from the existence of these nuisances', but the labouring classes were not blameless: 'many who are unfortunately obliged to live in dirty and otherwise objectionable tenements are by no means so limited in their resources as to be entirely helpless in the cause of sanitary reform'.[13] The system of biennial or triennial inspections instituted by the association continued until superseded by city administration and the appointment of a medical officer in 1874. Other signs of improvement from mid-century included the gradual provision of a safe water supply and the erection of new housing stock, notably artisan housing in west Carlisle in 1857 and middle-class housing in the east of the city, later in the century. This followed the publication of the great social reports, in which slums were recognised as such, rather than just an inevitable part of urban life.

Despite·the poverty, Carlisle and its environs were home to an increasing number of wealthy industrialists and professional men, who sought to emulate the minor gentry on their country estates. In his diary of 1826, James Losh wrote: 'proceeding to the Dukery, four or five houses belonging to some of the nouveaux riches at Carlisle. These are on the north side . . . at a distance of three or four miles and . . . the views are very fine'.[14] Villas were erected or remodelled, overwhelmingly in the Classical style, on the outskirts of the city at this time.[15]

Disease and mortality

More than 50 years before the great social surveys of Britain in the 1830s and 1840s, Dr. John Heysham of Carlisle recorded the annual births, marriages and deaths in Carlisle.[16] His demographic statistics cover the period 1779 to 1788, and their quality was confirmed by Milne, who based his 'Carlisle Life Table' on them. This was used by life assurance offices until the late 19th century, and is reproduced here as Table 3. Taken with Table 4, the horrendous child mortality rates are revealed, illustrating, for example, that if a child survived to the age of three, his life expectancy leapt from 39 to 53.

Table 3

Mortality rates and life expectancy of different age groups in Carlisle, averaged over the years 1779–1787.

Age	Mortality rate p.a.%	Life Expectancy
0)		39
1)		46
2)	8.23	50
3)		53
4)		55
5)		56
10	1.02	58
15	0.50	60
25	0.69	63
35	0.9	66
45	1.26	69
55	1.48	73
65	2.95	77
75	5.44	82
85	12.53	89
95	24.58	99

Smallpox was the only major epidemic disease of the 18th and 19th centuries which was contained by medicine, and inoculation was particularly effective in Carlisle, after initial hostility. Heysham claimed that in the second half of 1779 none of the several hundred who had been inoculated against smallpox, but 90 of the 300 infected with the disease had

Table 4
Tables of mortality for Carlisle 1779-1787
Causes of deaths for children under five years of age

Year	Smallpox	Scarlet Fever	Measles	Thrush	Consumption
1779	86	31		2	3
1780	3		28	12	4
1781	17		1	9	2
1782	28			10	7
1783	17			6	4
1784	9			6	1
1785	39			11	6
1786	1		26	11	3
1787	28		1	8	8
Total	228	31	56	75	38

Year	Weakness of Infancy	Other	Total all deaths	Child mortality rate p.a.%
1779	9	19	150	14.6
1780	37	19	103	10.1
1781	25	14	68	6.6
1782	19	14	78	7.4
1783	34	12	73	6.9
1784	23	7	46	4.5
1785	24	16	96	9.4
1786	39	29	109	10.3
1787	31	13	89	7.6
Total	241	143	812	7.8

The 812 deaths for the nine years for children under five is 44 per cent of the total number of deaths (1,840) for all age groups, of the total population. The total child population of the city was estimated as 1,029 in 1779 and 1,164 in 1787.

died. He lamented that 'so great is this prejudice against the salutary practice of inoculation amongst the vulgar, that few, very few, can be prevailed upon either by promises, rewards or entreaties to submit to this operation'.[17] When smallpox was rife again, in 1785, great numbers of the poor were inoculated at the Dispensary, and Heysham reported in 1787 that 'inoculation soon became general which prevented the disorder from raging with any great degree of violence'.[18] From 1798 vaccination began to replace the more dangerous inoculation, and in 1800 Heysham vaccinated his youngest daughter. The mortality rates in the city showed an encouraging downward trend by the turn of the century.[19]

Period	Mortality rate p.a. %	Population
1779-87	2.49	6,500
1787-95	2.6	7,000
1796-1800	2.33	8,500
1800-1810	2.33	10,000

In the low-lying districts of Carlisle typhus was endemic. There was a severe outbreak in 1781; in eight months 500 people were affected, and there were 48 deaths.[20] With the help of the dean and chapter, Heysham established in a small room over the abbey gate the city's first dispensary for the poor. It was moved later to St Cuthbert's Lane. In the 14 years from its foundation in July 1782, 11,382 patients were treated there. Between 1782

36.   Dr. Heysham.

and 1787 the cases of typhus treated increased from 26 to 252 a year, but the deaths in the city remained remarkably constant, at between 14-16 a year.[21] Typhus visited Carlisle again in 1837-8 and 1840-1, with a total of 1,223 recorded cases.

Cholera was a disastrous epidemic that was almost entirely confined to the most congested and insanitary parts of the city. In 1832 there were 448 recorded cases, with a mortality rate of one in three. A second epidemic in 1834 left 22 of the 33 patients dead.

There was no provision for in-patients in Carlisle before 1820, when a small infectious diseases hospital, the House of Recovery, opened in Collier Lane. The Cumberland Infirmary, projected in 1828, did not open until 1841, because of a dispute with the contractors, and prolonged litigation.

The registration of births and deaths from 1837 permits a comparison between the late 18th century Carlisle that Heysham knew and the larger industrial city of the mid-19th century. The mortality rate increased and life expectancy decreased, comparing badly with the national average. This was mainly due to an abnormally high child mortality rate in Carlisle.

	Mortality rate: percentage per annum		
	Heysham	Civil Registration	
	1780s	1838-44	1849-55
Carlisle	2.5	2.72	2.69
Nat. average		2.19	2.17

Neither Heysham nor Reid provided an analysis of life expectancy for the different social classes in Carlisle, but figures for a range of other industrial towns in the 19th century

NOVEMBER 5th, 1783.

Carlifle Difpenfary.

THE Small Pox, both natural and from Inoculation, being now pretty general in *Carlifle*, and likely to fpread ftill further, the Monthly Committee of the *Carlifle Difpenfary* are of opinion that a general Inoculation of the poor and indigent Inhabitants will be attended with very beneficial Effects.

PRESENT,

Rev. Mr. P A L E Y, Archdeacon of *Carlifle*, in the Chair.
    Mr. F O S T E R,
    Mr. M I T C H I N S O N,
    Mr. E L W O O D,
    Mr. M I L B U R N E,
    Dr. H E Y S H A M,
    Mr. B L A I N.

R E S O L V E D.

1ft. THAT all fuch Perfons as come recommended by a Subfcriber fhall be inoculated Gratis at the *Difpenfary*.

2d. THAT the fum of 2s. 6d. be given to the Parents who are moft indigent, and who have three or more Children inoculated, as a Reward for nurfing them properly during Inoculation.

3d. THAT a Subfcriber of One Guinea fhall have the Privilege of recommending three Perfons to be inoculated, with the Reward ; or five who do not require it : and fo in Proportion for any larger Sum.

4th. THAT the Privilege of being inoculated at the *Difpenfary* be continued till the 1ft of *January*, and no longer.

suggest that social status and financial resources of parents were all important, with life expectancy at birth for gentlefolk being double that of labourers.[22]

In his report of 1842 Edwin Chadwick attempted to explain how industrial towns could escape from the filth and degradation that created miserable living conditions and caused disease:

> As to the means by which the present sanitary conditions of the labouring classes might be improved . . . That the chief obstacles to the immediate removal of decomposing refuse of towns

and habitations have been the expense and annoyance of the hand labour and cartage requisite for this purpose. That this expense may be reduced to one-twentieth, or rendered inconsiderable, by the use of water and self-acting means of removal by improved and cheaper sewers and drains.[23]

The first positive step taken in Carlisle to obtain an adequate and unpolluted water supply, for domestic use and to service a sewage system of the type proposed by Chadwick, was the formation in 1846 of a joint stock company. This was to supply the city with water from the Eden, at Stoney Holme, adjacent to its junction with the River Petteril. A steam engine was erected there and after filtration the water was piped along Union Street and London Road to Gallow Hill, the highest ground in Carlisle. A reservoir was built here with capacity for an estimated 10 days' supply. In 1847 Mannix and Whellan reported that

> It has been ascertained that there are in Carlisle 4,481 dwelling houses varying in amount of rental from under £3 to upwards of £100 p.a.; and it is proposed that the poorest class of houses, viz. those under £3 rent, should have an unrestricted supply of water at the rate of 1d. per week; the price for the higher classes gradually rising in reasonable proportion to the rental.[24]

The total cost of the scheme was estimated at £15,000, to be raised in £10 shares, and the initial response to it was, according to Mr. Steel, chairman of the water company, rather muted: 'At first we had some difficulty in inducing people to dispense with private pumps . . . there was, on the establishment of the works, coldness or indifference, rather than opposition to us'.[25] It was not long, however, before the advantage of piped water was seen. By 1849, 760 private houses with a rateable value of £10 and above, and 2,619 under £10 were connected to the supply. This was 75 per cent of the total housing stock, but only 20 baths and 49 lavatories were connected by this time. Several years later, in 1865, Rawlinson was commissioned by the corporation to design a sewage system, similar to the water-carriage system proposed by Chadwick. Carlisle's was one of the earliest schemes carried out on this principle, and involved the laying of a graded main sewer that emptied itself into the Eden below the city. As the water intake was about a mile above Carlisle an effective separation of water supply and sewage was expected. Removal of the sewage downstream, however, did not satisfy everybody, as there were complaints from the Eden Fishing Board.

The appointment of a medical officer of health in 1874, and the council's acceptance of responsibility for the sanitary state of Carlisle led to important decisions, as was noted in 1896:

> . . . several insanitary areas have been scheduled in the course of town improvements; many noted 'fever dens' have disappeared .'. . . all private ashpits have been abolished; an improved method of house refuse disposal has been adopted, all private slaughterhouses have been closed, and public slaughterhouses have been erected . . . [The water supply] is abundant, and has been improved upon from time to time as a pure and wholesome water suitable for drinking and other domestic and manufacturing purposes.[26]

The mortality rate fell in Carlisle from 3.6 per cent in 1874 to 1.8 per cent in 1881, due to the provision of water and sewage services from mid century. The figure of 2.49 per cent in Heysham's day was only bettered c.1880, a reflection of the social consequences of the industrial revolution.

Law and Order

The early years of the 19th century were a period of violence and disorder, with society brutalised by the harshness of life and the squalor of slums. Industrial growth brought a rapid increase in material wealth and prosperity, but only for the privileged few. In a polarised society the pressure for change was acknowledged only grudgingly, but led to a transformation of the draconian theory and practice of law enforcement into a more pragmatic and humane system. This was still in the future, though, and in the early 19th century the situation in Carlisle was deteriorating. Crucial factors that led to this were the explosive population growth between 1790 and 1820 (from 7,000 to 14,000), the influx of Scottish and Irish immigrants with consequent loss of homogeneity in the community, and a depression of wages amongst the weavers. Dissatisfaction culminated in the food riots in 1795, 1812 and 1817, and the weavers' riots of 1826.[27] 1795 was a year of famine and widespread disturbance over much of Europe. Substantial rises in the price of grain and the suspicion that it was being exported by avaricious dealers led to rioting in Carlisle in July. Despite the seriousness of the riot, both magistrates and poor seem to have realised that there were limits to their behaviour which neither group could transgress. The 1812 riots were more intractable, and were coupled with unrest in the textile manufacturing industry. Warehouses at Sandsfield were looted and unwanted grain was destroyed, rather than being distributed in the city at a fair price, as had happened in 1795. Although prepared to negotiate at first, the city magistrates finally lost patience. When a large crowd gathered outside the Town Hall, they ordered troops to open fire, and a woman was killed. The attitude of the authorities began to harden during the riots of 1817. In that year two weavers, two women and a young girl stole bags of meal from the warehouses at Sandsfield. The two weavers were transported, the women sent to the House of Correction for six months and the girl imprisoned for a month. In the same year John Mattinson stole a piece of white calico from a drying ground and was sentenced to transportation for seven years. The 'right' of the poor to free or subsidised food was denied, and the magistrates were suspected of employing spies and agent provocateurs to uncover the planning of riots. They resorted to the offer of £50 rewards for the apprehension and conviction of rioters rather than confronting them face to face. The long-established system of law enforcement as advocated by Archdeacon Paley (see Appendix 5) was clearly breaking down.

A strong police force to counteract the increasing public disorder was unacceptable to the establishment in Carlisle: 'Whenever it was proposed to augment the civil force of two constables, it was always successfully opposed by the Corporation on the grounds that there was a garrison at hand in the Castle which the magistrates would call in when the two constables were overpowered'.[28] This attitude came under increasing pressure when the grievances of the weavers came to a head, and culminated with the notorious incidents of the 1826 election.[29] Sir Philip Musgrave, the Tory candidate, ventured into Caldewgate to address the voters, but his answers, particularly those concerning the corn laws, enraged the crowd. A riot ensued in which Sir Philip was put on a loom and forcibly given a lesson in the art of weaving, while his friends and members of the corporation were ducked in the mill dam. A body of 300 special constables was sworn in hastily by a magistrate, but the mayor decided not to use them when he discovered that most of them were weavers. The mayor, a magistrate and the entire police force, two constables, went to the scene and read the Riot Act, and the mob responded by capturing the mayor and ducking the constables. A detachment of troops was called in from the castle garrison, but they were stoned and some were severely injured. Shots were then fired by the soldiers over the heads of the crowd, and a woman watching from her window was killed. Four days later the mayor was assaulted and beaten so severely that for several days his life was in danger.

The city corporation came under pressure to put an end to civil disturbances in January 1827, when Sir Robert Peel, the home secretary, wrote to the mayor protesting about the situation. In the same year a committee of local Whig businessmen applied for a police act, and were elected as police commissioners with home office approval. This did not lead to harmonious relations with the magistracy drawn from the Tory-controlled corporation. Mr. Batty, from Manchester, was appointed superintendent of the new force – two day officers and 16 night-watchmen, at an annual expenditure of £700. Every effort was made to distinguish the constables from the hated military: they were dressed in top hats, blue swallow-tailed coats and stove-pipe trousers.[30] They were the old regime in all but name and uniform, though, and were incapable of serving as a preventative force.

The inauguration of the force was not auspicious. Mr. Batty had served as deputy to Joseph Nadin in the Manchester police, and had been involved in the notorious Peterloo Massacre. His credentials were anathema to the weavers of Carlisle, and Batty's first visit to Caldewgate showed the helplessness of a superintendent and two officers. Parson and White, writing in 1829, described what happened:

> Mr. Batty, and the officers under him, met with serious resistance from the Irish, Scotch and other weavers in Shaddongate when making their first survey of that part of the suburbs; when the then turbulent inhabitants, unused to the interference of an effective police, became so outrageous that it was necessary to call in the aid of the military and 150 special constables by which means the riot was quelled, and 30 of the ring leaders taken into custody and punished.[31]

The strength of the Carlisle police force was ludicrously inadequate throughout the 1820s, and was limited to four officers and 14 night-watchmen in the 1840s. A new headquarters was built on the West Walls in 1840, but it was not until 1857 that the force was increased to 34 men and based on the model of the Metropolitan Police.

From the late 1830s Chartism took a strong hold throughout the country. For a decade this movement, which supported parliamentary reform, including universal male suffrage, posed a great potential threat to the civil peace and stability of the country.[32] Chartism was inaugurated in Carlisle by the formation of the Carlisle Radical Working Men's Association in July 1838. This consisted almost exclusively of the working classes and in particular handloom weavers. In 1839 local Chartists were reportedly arming themselves with pikes and fowling pieces, and drilling at night. At Whitsun, about ten thousand people took part in a meeting on the Sands, but the arrest of the Chartist leaders and the presence in the city of two troops of the Second Dragoon Guards had a sobering effect. In August fears were roused by the prospect of a Chartist strike, and the Carlisle magistrates swore in 900 special constables, acting on the Home Secretary's instructions. In addition, 120 men of the Yeoman Cavalry were armed and two troops of Dragoons were stationed in the Crescent, but in the event the strike passed off quietly. The Yeomanry, infantry and 200 special constables were mobilised during the strike of 1842, but the emergency passed when the strike ended in failure. After this there was a collapse in support for the cause in Carlisle, and during 1848 the Chartist movement expired.

As an adjunct to the rise of a more efficient police force, improvements began to take place in the prison system. At the turn of the century, the county gaol at Carlisle was 'old, much out of repair, and without the regular means of supplying the different rooms with fresh air, so necessary in these receptacles of guilt and misfortune'.[33] John Howard, the renowned philanthropist, visited the gaol, and deplored the squalid conditions and lack of segregation between the sexes:

> The wards for felons are two rooms, down a step or two; dark and dirty. One of them, the day room, had a window to the street; through which spiritous liquors, and tools for mischief, might be easily conveyed, but it is now bricked up; the night room is only 11 feet by 9. At my last visit men and women were lodged together in it. Two rooms over the felons' wards, which have been used as tap rooms, seem to be intended for women only, but in one of these I also found three men and four women lodged together.[34]

If a prisoner had money, he was able to rent a room in the gaol, to purchase milk and vegetables, and at one time to obtain ale and spirits. This system was abused by the gaolers:

> Five rooms are for master side debtors; and as many on the common side. Few gaols have so many convenient rooms for common side debtors. It is more remarkable here, because there is no table signed by the magistrates to particularise the free wards. Some gaolers avail themselves of such circumstance and demand rent for rooms which were undoubtedly designed for common side prisoners.[35]

This prison was under the control of the secretary of state for the home department, but there was also a local prison housed over Scotch Gate, until the city walls and gates were demolished. This was the responsibility of the local justices, and in it the city debtors were confined. The prisoners took considerable licence during their incarceration, as they were allowed access to the turret of the gatehouse. From this position they demanded toll from countrymen who brought peat to the city, and if they refused they were bombarded with 'sundry stones which, from the decomposed effect of time, were ever ready at hand for such a purpose'.[36]

The gaols act was passed in 1825, and in 1829 a new county gaol and house of correction were erected in Carlisle on the site of the old gaol:

> The old County Gaol stood on the site of the lodge and offices containing the reservoir, and it is only a small edifice, with a court yard, eighty-five yards in length, and thirty-six in breadth. The new building consists of a centre and two wings, finished with an embattled parapet, and has several narrow Gothic windows to correspond with the court house to which it is united. Its front measures 340 ft., and the entrance is through a beautiful pointed arch, with massive iron-studded doors, and over the gateway is an excellent clock for the convenience of the inhabitants. The interior buildings consist of the governor's house, and six radiating prison wings, affording accommodation for thirteen classes of prisoners, with separate airing grounds, so planned and divided by walls and lofty wrought iron rails, that the governor, and his assistants have, from their apartments, a complete view of the whole; and the improved system of prison discipline and classification is adopted. The prison contains room for 150 prisoners but there are seldom more than eighty at a time.[37]

The striking design of the prison is evident from its ground plan on the 1852 map of the city. In the early 19th century pressure of public opinion led to a drastic reduction in the number of capital offences, and penalties such as transportation were often commuted to imprisonment. Carlisle's new gaol was a physical indication that reform of an offender's behaviour, through isolation from corrupting influences, was replacing harsher forms of punishment.

The Electorate

The 1832 Reform Act extended the franchise to all men owning, or renting, property worth £10 or more a year. Voting rights were given, therefore, to the 'respectable' working class, but the poor remained a separate lower order of society. Freemen retained their enfranchisement, but the right was not extended to newly-created freemen. In the 1832 poll list for Carlisle there were 330 freemen and 587 £10 householders – a total of 917 voters from a population of 20,000. In spite of the extended franchise, the landed magnates, the Earl of Carlisle, the Earl of Lonsdale and Sir James Graham of Netherby, still exerted considerable influence. The act did not affect the political balance in the city, and the Liberals, Philip Henry Howard and William James, retained their seats in 1835, 1837 and 1841. Sir James Graham was one of the Liberals elected in 1852, and he retained his seat after being elected First Lord of the Admiralty in 1853.

During the first half of the 19th century the great industrialists in Carlisle became increasingly influential in the city's political life. From 1812 the Dixons and Fergusons were prominent in local politics as supporters of the Liberals, and Caldewgate, the centre of the cotton industry, was a scene of great activity at election time. John Dixon was elected as M.P. in 1847, but was unseated as he held a government contract, and Joseph Ferguson was elected in 1852, holding the seat until 1857. It was chiefly as mayors that the industrialists made their mark, the two families almost monopolising the post between 1836 and 1845, and in the 1850s. The corporation itself was transformed by the Municipal Corporation Act of 1835. 'The Mayor, Aldermen and Burgesses of the City of Carlisle', as the new body was styled, consisted of 10 aldermen and 30 councillors. Under the act the city was divided into five wards, the citizens or burgesses of each ward electing six councillors for a three-year term of office. Aldermen were appointed by the councillors for a period of six years (the mayor was elected by the council) and were to be people of substance with estates valued at £1,000 or more. The electorate was made up of those resident within seven miles of the city who paid rates for the relief of the poor. The 1835 act gave corporations considerable powers to provide services, only restricted by the willingness of the electorate to foot the bill.

Religion

There are clear indications that the diocese of Carlisle was in a state of apathy, compounded by poverty, in the early 19th century. The clergy were badly paid, the average stipend being £175 compared with £289 for England and Wales, and Church property was in a state of disrepair. Not unconnected with these problems was the high incidence of pluralism: of 128 livings in the diocese in 1835, 56 were held by pluralists, and only 84 livings had a habitable church house.[38] Pluralism was widespread in the upper reaches of the Church hierarchy too. For example, the bishop of Carlisle from 1827 to 1856 was Hugh Percy, a rich man and connected by family ties to the Archbishop of Canterbury and Duke of Northumberland. He also remained chancellor of Salisbury, and occupied a prebendary stall at St Paul's while he was bishop of Carlisle.

Of more direct importance to the spiritual well-being of the diocese was the Church's seeming lack of interest in meeting the needs of the people in Carlisle's rapidly-expanding suburbs. Christchurch in Botchergate and Holy Trinity church were built in 1828-30, but four decades were to pass before reforming bishops were to take further steps to meet the needs of a rapidly growing city. St Stephen's, St James' and St John's were built in 1865-7 under the aegis of Bishop Waldegrave, and St Mary's was built adjacent to the cathedral in 1870. Housing expansion in the Warwick Road area did not get under way until late in the century, but was then well catered for by St Paul's church (1875) and St Aidan's (1902).

The Catholic Church was understandably slow in responding to the great influx of poor Irish immigrants in the early 19th century. According to an estimate in the *Carlisle Journal*, by 1827 a quarter of the city's 15,000-strong population consisted of unemployed Irish. The first Catholic church in Carlisle after the Reformation was built in 1799, but no expansion took place until 1824, when a church was built in Chapel Street. Half a century later, St Bede's, Silloth Street, was built (1878), followed by the more commodious Warwick Road church in 1893.

The growth of Methodism has already been discussed. The movement expanded rapidly, and the membership increased by 126 per cent in the period 1821-31. In the 1830s a crisis occurred as the Wesleyans sought to control a vast and diverse movement, and the circuits based on Carlisle, Appleby and Whitehaven lost half their membership as local preachers revolted against this centralising tendency.

Carlisle's physical development

By 1803 Carlisle's walls had become a hindrance to a developing city. The *Carlisle Journal* contended that

> So long as the old walls remain standing the city can never properly extend itself. The population increases rapidly yet we can number no new streets; every little corner is built upon, to the great discomfort of the inhabitants, whereas if all obstructions were removed the town would rapidly extend itself.[39]

The walls were not maintained and indeed were becoming disreputable. Dorothy Wordsworth visited Carlisle in 1803 with her brother and Coleridge. She recalled that they 'Walked upon the city walls which are broken-down in places and crumbling away and most disgusting from filth', and so they were to remain for the next decade.[40] Jollie's map of 1811, however, shows major developments. The citadel had been replaced by the court houses, designed by Robert Smirke.[41] Botchergate opened directly onto English Street, and the old English Gate had been superseded, as was Irishgate some months later. Infilling was taking place, and the Lanes area shows up as a high density development. By 1825 there were three workhouses. These were St Mary's, near Irishgate, erected in 1785; St Cuthbert's on Harraby Hill, 1805; and a workhouse in Caldewgate, 1825.

In 1811, Jollie commented on Carlisle rather selectively:

> . . . at the present day Carlisle in the openness of its principal streets, neatness and elegance of its buildings, and the decency and respectability of its inhabitants is excelled by few, if any, towns of equal size in Great Britain. Shops are numerous, many show a degree of taste and elegance, well furnished with every necessity of life, and not a few of its luxuries.[42]

A major transformation took place in 1813, when the city walls were finally demolished, and Lowther Street was built on the line of the east curtain wall. Although the city had already extended into extra-mural industrial areas, the demolition symbolised the final transition of Carlisle from an insular enclosed community to a fully-fledged modern city, dependent upon and willingly embracing the outside world. Sir Walter Scott, however, complained in 1828 that 'I have not forgiven them for destroying their quiet old walls and building two lumpy things like mad-houses [the law courts]'.[43]

The new Eden Bridge was built in 1817, to replace the obsolete stone-built 17th-century bridge over Priest Beck. This had proved inadequate for the growing volume of traffic, but the decision to build was taken because of national rather than local concerns. The uncertain state of Ireland meant that the new road between Carlisle and Port Patrick was of strategic importance, and the bridge was given a government grant of £10,000. Scotchgate was demolished, and the stone was used to fill part of the causeway between the new and old bridges, over the original channel of the Eden. Work continued until 1827 to obviate the inconvenience of two channels, an embankment being built and one channel being filled in below the old bridge.

In 1819 an act for lighting Carlisle and its suburbs by gas was passed, and the Carlisle Gas, Light and Coke Company was formed 'to supply the City with inflammable air or gas, and making and maintaining the works necessary for that purpose'.[44] The Gas Works was built at the junction of Collier Lane and the former Brown's Row. Within 10 years streets, shops, factories and some private houses were gas-lit.

38. City Gates, *c.*1800. (M.E. Nutter.) a. Scotch Gate, with debtors' prison above. b. English Gate, and the old county gaol. c. Irish Gate, and the Georgian buildings in Abbey Street.

39.   Subscription Newsroom and Library, *c.*1830. (Thomas Rickman.)

The city was changing rapidly, not least in the increasing provision of cultural facilities. Although the Macready theatre closed in 1848, partly because the lessee alleged that 'certain reverend gentlemen allowed their sacridotal zeal to outrun their Christian Charity',[45] the subscription news room and library was built at the corner of English Street and Devonshire Street in 1831, and the Athenaeum (now the Trustee Savings Bank in Lowther Street), with its lecture rooms, exhibitions and assembly or concert hall, opened in 1840.

Chapter Ten

The Mature City

The Railways

By the late 1820s the Carlisle canal was well established, but had never been extended to the east coast. In 1824, a committee was formed in Newcastle, and commissioned Chapman to provide estimates for both canal and railway from Carlisle canal basin to Newcastle. These figures, £252,000 for a railway and £888,000 for a canal, confirmed that a canal was no longer viable.[1] An act for making a railway or tramroad from the north-west corner of the canal basin to Newcastle was passed in 1829, but a railway in the present sense was not intended. The legislation was specific: 'No locomotive or movable steam engine shall be used – for drawing wagons or other carriages . . . No steam engine shall be erected or used within view of the Castle of Naworth or Corby Castle . . .'.[2] The act authorised the raising of £300,000 in £100 shares, and provision was made for the borrowing of a further £100,000 by mortgage if necessary. In 1836 the Carlisle to Blenkinsop Colliery, Greenhead, was completed, and the whole line opened in 1839. The significance of the Liverpool to Manchester railway, which had been opened in 1830, was noted, however, and the act was modified to allow steam locomotives.

The Newcastle to Carlisle railway had a dramatic effect on the price of coal, which dropped from 17s. to 10s. a ton in Carlisle.[3] It had a beneficial effect on the canal company too, which had encouraged the termination of the line at the canal basin. Tolls taken on the canal doubled between 1836 and 1840, and there was a dividend increase from one to four per cent. The new link permitted the movement of goods from the north-east coast and also from the continent to north-west England and Ireland. The route was also used by a wave of German emigrants on their way to Liverpool and America. In the late 1830s, the fortunes of the company reached their peak:

> The number of vessels belonging to this port [Port Carlisle] is forty-four. The vessels employed in the coasting trade in 1836 were 831, the tonnage amounting to 68,855; in 1837 the number of vessels was 1,186 and the tonnage 84,910. This increase is to be attributed to the railway communication with the Earl of Carlisle's and the Blenkinsop coal-mines.[4]

It is noteworthy that the original concept of the import of coal was reversed, with its export from east Cumberland to the port, and thence to Scotland and Ireland. By 1847, the canal was also becoming increasingly beneficial to industrialists, particularly to textile manufacturers and traders:

> [The canal] contributes greatly to the wealth and prosperity of the city by affording a communication with the Western ocean . . . It has a good trade in timber, iron, slates, etc., etc., and the exportations consist principally of grain, flour, meal, oak bark, alabaster, freestone, lead, staves, etc. The cotton wool manufactured here is brought directly from Liverpool, whither a great part of it is returned in a manufactured state for exportation.[5]

While the full significance and capability of the railway was only slowly recognised, the vulnerability of the canal as a trading artery was becoming apparent by the mid-1840s. The Maryport and Carlisle Railway Company, authorised in 1837 and commissioned in

40.   Newcastle and Carlisle Railway, the Conran Cut. The line was opened in 1837, and the picture shows an early locomotive and a combined passenger and goods train. The carriages for third class passengers are open.

1845, had a superior port, and challenged the canal. The greatest threat, though, was that of north-south rail routes, combined with the intricacies of railway politics.

Carlisle's industrialists had invested considerable sums in the canal, and also in the Carlisle to Newcastle railway, though not enough to exert influence on its future policy. Their financial interest in the Carlisle to Maryport line was minimal, and control was in the hands of the west Cumbrians. When the chance came to invest in the proposed Carlisle to Lancaster line, as part of the link between London and Scotland, the scheme was met by apathy. After a year's delay, landed families and the Dixon family finally invested, but not enough to control future company policy. In the long term, the policies of the North-Eastern Railway Company (N.E.R.C.) were to prove damaging to Carlisle's interests, while the opportunism of the western railways, soon to be merged into the London and North Western (L.N.W.R.), did not protect the Carlisle economy.

The north-south route through Carlisle had a national significance, unlike the links to Maryport and Newcastle. In the mid-1840s it was debated whether the London to Scotland railway should follow the east or west coast. By 1840 the west coast line ran as far as Lancaster, while the eastern line had reached York. A royal commission examined the alternative routes from this point, and their report, published in March 1841, favoured the western, if the Lancaster to Carlisle link was built. The response in Cumberland and Westmorland to this challenge was apathetic:

It required much time, much argument, and much canvassing to induce persons to take up shares; and it was not until the London and Birmingham and the Grand Junction Railways had undertaken to take shares to this amount of £350,000, on condition that other sums should be raised in the counties of Lancaster, Westmorland and Cumberland, that the scheme could be said to be fairly afloat. The North Union and the Lancaster and Preston Railway Companies also subscribed £60,000 each.[6]

During 1842 three alternatives were put forward for the route from Lancaster to Carlisle. It was decided that the line should run via Kirkby Lonsdale and Penrith, but this was later amended so that the line would embrace Kendal, crossing over from the valley of the River Kent to that of the River Lune at Grayrigg. The parliamentary bill was delayed for a year, due mainly to the difficulty in raising share capital in Cumberland and Westmor-

41a & b. Newcastle and Carlisle Railway notice of initial services, and a draconian trespass warning.

land, but the quota was guaranteed by the end of 1843. The bill was passed in February 1844, and the Lancaster and Carlisle Railway Company was formed. Of its 12 directors, six were nominees of the railway companies who had invested in the new venture, four were taken from the two counties' landed gentry, and the others were Carlisle citizens – John Dixon, the industrialist, and G. H. Head, the banker. Joseph Locke was appointed engineer-in-chief, and the resident engineer was J. E. Errington. The contractors were Messrs. Stephenson, Brassey and MacKenzie.

The engineering problems presented by this 70-mile stretch of line were immense, and the labour force peaked at 10,000 men with 930 horses.[7] Because of the great demand for labour, the average wage of a labourer quickly rose from 2s.6d. a day at the start of the enterprise to 3s.6d.[8] The deploying of a workforce of 10,000 men in a sparsely populated countryside, with virtually no preparation for their accommodation, caused grave problems. The navvies spent a high proportion of their generous wages on alcohol, and this led to rioting and general disorder. The worst outbreak took place near Penrith on February 1846, when 'armies' of Irish, Scottish and English navvies clashed, order finally being restored by the Cumberland and Westmorland Yeomanry.

The line was finished in two years and five months, at a cost of £17,000 per mile of double track. This was below the estimated cost, and took only five months longer than expected, despite the delays caused by the unexpected amount of excavation and problems in purchasing some of the land. The line was opened on 15 December 1846, and the people of Carlisle took the opportunity to have a general holiday. Critics were silenced when the first train, with 200 passengers aboard, ascended the steepest gradient on Shap, one in 75, at a speed of 22 mph. Carlisle now had a direct rail link with London, and the connection with Glasgow followed soon. The Caledonian Railway Company, with the same engineers and contractors as the Carlisle and Lancaster, opened their line as far as Beattock summit in September 1847, and to Glasgow in February 1848, over two years before the rival east coast route to Edinburgh was completed. By the end of 1848 Carlisle had important rail connections to London, Glasgow and Edinburgh, and the railways had become an industry in their own right in the city. Soon the citizens could reach London in 11 hours, and Glasgow and Edinburgh in three hours.

With increasing competition from the railways, the canal company was soon in financial difficulties. The company's directors resorted to desperate expedients in order to compete, but after early successes these were disastrous. Port Carlisle had become obsolete, because of its dependence upon tides and restricted harbour facilities, but this was not accepted at first. In 1854 the canal was filled in and a railway was laid on the same course. This venture was doomed, but was soon incorporated into a much larger scheme, already under consideration. A meeting was convened in July 1853 by the mayor of Carlisle, attended by leading citizens, to consider an alternative port at Silloth. The merits of a harbour there were compelling. It would be accessible in all weathers, less time would be wasted waiting for high water and a steamer could land passengers three or four hours sooner than at Port Carlisle. In conjunction with railways, the shortest route from Dublin to Edinburgh and Glasgow was via Silloth, and vessels from Belfast would reach Silloth sooner than Liverpool. At this early stage the co-operation of the railway companies seemed to be certain. The committee that formed to discuss the proposals was reassured by the favourable response from the Newcastle and Carlisle Railway Company (N.C.R.C.), and the chairman of the Hawick line.

The first bill to promote the Carlisle and Silloth Bay Railway and Dock Company (C.S.R.C.) was rejected in 1854, but the second application, in 1855, received parliamentary approval. It had almost unanimous support from Carlisle's leading citizens, and 201 of the 245 shareholders accounted for £94,000 of the £112,000 subscribed. The shareholders included 29 city councillors, members of the Dixon and Ferguson families, and J. D. Carr, the biscuit and flour manufacturer.[9] Building the line presented no problems as it was over flat terrain and was only 12 miles long, from Silloth to its junction with the Port Carlisle line at Drumburgh, nine miles from Carlisle. The railway was opened on 29 August 1856, and was an occasion of great celebration. Shops closed for the day and 'the swarming population of Caldewgate seemed to have taken a holiday'.[10]

The directors were anxious that the port should be opened up to the national railway network. In 1853 the Caledonian Railway Company, that had a close working relationship with the Carlisle to Lancaster Company, failed to obtain parliamentary approval for a connecting line to the Silloth railway, because the House of Commons committee considered that the proposal did not give facilities for the traffic of the district. This opinion was shared by the directors of the C.S.R.C., who had strong suspicions, to be confirmed in later years, that discriminatory freight charges would siphon off traffic from the Silloth to Liverpool route. The directors expressed a strong preference for an arrangement with the North British Railway Company (N.B.R.C.), who wished to connect Hawick with Carlisle, so as to give an outlet to the sea at Silloth for their mineral and passenger traffic. This was mutually advantageous for the C.S.R.C., giving them access to Edinburgh, the Scottish border towns, and two ports facing the continent – Leith and Berwick.

Before the dock was completed the committee, seeking other means to obtain revenue to meet interest charges, built up passenger traffic with great success. During July and August

42.   Port Carlisle Dandy. In 1857 steam motive power was withdrawn from the Port Carlisle to Drumburgh Junction line, and replaced by a horse-drawn carriage until the line's closure in 1914. First-class passengers travelled inside the coach; third-class outside.

1857 the number of passengers using the railway to Silloth averaged 1,450 a week. At the same time the company attempted to build up a holiday resort. They purchased common land, consisting of little more than sandhills and rabbit warrens, laid out a street network and started to sell building plots. In effect the company was attempting to create a new town to the north of the railway and docks. Early optimism was soon shown to be premature, as an ominous development was taking place. For 30 years, considerable traffic in cotton, grain, alkalis, groceries and general merchandise, latterly over 14,000 tons a year, had flowed between Newcastle and Liverpool. A greater part of it had been transported by the Newcastle to Carlisle railway to Port Carlisle or latterly Silloth, and then by steamship to Liverpool, two or three times a week. The N.C.R.C., however, agreed with the N.E.R.C. that they would divert this lucrative traffic from the north east to Liverpool and Ireland via a southerly route through Yorkshire and Lancashire. This had the effect of excluding the Port Carlisle and the Silloth railways, and created a monopoly for the longer and more expensive routes. As a direct result of this, the carriage charges on some classes of goods increased by 50 per cent. The Port Carlisle and Silloth railways submitted a complaint to a parliamentary committee about the interference to free flow of traffic, but their protest was not upheld, and Liverpool traffic over the Newcastle to Carlisle railway ceased in April 1857.

By the summer of 1860 Silloth was a thriving resort, with four hotels and 38 lodging houses, and a weekly newspaper, the *Silloth Gazette*. This published a list of the visitors staying in the town. They were mostly local holidaymakers but some were from as far away as London and Edinburgh, even America. Visitors included members of the aristocracy, such as Lord Scarsdale of Kedleston Hall and the Curzons from Derby. The appearance of Silloth, with its orderly and spacious plan, broad streets, well-built and properly-sewered houses, and landscaped open space, the Green, between town and sea, was impressive and a dramatic contrast with the congestion and squalor still prevalent in Carlisle. The Silloth street map of 1860 and the amenities listed in the *Gazette* reveal that apart from the loss of the pier the town has hardly changed for the last 130 years.

The establishment of a thriving resort in just four years was a remarkable achievement, but it resulted from an unauthorised venture of dubious legality by a company close to bankruptcy. When the new dock was opened in August 1859 the flow of freight and passengers was disastrously below the planned capacity, and in 1862 the Port Carlisle railway and Carlisle and Silloth railway were taken over by the N.B.R.C. The financial position of the Silloth company had become increasingly untenable. Share capital had been £165,000, and the original act empowered them to borrow £55,000.[11] Expenditure on the railway, docks and the new town had been £290,000, and the deficit had been borrowed by the directors on personal guarantees. To pay off the debt and complete unfinished works required nearly £90,000 in extra capital. In the deal between the companies it was agreed that the N.B.R.C. would pay interest on the original share issue, and give the Silloth company £2,000 as annual rent. At the same time they leased the Port Carlisle company with the transfer of debts and liabilities, leaving them only their original capital. When the Hawick link was opened in June 1862, the N.B.R.C. began to work the whole Edinburgh to Silloth route as one line. The Carlisle industrialists who had invested heavily to ensure reliable communication with Liverpool and Manchester were rescued from their grave financial predicament, but lost their independent connection with Liverpool. Henceforth they had to rely on identity of interests with the L.N.W.R.

The Settle to Carlisle Railway
The last great railway project undertaken in the Victorian era was the Settle to Carlisle line. Although a triumph of engineering and a spectacular route it was of dubious financial

viability. The railway had an inauspicious birth. During the 1860s, in the second railway boom, the Midland Company sought to compete with their great rivals, the L.N.W.R. and the L.N.E.R., for the lucrative Scottish traffic. Their line reached only as far north as Ingleton and after failure to reach agreement with the L.N.W.R. for the joint use of the line from Lancaster to Carlisle, they decided to extend their own line to Carlisle. In July 1866 the Settle-Carlisle Railway Bill was approved by parliament, and work started in September. This stopped at the end of December for almost two years, because of financial difficulties, and while joint use of the Lancaster to Carlisle line was agreed. An application to parliament for an abandonment bill in April 1870 was refused, and work on the Settle line began again. The project was a triumph for the engineer but a financial gamble for the company. It took six and a half years to complete, and cost £3½m., the labour force peaking at 6,000 men.[12] Express trains were running to Carlisle, and then to Glasgow via the Glasgow and S.W. Scotland Co., and to Edinburgh via the N.B.R.C. by 1876.

The efforts of Carlisle's industrialists to safeguard their trade routes had not turned out as planned, but the city's development as a major rail centre was to be of prime importance in ensuring the city's industrial future. This was acknowledged by the *Carlisle Guide* of 1881:

> There are few towns which have more largely shared in the national prosperity resulting from the development of the railway system than Carlisle . . . It is an undoubted fact that the last 10 or 15 years have been more productive of material progress than any previous period of the same length – if not, indeed, of the half century. There were certainly never so many streets laid out, or houses built, or manufactories erected, or improvements made, as in the time denoted. Railways gave the impetus to these strides of prosperity, which have gone on contemporaneously with the prosperity of the system that called them into existence. Carlisle is now a great centre of railway communication. East, West, North, South the iron roads radiate from it. It is placed on two of the three great trunk lines which run from one end of the kingdom to the other, and has short and easy access to the eastern and western seas.[13]

The Citadel Station

A physical symbol of the importance of the railways to Carlisle is the citadel station, designed by Sir William Tite in the Tudor style, and built in 1847-8. In the early days each railway company had its own station: the Carlisle to Newcastle on the London Road, the Carlisle to Maryport at Crown Street, and the Silloth line at the canal basin. The L.N.W.R. and the Caledonian had built the citadel station and shared the premises. The other companies were gradually admitted to this station. Rail traffic increased dramatically, and by 1870 as many as 138 passenger trains were arriving and departing from the station every day.[14] In addition to this there was an enormous through goods traffic. This was both inconvenient and dangerous, and an act was obtained in 1873 to separate the goods traffic by diverting it to the west of the station, between the inner city and the Denton Holme and Caldewgate suburbs. In 1873-6 the passenger station was enlarged. The single platforms and two bays, to accommodate the traffic that terminated in Carlisle, were replaced by three long platforms for north-south passenger traffic and six bays. A joint-stock undertaking ran the station, its shareholders being the individual railway companies: the L.N.W.R., Caledonian, Midland, N.B.R.C., L.N.E.R., and Glasgow and South Western. The Carlisle to Maryport Company was only a tenant. At the end of the 19th century the station must have presented a magnificent spectacle, with the different company liveries and the formal uniforms of station staff being a far cry from the anonymity of today.

43.   Carr's biscuit works *c.*1834. The picture shows ships in the canal basin.

Carlisle Industry

By the 1860s the cotton industry was in decline, although the specialised firms such as Ferguson's and Stead McAlpin prospered into the 20th century. The number of handloom weavers was dwindling rapidly and Dixon's, as mentioned above, was declared bankrupt in 1872. Railways gave employment in their own right and also opened up markets for firms that were to come to prominence in the second half of the 19th century.

Carr's of Carlisle: Founded by a Quaker, Jonathan Dodgson Carr (1806-84) in 1831, it supplemented his bakery with four flour mills and a small fleet of coastal vessels. A new biscuit factory was built *c.*1834 adjacent to the canal. Jonathan was succeeded by his three sons, and in time the company passed to his grandson, Theodore, who laid the foundations for future prosperity. A major development was the opening of the flour mill at Silloth, alongside the recently-opened inner dock. The mill was enlarged in 1904. Carr's was a good employer, and the biscuit factory had a reading room, school room, a library and a bath with hot water. Hours worked were moderate by the standards of the day: 63½ hours a week in 1848, and 55½ by the 1870s. Women made up a large proportion of the labour force, decorating and packing the biscuits. By the 1920s, 3,000 people were employed by the firm.

Cowans Sheldon: In 1846, John Cowans and Edward Sheldon, who had served apprenticeships with Robert Stephenson, founded their engineering firm at Woodbank Upperby. The time was propitious as the Lancaster to Carlisle line was nearing completion. Orders were taken to make forgings for the wheels of locomotives, and for points and crossings. The company expanded in 1857-8, moving to a site between Nicholas Street and London Road. Here they started to build cranes, railway turntables and locomotives. When a limited company was formed in 1873, the factory had built 530 cranes and 64 steam engines. In

1891 they built the largest dockside crane in the country (130 tons) and in 1907 constructed their first floating crane. These were to become the company's speciality, supplying customers worldwide.

Hudson Scott: The small printing business set up in 1799 in English Street by Benjamin Scott was developed by his nephew Hudson Scott, who installed a steam litho press. In due course he was joined by his two sons, Benjamin and William, to run a firm of printers of stationery, specialising in lithography. Demand for biscuit packaging led them to produce decorated tins for Carr's and Peak Freen. A new factory was opened in James Street in 1868, where they provided a complete packaging service. At this time there were 370 employees. In 1898 a limited company was formed, and by 1902 it had a turnover of £150,000, which was split between tins and stationery. Further expansion followed, and by 1906 the firm employed 1,200 people, half of whom were women or girls. In 1922 they grouped with other firms to form the Metal Box Company.

Stead McAlpin: Thomas McAlpin left his Wigton works in 1835 and took over a disused mill at Cummersdale. He renovated the mill and installed a new water-wheel for power, engraved copper rollers for printing, and opened up a vast market for mass production. John Stead, his stepson, joined him in 1837, and on Thomas's death the firm became known as McAlpin Stead. They employed gifted artists and retained a niche for hand block printed chintz, which gained an international reputation.

Morton Sundour: The firm was established when James Morton came to Carlisle in 1900, and helped his father set up a factory at Denton Hill. James employed artists to create original designs for their fabrics, and specialised in the application of fast dyes to textiles. The firm became an acknowledged leader in high-quality fabrics.

John Laing and Sons: A small building firm was set up in 1848. It became one of the country's great building and civil engineering contractors. The head office was moved to London in 1922.

Buck's: Manufacturer of fancy flannel shirting at Atlas Works from 1883.

William Carrick: Manufacturer of felt hats at Norfolk Street Works.

Teasdale: Founded in 1835. Manufacturer of sugar confectionery and medicated pastilles.

Pratchett Bros.: Founded in 1859. Manufacturer of portable steam engines and pumping machinery at Denton Iron Works.

On a smaller scale, a number of iron and engineering trades played an important rôle in the second half of the 19th century, particularly connected with the railways. The L.N.W.R. built an engine works at St Nicholas, the Caledonian Company built a repair workshop at Etterby and, at a later date, the Midland Railway Company built their workshop at Durran Hill. Other firms included the Waterloo and the Victoria foundry companies, and Porter, Hinde and Porter in Blackfriars Street.

Occupational Structure in Carlisle

Appendix Three shows some of the more significant occupational changes during the last 40 years of the Victorian era. In 1861 the textile industry was by far the greatest source of employment in the city both for men and women. By 1901 the workforce had shrunk to a third of its former size and those remaining were overwhelmingly female. The men were working on the railways, and in the engineering and building industries. Over this period the service and retail sectors grew massively, with young women leaving the factories for domestic service. The 1861 census shows that agriculture still played an important rôle, while the dominance of women in teaching and the emergence of commercial clerks, strictly a male preserve, are both shown in the census of 1901.

11, ENGLISH STREET, CARLISLE,

AT

HUDSON SCOTT'S

General & Commercial

PRINTING OFFICE,

ENGRAVING,

Lithographic & Copperplate

PRINTING,

EXECUTED ON THE PREMISES BY FIRST-RATE WORKMEN.

ACCOUNT BOOKS

RULED OR PRINTED TO ANY PATTERN.

CARD PLATES

ENGRAVED AND PRINTED

ON THE SHORTEST NOTICE.

AGENT FOR MILNER'S

PATENT SAFES & FIRE PROOF
BOXES.

44.   An advertisement for Hudson Scott's printing and engraving business.

The Political Scene

The passing of the Second Reform Act in 1867 gave the right to vote to male householders and £10 lodgers in boroughs. In comparison with the election of 1865, the votes cast in the 1868 parliamentary elections in Carlisle had increased by 230 per cent – an increase from 1,816 to 6,042. The result of this was that a Tory member lost his seat to a Liberal. In 1872 secret ballots were introduced, so that newly-enfranchised workers could not be influenced by their employers. There was, however, no noticeable change in the voting pattern in Carlisle after this date. With the Redistribution of Seats Act in 1885, the city lost its right to return two members of parliament. They were selected from the upper echelons of society, and included over the years Philip Henry Howard and Sir James Graham, members of the Dixon and Ferguson families, county gentry and barristers. In a more humble stratum of society, the Carlisle Labour Party was founded in 1889, the first local labour party in England. In local government the leadership was strongly liberal, with industrialists, such as the Dixons, Fergusons, Benjamin Scott and F. W. Chance, very prominent. At the end of the century a small number of 'established notables' dominated the town council, together with small tradesmen and businessmen.

Education

The earliest school for which there is firm information in Carlisle is the grammar school. This was founded in the 16th century to provide a classical education, but by the 18th century grammar schools across England were in decline: late in the century there are said to have been only four boys at the Carlisle school. A revival took place in the early 19th century, when the school had 40-50 pupils, and the growing numbers by mid-century forced a move to the present building in 1883.[15] Systematic attempts to provide an elementary education began in the late 18th century, when charity schools and Sunday schools appeared. Charity schools were established for the education of the poor, and free instruction, together with free meals and clothing, provided a basic level of literacy and, sometimes, numeracy. The first reference to a charity school in Carlisle is in 1790, when a school for the daughters of poor freemen was in existence. This provided clothing, and taught the girls to read, knit and sew.[16] Sunday schools, though, played a more important rôle. They began to proliferate in England from c.1780, with their professed purpose being to teach children to read the Bible and to accept their position in society. The schools' educational value was augmented over time as more emphasis was placed on the teaching of writing, and some arithmetic. It is not known how many such schools there were in Carlisle at the turn of the century, but the *Universal British Directory* of 1790 and Jollie's *Directory* of 1811 both refer to them in the plural. A form of education in the city at the turn of the century which had a more explicit social context was the School of Industry, where 30 girls were taught to sew, read and write.

In the early 19th century the Church and voluntary organisations accepted the challenge to provide primary education. They introduced radical concepts, both in the teaching methods themselves and in the design of school buildings. Two notable pioneers were Joseph Lancaster, a Quaker, who set up the British and Foreign Schools Society, and whose teaching was undenominational, and Andrew Bell, a Church of England clergyman, who founded the National Society.[17] In Carlisle a Lancasterian School opened in 1811, with a large room in Watergate. It moved to two rooms in Mary Street in 1834, where on average 100 boys and 70 girls were taught. The National School was built in 1812 on West Walls, adjacent to the Sallyport. It was named the Central School, and two rooms accommodated 220 boys and 180 girls. In 1826 St Patrick's Day and Sunday School was opened, with 200 pupils of all denominations, although it was a Catholic school.

In 1829 there were 905 pupils at the elementary day schools and 1,360 at the Sunday schools.[18] In addition to the facilities provided by the large educational institutions, schools were also established for those who were prepared to pay. Parson and White's *Directory* of 1829 lists many establishments based upon modestly-sized private houses. There were three gentlemen's boarding schools, each run by a clergyman, two ladies' boarding schools and 22 additional day schools. In 1843 there was the first mention of a state grant for education, when two national schools were built. These were Trinity School in Caldewgate and Christ Church School in Botchergate, and the latter received a parliamentary grant for a school house in Crown Street. There was also a welcome sign in that playgrounds were provided for the first time.

Until the establishment of the 'Ragged Schools Union' in 1844 under the presidency of Lord Ashley, the children of the very poor had failed to find a place in the education system. It would seem that the ragged schools in Shaddongate were founded at almost the same time as the Union, as they are recorded in the 1858 *Directory and Guide to Carlisle.*

The 1851 census, and published report on education is unique in its wealth of detail. It recorded that there were 47 schools in Carlisle, of which 10 were public and 37 were privately-owned. In the day schools there were 3,233 registered scholars, 2,233 in 'public' schools, and in the Sunday schools 2,603 were registered. In a count on the 30 and 31 March attendance was disappointing: only about seventy-five per cent of the children were present.

By 1870 nearly 5,000 children were being educated at the city's schools, albeit irregularly and for short periods. In that year the government introduced momentous changes in the educational system, with a doubling of the grant to Church schools, both Church of England and Catholic, while introducing board schools, which were funded by the rates. Between 1872 and 1900 two Church of England schools (St John's and Goodwin Memorial) and a Catholic school (St Cuthbert's) were built, together with 18 board schools. From 1880 compulsory attendance was required for all children aged between five and twelve.

Three sets of statistics indicate, in the most general terms, that higher educational standards were achieved as schooling increased. The growth of the professional classes in Carlisle imply that this was so: 25 in 1790, 35 in 1811, 80 in 1847 and 129 by 1858.[19] The increased circulation of newspapers suggests that literacy was increasing, although there is no way of knowing how many people read each paper and thus how many literate people there were in the city:

	Estimated Weekly Circulation		
	Carlisle Journal	Carlisle Patriot	Total
1837	1,879	546	2,425
1841	2,216	962	3,178
1845	2,837	731	3,568[20]

The third measure is more basic and precise, and is the ability to sign the marriage register. The Carlisle figures compare well with the national average:

		Carlisle		England	
	Marriages	% signing		% signing	
		Men	Women	Men	Women
1855-9	1,376	87	65	72	60.9
1872-6	2,098	90.1	74.7	82.4	75.7[21]

The number of children attending school in Carlisle doubled between 1870 and 1902, when the school boards were abolished and elementary education became a function of the local council. This remained the case until 1914, when the city became a county borough, and thenceforth administered secondary and technical education as well.

Landscape of the city

Mannix and Whellan recorded their general impressions of the city in 1847:

> . . . now contains many elegant houses and public edifices. English Street, Scotch Street and Castle Street diverging from the market place are spacious and contain many well stocked shops . . . The market place is lined with well stocked retail shops, and the city possesses several commodious and comfortable inns with 3 excellent hotels, and within a circuit of 10 miles round Carlisle are numerous beautiful castles and villas.[22]

45.   Green Market in the late 19th century, showing the Guildhall and the rear of the Town Hall. Note stalls outside shops, limited gas lighting and the cobbled road surface.

Mannix and Whellan emphasise the number of shops, and this is confirmed by the city directories (see Appendix Two). Most of them must have been very small, on the evidence of the 131 grocers and 47 butchers in 1858. The 'public edifices' that Mannix and Whellan mention included the Athenaeum (1840) and the Reading Room (1831), both already mentioned, and the long-delayed Cumberland Infirmary (1841). The original building, on high ground above the canal basin, still exists, but is now part of a much larger complex. Jefferson described it as 'an extensive and very handsome white free stone building erected by subscription . . . It is a tetrastyle, with a portico with four Grecian Doric Columns; and it is the only example of the ancient or classical architecture exhibited in the public buildings of Carlisle'.[23]

Carlisle was transformed not only by the increasing number of public buildings and shops but also a corresponding increase in the number of houses. Whellan emphasised this in 1860:

> There are few towns in England that have made more rapid strides in social and material advance-ment than Carlisle. In a single decade the face of the town has been almost entirely changed . . . streets of houses, of massive form, with all the conveniences that modern art can suggest . . . have sprung up as residences for the merchant and the manufacturer, and the tradesman. Streets of houses, too, have been erected for the working man, in lieu of dingy alleys, creaking garrets, and

46. Working-class housing. a. Milbourne Street. b. Denton Street.

fever stricken yards. The clerk, the merchant, and even the labourer, has had his dwelling improved and now enjoys the freshness of the fields and the recreation derived from the cultivation of his little plot of garden ground.[24]

The housing referred to here must be the closely-interwoven houses and industrial premises that were built after the Denton Holme estate was sold off by the Dixon family. This followed the construction of Nelson Bridge in 1853 across the Caldew, connecting Denton Holme to the heart of the city. This was crucial to the success of the scheme, and was financed largely by proprietors of land and factories, especially the Dixons who contributed £1,000.[25] The estate came under the supervision of the local Board of Health, set up in 1850, so standards for minimum room size and wall thickness were enforced. Back-to-back houses were prohibited by the 1859 by-laws, but this was too late to prevent some being built in the Milbourne Street area. They were converted to through houses in 1932-40. The speed of development can be gauged by comparing the 1850 map with the Ordnance Survey map of 1865, which shows the most important streets on the estates. Major developers were the Dixon and Ferguson families, speculative builders and two building societies. These were the Co-operative Benefit, who consigned sites by ballots to 71 of its members, and the Carlisle and Cumberland Benefit Building Society. The houses were built to a consistent architectural style, with uniform frontages, and were largely occupied by artisan classes who were attracted from the lanes and courts by proximity to their work and superior living conditions, as the medical officer of health testified: 'The houses consist entirely of cottage property occupied by the artisan class and are, in their sanitary arrangements, and structural aspects, unsurpassed by any similar property in Carlisle'. Population statistics for Denton Holme indicate clearly the suburb's rapid growth. In 1841 there were 460 inhabitants, 780 in 1851 and 2,800 in 1861.[26]

47. 'Genteel' housing: Howard Place.

Between 1862 and 1901 the Ordnance Survey sheets reveal the development of dense working-class terrace housing on both sides of Botchergate, although the street itself became a shopping area. In Stanwix, grand detached houses overlooking Edenside, and terraces in the Scotland Road and Etterby Street areas were built. The residential area to the east of the city was developed late in the century. In 1865 the beginning of Chiswick Street was shown on the Ordnance Survey map, and by the turn of the century Warwick Road had been extended eastwards to Brunton Avenue. The housing was generously laid out, with back lanes running along terrace blocks, and sufficient open land for bowling greens. The three-storey housing in Howard Place, for example, provided genteel residences, with accommodation for the domestic servants on the top floor and rear access for tradesmen. The development in Portland Square and Chatsworth Square was on a grander scale, with formal gardens for the residents.

In the closing decades of the 19th century, there were welcome signs of civic initiatives in the city, albeit with some opposition to council spending. Public baths were opened in St James Street in 1884, and extensions were made to Tullie House in 1895, to provide a library, museum and school of science. In 1895-6 the Lowther Street improvement scheme was undertaken, in which the horse, pork and poultry markets were removed and a fine north-south thoroughfare was constructed. The opening of the magnificent covered market on 2 October 1889 occasioned some of the greatest celebrations ever seen in Carlisle, as 8-10,000 people thronged the streets. A concert was given in the market hall, attended by nearly 10,000 people, and this was followed by a torchlight procession and a fireworks display in front of the Town Hall.

The 19th century ended on a note of optimism after the solid progress of the Victorian era. With the help of a rapidly developing transport system, Carlisle's industrial base was more balanced and diverse, while housing, sanitation and water supply had all improved greatly since the beginning of the century.

Chapter Eleven

Twentieth-Century Carlisle

The new century was to witness two world wars that were profoundly to affect the lives of Carlisle people, but the fabric of the city was untouched by enemy action. Wars are great catalysts, though, and they stimulated changes in industry, in the development of new technology that transformed daily life, and in social and political attitudes.

The turn of the century saw the birth of industry that was to enhance life in 20th-century Carlisle. The Corporation Electric Light and Power Station was opened at James Street in 1899, to provide lighting for the principal streets, pumping for the town's sewage and power for the electric tramways which replaced the horse-drawn omnibuses in 1900. Two other momentous inventions, the internal combustion engine and the cinema, were in their gestation period, and made their appearance in Carlisle at the same time. The first 'picture house', the *Public Hall*, occupying the former Catholic church in Chapel Street, opened in 1906, the year in which the first motor bus service began. These, together with the opening of the National Telephone Company's exchange in 1885, were fitting symbols of the great cultural and technical changes that were to transform Carlisle in the 20th century.

Carlisle's Economy and Occupational Structure

Many of the great firms that had revitalised Carlisle in the 19th century began to decline, or lost their identity, in the present century. The evolving economy is illustrated by the city's changing occupational structure, which was a product of the stable and broad-based economy founded upon transport, food processing, engineering, textile and service industries and public administration.

In the first half of the century, the railways, engineering and metal trades were the major industries. A secondary but important employer was the building industry which, although in decline between 1901 and 1921, revived strongly in the late 1920s. The textile industry, in which women were predominant, was in severe recession at the beginning of the century. It made a limited recovery during the inter-war years, but after 1945 it was a shadow of its labour-intensive 19th-century self. Women were employed increasingly in shops and in clerical work, while domestic service all but disappeared. These trends are illustrated by the census returns for 1921 and 1951. (See Appendix IV.)

Carlisle is now an important administrative centre for the county and city councils, and for service industries (administration and distribution) which employ 62 per cent of the workforce. Industry employs 29 per cent, and nine per cent are employed by the construction industry. The city's population has continued to increase: in 1981 it was 70,000, with 101,000 in Carlisle District. The population within a 25-mile radius of the city is about two hundred thousand.[1]

Industry (1945-90)

Carlisle's industry was drastically transformed after World War Two, with the disappearance of major firms and changing ownership of others. In a period of takeovers and mergers, Carlisle firms became engulfed in vast conglomerates, which had overriding commercial and financial targets but minimal loyalty to the city.

Major firms have been closed down. For example, Buck's was taken over by Bonsoir in 1984 but closed in 1986. Morton Sundour was taken over by Courtaulds in 1963, and shut

123

in 1980. Cowans Sheldon was taken over successively by Clarke Chapman, N.E. Industries and Cowan Boyd. The last crane was built in 1987, and the firm, except for its design office, has now left Carlisle. Other firms have kept their names but are now parts of larger concerns. In 1921 Hudson Scott became part of Metal Box, which is now owned by Carnad, the French company. Carr's became part of Cavenham Foods in 1964, and was taken over by United Biscuits in 1972. Carr's Flour Mills remains at Silloth, however, as an independent concern. Ferguson merged with Viyella, also in 1964, Stead McAlpin is now part of the John Lewis Partnership and Pratchett is now A.P.V. Mitchell. British Rail is still a large employer, but has been slimmed down drastically since pre-war days. Losses in Carlisle's older industries have been counteracted to some extent by the growth of several new firms. These include B.S.R.A. (Kangol), Pirelli and Nestlé.

Housing

Throughout the 19th century industry prospered and the population grew, but little regard was paid to the social consequences of an inadequate housing stock. It is true that large industrialists, such as the Dixons and Fergusons, built new housing for their workers, building societies were able to provide a limited number of houses for their members, and speculative builders catered for the well-to-do, but these measures did not meet the needs of the masses.

The Housing Act of 1890 aimed to establish standards for existing buildings and initiated slum clearance. It was only after the introduction of a housing subsidy in the Housing and Town Development Act of 1919 that Carlisle Corporation embarked on the building programme that produced 5,068 corporation houses between 1919 and 1938.

The first efforts were piecemeal in character, with limited development in Denton Street, Longsowerby, Bousteads Grassing and the Garden City estate in Stanwix, and a few years later in the Blackwell Road and Wigton Road areas. These tentative schemes were followed by ambitious large estate development at Raffles (1926) and Botcherby (1928), where the earlier compact rectangular layout gave way to informal plans. The Ordnance Survey map of 1937 shows that the Raffles estate included a mixture of short terrace blocks and semi-detached houses with front and back gardens, 12 houses to the acre. The road layout was more suited to pedestrians than to the growing volume of motor traffic. Building resumed at the end of World War Two with increased urgency and, by September 1958, 4,573 new houses had been built. Forty-four per cent of the housing stock in 1958 had been built since 1919 (9,638 houses), and was inhabited by 55 per cent of the total population. The main estates were Botcherby (546 houses), Currock and Upperby (1,848), Raffles and Wigton Road (2,352), Stanwix (644), Harraby (2,029) and Morton (754). The latter two were post World War Two. Private sector housing was on a considerably smaller scale, totalling 3,260 houses between 1919 and 1958.[2] A feature of post-war development was the provision of a limited number of shops and garages. Industry was kept out of residential areas by planning laws, and industrial estates developed at Durranhill and, later, Kingstown.

In recent years the supply of council housing has been restricted by financial constraints and changes in legislation, but a large-scale improvement scheme for pre-war houses was 85 per cent complete by 1988. The programme has now been extended to the 5,000 post-war houses, with an expected completion date of the year 2000. From 1981 government policy has encouraged occupiers to purchase their council houses, and although 2,500 have been sold, the proportion of council houses in Carlisle is still above the national average: in 1988 about 35 per cent of households were in local authority housing and 64 per cent were owner-occupiers. Since the 1970s private sector housing has been concentrated to the north and west of the urban area.[3]

The Infrastructure of Twentieth-Century Carlisle

Rapid growth in population at the turn of the century and the expectation of higher living standards necessitated a better service network. By 1900 the city's water supply was inadequate, and the corporation used its powers under the 1898 Water Act to secure a supply from springs and streams in the Geltsdale valley. The water was piped to a new storage reservoir at Castle Carrock and then to Carlisle via the Cumwhinton reservoir. The supply from the Eden was discontinued. After 1945, however, additional supplies were taken from the Eden at Wetheral, as the storage capacity at Castle Carrock proved inadequate in times of drought.[4]

As mentioned above, the Electric Light and Power Station was opened in 1899. In 1927 a new power station was erected at Willow Holme, and was connected to the national grid. The oldest municipal department, the gas-works adjoining Victoria Viaduct, purchased by the corporation in 1850, was superseded by a new works at Boustead Grassing in 1922.

The electric trams which ran through the streets from the city centre to the suburbs started operating in 1900. Most of them were double-deckers, but single-deckers were necessary in Denton Holme because of a low railway bridge. The gauge was narrow, 3ft. 6in., springing was rudimentary and the ride bumpy and noisy. On the lower deck the passengers sat facing each other on longitudinal wooden seating. Balfour Beatty bought the tramway system in 1912, but by 1931 it was judged that the trams were causing congestion, and they were taken out of service. There was some debate whether the corporation should run the services, but city transport was taken over by the Ribble and United bus companies.

Today, in 1991, severe traffic problems plague the city. The M6 skirts Carlisle on the east, but there is not a satisfactory route from it to West Cumberland through the west of the city. Although the Department of Transport has commissioned a study of M6 to A69 (Brampton and Newcastle) and M6 to A595 (Wigton and West Cumberland) links, implementation of a major scheme is not expected until after 1996.

Railways

The main legislation that affected the railways in the 20th century has been the 1921 Railway Act, which amalgamated the multitude of railway companies into four main groups, and the 1947 Transport Act, which nationalised the railway system. Carlisle was also affected by the closure of two unprofitable lines, advocated by the Beeching plan of 1963.

Before the 1921 grouping the citadel station must have presented a colourful and romantic sight. After the amalgamation and especially after nationalisation this diversity was lost. At the same time increasing road competition destroyed the viability of some lesser-used lines. The Carlisle and Silloth railway closed in 1964 and the Waverley line (Carlisle to Edinburgh) in the following year. A changing pattern of distribution was disastrous for the vast Kingmoor marshalling yard, which was completed in 1963 but never worked to full capacity, as block trains were substituted for single wagon freight trains. The relative importance of the railway to Carlisle's economy and employment is now at a much lower level than at nationalisation, mainly because road transport has to a considerable extent supplanted rail.

The Political Scene

In the early years of the century the parliamentary elections in Carlisle were usually straight fights between Liberal and Conservative candidates with a Liberal victory virtually inevitable. In 1918 the Fourth Reform Act increased the electorate threefold, when the franchise was extended to men over 21 and women over thirty. During the inter-war years

48.   The Town Hall and street market in the late 19th century.

the Labour party rose to prominence and increasingly the Liberal candidate was relegated to third place. The Equal Franchise Act was passed in 1929 and Carlisle's electorate was increased by a further 33 per cent, votes being given to women over 21 (the 'flapper' vote).

During the General Strike of 1926, contingency plans were set in place, and these are illustrated by the photograph of a formidable-looking posse of leading citizens, led by the mayor and chief constable, mobilised as special constables. In Carlisle, however, the strike did not affect the 1929 election, as it did in many other areas.

George Middleton, the city's first Labour M.P. in 1932, was for a decade to contest the seat with General Spears. Spears, Carlisle's M.P. during the war years, brought de Gaulle to Britain on the fall of France, and became head of the military mission to the Free French forces in Africa. In the post-war years the political contest followed the same pattern, but eventually Carlisle became a safe Labour seat.

In municipal elections the most marked innovation was the introduction of women into local government. In 1918 Mrs. Eliza Buchanan took her seat on the council. The first female magistrates were appointed in 1920, and in 1945-6 Carlisle had its first lady mayor, Mrs. Isa Graham. The greatest structural changes in local government took place when the Local Government Act of 1972 led to the abolition in 1974 of some county boundaries. Cumberland and Westmorland became Cumbria, and Carlisle became a district council with boundaries extended to include Brampton, Longtown and Dalston. The population was increased from 73,000 to 103,000 by this. It was inevitable that advances in transport and the community of interests between neighbouring districts would lead to large-scale planning and the control of services such as police, fire brigade, education, social services and libraries by the county.

Education

In 1902 primary education became a function of the local council and the first council school, the Robert Ferguson School, was taken over from the old school board. When Carlisle became a county borough in 1914, the responsibility for secondary education was given to the borough as well. In 1944, when the Education Act raised the school-leaving age to 15, secondary schools in the city fell into three categories. The grammar school for boys and the high school for girls, secondary modern schools, and the technical school. At this time the technical school and the school of art were housed in very cramped quarters at Tullie House, but in 1950 the school of art was moved to Homeacres on Brampton Road and a commodious technical college was built in Victoria Place.

In the 1960s the tripartite division and ranking of schools became a controversial political issue. Carlisle Grammar School and High School were integrated into the comprehensive co-educational system, the former becoming Trinity School and the latter St Aidan's, in 1970. In 1991 the future remains controversial, as proposals have been made for some schools to opt out of council control.

Leisure and Amenities

In the first half of the century Carlisle had two theatres. Her Majesty's Theatre opened c.1880 and the Palace Music Hall was established in 1906. Neither could compete with the cinema later in the century, and the Palace became a cinema in 1930. Her Majesty's Theatre struggled on until 1960 when, on the brink of financial collapse, it was taken over by the council. Municipal control was no more successful, and it finally closed in 1963.

The great source of mass entertainment in the early and mid-20th century was the cinema. It was a cohesive force socially, truly mass culture, attended by people of all ages and backgrounds. The Public Hall, formerly a Catholic church, was opened as a cinema in 1906, and the next two date from World War One, the City and the Botchergate. The palatial Lonsdale opened in 1931 and is now the only one left, albeit sharing its premises with a bingo hall. As theatre was affected by cinema, so was cinema affected by television.

49. General Strike, 1926. A formidable posse of leading citizens, led by the mayor and chief constable, were mobilised to escort essential services.

A great surge in television ownership followed the Coronation broadcast in 1953, and in 1961 Border Television began to compete with the B.B.C.

Spectator sport in Carlisle began with horse-racing on the Swifts, but the Duke of Devonshire declined to renew the lease when it expired in 1904, and the course was removed to its present site at Blackwell, two miles from the city centre. The other major spectator sport was football. Carlisle United, formerly Shaddongate United, was formed in 1904 and moved to its present home at Brunton Park in 1909. The club was elected to Division Three (North) in 1928, but the great period of glory began in 1974, with promotion to the first division. After winning the first three games, without conceding a goal, they were in an unassailable position at the top of the league. Sadly this was too good to last.

On a more intellectual plane Tullie House library was established in 1873. William Jackson donated a valuable collection of 2,500 volumes on local history, and when the Working Men's Room in Lord Street was closed in 1891 its 5,000 books were transferred to Tullie House. This was followed by stock from the subscription library in Devonshire Street which closed in 1896.

The fabric of the city

Dynamic growth in 20th-century Carlisle was concentrated in the vast new residential suburbs. The basic structure of the city remained intact, but secondary features were transformed. Motor traffic and competitive retail trade were the major catalysts for change.

In the inter-war years an ever-increasing volume of traffic necessitated major bridge-widening schemes: Caldew Bridge in 1926, St Nicholas Bridge in 1927, and Eden Bridge was doubled in width in 1932. Other concessions to the growing traffic were the closing of the open market in front of the Town Hall (1927), demolition of the Gaol Tap block (1930), replacement of cobbles by asphalt in practically all the main streets, and the replacement of trams with buses (1931).

Another aspect of the changing face of Carlisle was the gradual replacement of small, locally-based shops by department stores and other large multiple shops. Robinsons in English Street developed during the early decades of the century to become the major store in Carlisle, but was taken over by Binns in 1933. Burtons and Boots appeared, and Marks and Spencer and Woolworths played a leading rôle when they abandoned their down-market origins. The gaol wall was demolished in 1932, not without protest, and Burtons and Woolworths built on the site. Carlisle's first supermarket opened in 1962.

The strident commercialism of some of the new shop fronts had critics. The Design and Industries Association's 'Cautionary Guide to Carlisle' published photographs of some of the more aggressive displays which detracted from modest but dignified buildings.[5] In the 1930s motley advertisement hoardings around vacant sites and unsightly advertisements painted on gable ends greeted visitors as they entered the city.

The problem of traffic congestion arose again with the build-up of motor vehicles after World War Two, mainly because of the great volume of traffic passing through Carlisle on the journey between England and Scotland. The situation was aggravated, temporarily one hopes, by the pedestrianisation of the city centre in 1989. This scheme has, however, transformed the central shopping area, and the maturing of the numerous trees that have been planted will undoubtedly soften and enhance the urban scene.

The most noteworthy development in the city centre since 1945 has been the Lanes shopping precinct, which was built in 1984 on the site of increasingly derelict 19th-century lanes and courts. After considerable and prolonged controversy about what was architecturally suitable for this sensitive site, a design was chosen in which the frontage was on the same scale with, and sympathetic to, the old city streets. The scheme has

50.   Globe Lane, photographed *c.*1980, but retaining its 19th-century ambience. The lane was demolished to make way for the 'Lanes' shopping precinct.

delighted the local people, and won national acclaim when it was voted 'Best in Britain' by the British Council of Shopping Centres. Another development was the Sands centre, which has provided much-needed sporting facilities, and a concert hall/theatre.

Today Carlisle is a successful city with a generous mix of industries. Of the 2,500 registered businesses, at least six employ over 1,000 workers, but the great majority employ 10 or less. The unemployment rate is half the rate for northern England, and 20 per cent lower than the national average.[6] Carlisle can look to the next decade with a balanced economy which is no longer perilously dependent on the textile and railway industries. Hopes have been raised that the city will be drawn deeper into Europe after the channel tunnel has been opened and the west coast railway has been upgraded, but this may prove to be a chimera. Perhaps Carlisle's industrial base and administration services are best supported by tourism, for which it has long been a centre, being centrally placed for access to the Lake District, the Scottish border country, Pennine foothills and Hadrian's Wall, and an unspoilt Solway coastline. It is hoped that the recent opening of Tullie House Museum, which acts as a focus for Carlisle's fine heritage, is a sign that the city is becoming a tourist centre in its own right.

51a & b.   The award-winning 'Lanes' shopping precinct – exterior and interior views.

Appendix I

Population of Carlisle

1763	4,158[1]	1871	31,074
1780	6,299[2]	1881	35,884
1796	8,716[3]	1891	39,176
1801	9,555	1901	45,486
1811	11,554	1911	52,225
1821	14,531	1921	57,304
1831	19,069	1939	67,835
1841	21,964	1951	67,798
1851	26,598	1961	71,101
1861	29,417	1971	71,582
		1981	71,493

1. Inhabitants numbered at Lord Bishop of Carlisle's request (Hutchinson's *History*, p.667).
2. 1,605 families, 891 houses: Abridgement of the 'Observations on the Bills of Mortality in Carlisle from 1779 to 1787' (Hutchinson's *History*, p.667).
3. *Jollie's Directory*, p.9. Later enumerations were carried out according to Act of Parliament.

Appendix II

Professions, traders and domestic manufacturers in Carlisle

	1790[1]	1811[2]	1847[3]	1858[4]
Population	8,000	11,500	28,000	36,000
Professions				
Physician	4	8	5	20
Chemist and druggist	2	3	16	16
Dentist	–	–	2	7
Architect and surveyor	–	3	3	10
Attorney and solicitor	19	14	22	21
Accountant	–	–	–	5
Auctioneer	–	1	5	5
Insurance agent	–	6	27	45
Traders				
Baker and flour distributor	1	9	25	6
Confectioner	3	6	18	14
Butcher	7	38	38	47
Fishmonger	–	–	6	10
Grocer and tea dealer	37	62	66	131
General dealer	–	–	75	33
Dressmaker and milliner	8	16	38	36
Draper	11	20	23	37
Clothier	–	–	14	14
Tailor	9	12	17	17
Demostic manufacturers and retailers				
Boots, shoes, clogs	12	30	74	40
Clocks and watches	2	5	9	11
Building Trades				
Bricklayer and stonemason	1	3	6	9
Slater	–	3	5	2
Joiner and Cabinet-maker	3	16	13	12
Painter, Glazier, Paperhanger	3	7	–	12
Hotels and Catering				
Inns, Taverns, Beerhouses	117	103	137	154
Eating houses	–	–	–	10
Literary and Cultural				
Newsagent	–	–	1	3
Reading rooms	–	3	5	9
Stationer and bookseller	3	2	9	12

The sources for the statistics are:

1. *Universal British Directory* (1790)
2. *Jollie's Directory* (1811)

3. *History, Gazetteer & Directory of Cumberland*, Mannix & Whellan (1847)
4. *Directory and Trade Directory*, published by Scott, Hudson (1858)

The 1790 and 1811 entries are for individuals, but two entries for one address are listed as one business.

While the trend of the figures is unmistakable, their precision must be treated with caution because of possible differences of classification in the various directories.

The Carlisle directories give evidence of the increasing complexity of the Carlisle economy. An increasing number of professional people, domestic manufacturers and shops contrasted with the largely self-sufficient families of 1745.

Throughout the period under review Carlisle was very much a city of small shopkeepers and of domestic manufacturers not yet supplanted by the large scale manufacturers. People were becoming more literate as an increasing number of bookshops and reading rooms testify. There were also two weekly newspapers, the *Carlisle Journal* (Whig) founded in November 1798 and the *Carlisle Patriot* (Tory) founded in January 1815. The latter was renamed the *Cumberland News* in 1910.

Appendix III

CARLISLE OCCUPATIONS

1861 CENSUS

Male Workers	10,826	Female Workers	7,936
Transport		Domestic Service	1,000
Road	161		
Railway	574		
Metal workers	743		
Building	860		
Textiles	1,973	Textiles	2,252
Dress and Footware	620	Dress and Footware	746
Food, drink, tobacco, lodgings	799	Food, drink, tobacco, lodgings	382
Teachers	51	Teachers	74
Agriculture	563		
Scholars	2,468	Scholars	2,532
Clerks	64		
Others	1,950	Others	950

1901 CENSUS

Male Workers (10 yrs and over)	No	% of total	Female Workers (10 yrs and over)	No	% of total
Total occupied	13,579		Total occupied	6,486	
Transport	2,974	22	Domestic servants	1,407	21.6
Engineering, Metal working	1,274	9.3	Laundry	147	2.3
Building and con-struction	1,587	11.7	Teachers	257	4.0
Textiles	311	2.2	Textiles	1,097	16.9
Dress	721	5.3	Dress	924	14.2
Food, drink, tobacco, lodgings	1,470	10.0	Food, drink, tobacco, lodgings	1,085	16.7
Clerks	315	2.3			
Agriculture	207	1.5			
Others	4,720	35.7	Others	1,569	24.2

Appendix IV

CENSUS RETURNS OF 1921 and 1951

1921

	Male		Female	
Population	24,485		28,245	
Occupation	Occupied persons 12 yrs & over			
	16,581		8,245	

	Total	%	Total	%
Agriculture	363	2.2	48	–
Engineering and Metal Working	1,991	12	854	3
Textiles	796	4.8	1,155	14
Dress & Footwear	387	2.3	674	8
Food, Drink & Tobacco	493	3	787	9.4
Builders	683	4.1	–	–
Painters & Decorators	293	1.8	–	–
Woodworkers	687	4.1	–	–
Transport-Rail	2,668	16	–	–
Road	577	3.5	–	–
Commercial	1,645	9.9	1,007	12
Clerks	796	4.8	663	7.9
Professionals	404	2.4	479	5.7
inc. (teachers)	(96)		(304)	
Domestic servants	–	–	952	11.3

1951

	Male		Female	
Population	32,097		35,701	
Occupation	Occupied persons 15 yrs & over			
	21,902		10,977	

	Total	%	Total	%
Agriculture	304	1.4	33	–
Engineering and Metal Working	2,963	13.3	433	4
Textiles	445	2	853	7.8
Dress & Footwear	118	0.5	416	3.8
Food, Drink & Tobacco	315	1.4	339	3.1
Builders	1,264	5.8	–	–
Painters & Decorators	510	2.3	–	–
Woodworkers	623	2.8	–	–
Transport-Rail	2,380	10.8	–	–
Road	1,134	5.2	117	1
Commercial	2,103	9.6	1,441	13.2
Clerks	1,502	6.9	2,034	18.6
Professionals	928	4.2	867	7.9
inc. (teachers)	(144)		(304)	
Domestic servants	–	–	178	1.6

Appendix V

William Paley (1743-1805), archdeacon of Carlisle and famous theologian, was the philosophical exponent of government law enforcement policy in an age when property was sacrosanct. His influential book *Principles of Moral and Political Philosophy* (1785) was written during the time he was carrying out his pastoral duties in Carlisle. His policy was explicitly directed to the prevention of crime and the protection of property. He wrote 'the proper end of human punishment is not to the satisfaction of justices but to the prevention of crime'. From this premise he could rationally argue

> Crimes are not by any Government, nor in all cases, ought to be punished in proportion to their guilt but in proportion to the difficulty and necessity in preventing them.

He sought to impose upon the judges the duty of making arbitrary judgements so that only a small proportion of malefactors would be singled out to suffer the penalty of death, yet no one would take 'adventure upon the commission of any enormous crime from a knowledge that the laws have not provided for its punishment'. Thus Paley maintained that of those who received the sentence of death, only one in ten was executed.

Paley showed more prescience for problems of social order, foreseeing the danger of outward repression without gaining the acquiescence of the people:

> Let the civil government learn from hence to respect their subjects; let them be admonished, that the physical strength resides in the governed; that this strength only wants to be felt and roused to lay prostrate the most ancient and confirmed dominion; that the civil authority is founded in opinion; that the general opinion therefore ought always to be treated with deference, and managed with delicacy and circumspection.[47]

Paley identified the danger of the poor combining against their oppressors. The danger would be intensified if large numbers of dissatisfied men settled in the same districts of the city, especially if they were engaged in the same trade.

> the most frequent and desperate riots are those which break out amongst men of the same profession, as weavers . . . hence also the dangers of those great cities and crowded districts into which inhabitants of trading countries are commonly collected . . .

In Carlisle his presentiment was fulfilled at the notorious 1826 hustings riot in Caldewgate. William Paley is buried in Carlisle Cathedral in the north aisle.

Notes

Chapter 1

1. Tacitus, *The Agricola and the Germania*, ed. S.A. Handforth (1970), p.68.
2. ibid., pp.29-38.
3. Petriana is in modern Stanwix, across the Eden. 'Ala', literally a wing, is a cavalry regiment of 500 or 1,000 horsemen.
4. Cameron, K., *English Place Names* (1961), p.35. 'The Romano-British name of Carlisle was Luguvalium, meaning Luguvalo's town. The Celtic form was borrowed into English where in earlier sources it is spelt Luel. By the 9th century Celtic Cair, 'Fortified Place', has been prefixed to the old English form and this has evolved into the modern Carlisle.'
5. The Flavian emperors were Vespasian (A.D. 69-79), Titus (A.D. 79-81) and Domitian (A.D. 81-96).
6. McCarthy, M., *Carlisle, a Frontier City* (1980), p.8. This includes a speculative but informative reconstruction of the gate and rampart of the fort.
7. Charlesworth, D., 'Roman Carlisle', *Archaeological Journal* no. 135 (1978), p.115. A plan of the platform is reproduced from a survey dated 20 March 1892.
8. Shaw, R.C., 'Romano-British Carlisle: its Structural Remains', *C.W.* no. 24 (1924), p.100.
9. Ferguson, R.S., 'On a massive timber platform of early date uncovered at Carlisle, and on sundry relics connected therewith', *C.W.* no. 12 (1893), pp.344-64.
10. McCarthy, M. and Dacre, J.A., 'Roman Timber Buildings at Castle Street, Carlisle', *Antiquaries Journal* (1983), part 1, p.130.
11. McCarthy, M., 'Thomas, Chadwick and Post Roman Carlisle', in Pearce, S. (ed.), *The Early Church in Western Britain* (1982), p.244.
12. Caruana, I., 'Carlisle', *Current Archaeology* no. 86 (1983), pp.77-81.
13. Caruana, I and Coulston, J.C., 'Roman Bridge Stone from R. Eden', *C.W.* no. 87 (1987), pp.43-51.
14. McCarthy and Dacre, op.cit., pp.124-30.
15. McCarthy, M., 'Roman Carlisle', in Wilson, Jones and Evans (eds.), *Settlement and Society in Roman North* (1984), p.73.
16. Charlesworth, op. cit., p.123.
17. Rivet, A., 'British Section of Antonine Itinerary', *Britannia* (1970), p.42, and Richmond, I.R. and Crawford, O.G.S., 'British Section of Ravenna Cosmography', *Archaeologia* (1937), p.36.
18. Charlesworth, op. cit., p.123.
19. McCarthy, M., *Carlisle, a Frontier City*, p.13.
20. McCarthy, M., letter of April 1984.
21. Bede, *Lives of the Saints*, ed. J.F. Webb (1965), chapter 27.
22. Frere, S.S., 'The End of Towns in Roman Britain', in Wacher, J.C. (ed.), *Civitas Capitals of Roman Britain* (1966), p.88.
23. McCarthy, M., *Carlisle, a Frontier City*, pp.9-11.
24. McCarthy, M., 'Thomas, Chadwick and Post Roman Carlisle', p.249.

Chapter 2

1. Zosimus, *History of Count Zosimus*, Oxford edition (1814), pp.174-5.
2. ibid., p.177.
3. Bede, *History of the English Church and People*, ed. L. Sherley-Price (1968), p.53.
4. Gildas was a Briton and probably a monk. He wrote *De excidio c.* 530-44, relying on oral tradition for the fourth and fifth centuries in the absence of written records.
5. Camden, W., *The Destruction of Britain*, ed. E. Gibson (1722), vol. 2, col. cxviii.
6. Bede, op. cit., p.146.
7. The battle was dated 573 in Nennius' *Annales Cambriae*.
8. These sources were transmitted via Wales.
9. This view is held by Chadwick, N.K., 'The Conversion of Northumbria' and Jackson, K., 'Celtic

Background of Early Anglo-Saxon England', both from *Celtic and Saxon studies in the Early British Border* (1962), p.159 and pp.329-30 See also Nennius *Welsh Annals*, 66a.

10. Bede, op. cit., p.92.

11. Jackson, K., *Language and History of Early Britain* (1953), p.218.

12. Bede, *Lives of the Saints: Cuthbert*, chapter 27.

13. Colgrave, B. (ed.), *Two Lives* (1940), p.122.

14. Pevsner, N.,*Cumberland and Westmorland* (1967), p.68.

15. Symeon·of Durham, *Historia de Sancto Cuthberto*, ed. T. Arnold (1822-5), vol. 1, p.199.

16. After Ecgfrith's death, Cuthbert continued to develop the Church in Carlisle, possibly founding a monastery, a nunnery and a school.

17. Bede, *History of the English Church and People, pp.331-2.*

18. *Anglo-Saxon Chronicle*, ed. G.N.Garmonsway (1972), A.D.793.

19. ibid., 875.

20. Symeon of Durham, *Historia Regum*, ed. T. Arnold (1882), p.220. Symeon entered a Benedictine monastery at Jarrow *c*.1071 and moved to Durham in 1085. He died *c*.1130-8.

21. Symeon of Durham, *Historia de Sancto Cuthberto*, p.210.

22. Ekwall, E., *Scandinavians and Celts in N.W. England* (1918), p.2.

23. The origin of 'dale' is equivocal. It could have an Old English or a Norse root, but in the context of N.W. England the Norse origin seems probable. See Rollinson, W., *History of Cumberland and Westmorland* (1978), p.29, map 4, for the spread of Scandinavian place-names.

24. Goidelic refers to one of the two branches of the Celtic language, i.e. Irish, Manx, Gaelic and Brythonic; the other branch includes Welsh and Cornish.

25. Bailey, R.N., 'Aspects of Viking Age Sculpture in Cumbria' and Fellows Jensen, G., 'Scandinavian Settlement in Cumbria and Dumfriesshire, The Place Name Evidence', both in Baldwin, J.R. and Whyte, D.A., *Scandinavians in Cumbria* (1985) pp.58-9 and 72-3.

26. *Anglo-Saxon Chronicle*, 926.

27. Quoted in Armstrong, Mower, Stenton and Dickens, *Place Names of Cumbria* part 2 (1952), p.xxvii. Gospatric's writ was preserved among the Earl of Lonsdale's muniments in Lowther Castle.

28. Pevsner, op. cit., p.16.

29. Correspondence with Professor Bailey, January 1989.

30. Caruana, I., 'Carlisle', *Current Archaeology* (August 1986), p.177.

31. Keevill, G., *Carlisle Cathedral Excavations 1988 Interim Report.*

Chapter 3

1. *Anglo-Saxon Chronicle*, p.227.

2. When Carlisle was rebuilt as a plantation town the street pattern was constrained by the Roman plan rather than being laid out anew on a rectilinear grid.

3. Todd, H., *Account of the City and Diocese of Carlisle* (1699), pp.11-12. Todd seems to have relied on Denton's earlier works.

4. Jones, B.C., 'Topography of Medieval Carlisle', *C.W.* (1976), p.84.

5. Symeon of Durham, *Historia Regum*, p.267. The pipe rolls of Henry I, however, suggest that the city wall was built in 1130-1.

6. For instance, in 1086 only two of the 180 barons in the land were Anglo Saxon, and there was only one English bishop.

7. Henry, the son of King David held Cumberland as a fief of England from 1136.

8. Howlett, R. (ed.), *Chronicles of reigns of Stephen and Henry II* vol. 3 (1886), pp.253-69.

9. *Acts of Parliament of Scotland* vol. 1., Appendix to Preface, p.3.

10. Bliss, W.H. (ed.), *Calendar of Papal Registers*, Papal letters 1 (1198-1304), p.48.

11. Jones, op. cit.

12. ibid. See also Hogg, R., 'The Historic Crossings of the R. Eden', *C.W.* no. 52 (1952), p.131.

13. Nicolson, J. and Burn, R., *History and Antiquities of Counties of Westmorland and Cumberland* (1777), p.456. (Volume no.2).

14. Jones, op. cit.

15. Charter Edward II 1316.

16. Nanson, W., 'On the Customary Tenure at Carlisle called the Cullery Tenure', *C.W.* (1883), pp.305-18.

17. The Moot Hall was located where the old town hall now stands. Baxter Row and the Shambles were on opposite sides of the market-place. The land formerly occupied by the ditch was on the north side of the former Annetwell Street and Finkle Street.

18. Shirley, W.W. (ed.), *Royal letters of Henry III vol. 2, 1236-72* (1862-6), p.124.
19. Bain, J. (ed.), *Calendar of Documents relating to Scotland 1108-1272* (1895), p.391.

Chapter 4

1. *Chronicle of Lanercost 1272-1346*, ed. H. Maxwell (1913), p.88.
2. Duckworth, J., *The Carlisle Parliaments of Edward I* (1930), p.6. The writs were issued to 11 earls, 106 barons and to the sheriffs throughout the county.
3. Nicolas, H., *Siege of Caerlaverock* (1828), pp.3-5.
4. Nicolson, J. and Burn, R., *History and Antiquities of Counties of Westmorland and Cumberland*, (volume no.2) p.177. They draw upon parliamentary records for 1305: 'that town together with the way leading to it is carried away by the sea . . .'.
5. Ferguson, R.S., *History of Cumberland* (1890), p.228, quoting from Holinshed.
6. I should like to thank Professor M.C. Prestwich for his helpful suggestions on the question of identification. In correspondence he draws attention to two sketches of the king from memorando rolls, and the picture from Westminster Abbey reproduced in his book *Edward I*, which bear some relation to the Carlisle sculpture. He warns, though, that certain identification is impossible.
7. *Chronicle of Lanercost*, p.197.
8. ibid., p.205.
9. Hobelars were men mounted on 'hobbies' (fell ponies).
10. A church just outside the city walls. Not the 19th-century Holy Trinity church.
11. A simple version of the onager, which threw stones or darts.
12. *Chronicle of Lanercost*, pp.213-5.
13. ibid., p.228.
14. Bain, J. (ed.), *Calendar of Documents relating to Scotland*, p.799.
15. *Chronicle of Lanercost*, pp.237-9.
16. ibid., pp.141-2.
17. ibid., p.245. The parliamentary writ, however, states that the earl's quarters were bound for Carlisle, Newcastle, York and Shrewsbury.
18. ibid., p.245.
19. Bouch, C.M.C., *Prelates and People of the Lake Counties* (1948), pp.68-9.
20. *Calendar of Patent Rolls*, 1 Edward II pt. 1 m.15, 16 and 18.
21. ibid., 9 Edward III 1335 and 28 Edward III 1355.
22. *Chronicle of Lanercost*, p.257.
23. Wilson, J. (ed.), *Victoria County History of Cumberland* vol. 2 (1905), p.42.
24. *Chronicle of Lanercost*, p.228.
25. *Calendar of Patent Rolls*, 1343-5 m. 16d.
26. Lumby, J.R. (ed.), *Chronicon Henrici Knighton 1348-9* Roll Series (1895).
27. Ferguson, R.S., *Royal Charters of Carlisle* (1894), p.25. Charter 25 Edward III (1352).
28. Ziegler, P., *The Black Death* (1970), p.191.
29. Nicolson and Burn, op. cit., p.5.
30. Bain, op. cit., p.347.
31. ibid., p.320 and p.324. And *Calendar of Patent Rolls*.1377–81, Rich. II pt. 2, 1380.
32. The episode was used by Shakespeare in *Richard II*, Act IV.
33. Ferguson, R.S., *Royal Charters*, contains details of all Carlisle's charters.
34. *Calendar of Papal Petitions*, p.437.
35. Bulman, C.G., 'Carlisle Cathedral', *C.W.* no. 49 (1949).
36. Bouch, op. cit., p.79.
37. *Calendar of Patent Rolls* m.13 1393.
38. Wilson, op. cit., p.41, quoting from *Carlisle Epistolary Register*.
39. Jones, B.C., 'Topography of medieval Carlisle', *C.W.* (1976). Most of the topographical data in this section is based on Jones' article. See also Perriam, D.R., 'Unrecorded Carlisle church: the church of the Holy Trinity Caldewgate', appendix by Jones, *C.W.* (1979).
40. Gosling, P.F., *Carlisle an Archaeological Survey of the Historic Town* (1970), p.170.
41. Bouch, C.M.L., op. cit., p.99.
42. Gosling, P.F., p.171.
43. Jones, B.C., 'House building in the middle ages', *C.W.* (1986).
44. Ferguson, R.S., 'Testamenta Karleolensis of 1353-86', *C.W.* extra series (1892).

Chapter 5

1. *Letters and Papers* vol. IV, 20 Henry VIII. 5,055 20 December 1528: Earl of Northumberland to Brian Tuke.
2. ibid., 28 Henry VIII 687 20 March 1537 'The Northern Rebellion'.
3. ibid., vol. XII, Henry VIII 498 24 February 1537: Norfolk to Henry VIII.
4. ibid., 28 Henry VIII 478 21 February 1537: Norfolk to Cromwell.
5. Bain, J. (ed.), *Hamilton Papers 1532-1590* (1890-2), l.xxxiii-lxxxvi. A Remembrance made by Sir Thomas Wharton to the Earl of Hertford.
6. Mary Stuart was a granddaughter of Henry VIII's sister Margaret, who had married James IV of Scotland. She ascended to the throne of Scotland when her father James V died, in 1542.
7. Nicolson, W., *Leges Marchiarum* (1747). Letters from Lord Wharton, p.148.
8. Keeling, S.M., 'Reformation on the Anglo Scottish Border Counties', *Northern History* (1979), p.27 and p.36.
9. *Calendar of State Papers relating to Scotland 1509-1603*, 18 May 1568, Carlisle, ed. M.J. Thorpe (1858).
10. ibid., 22 May 1568 Carlisle.
11. ibid., 8 June 1568: Knollys to Cecil.
12. ibid., Domestic Addenda, 11 July 1568.
13. ibid., Knollys to Cecil, 11 June 1568. 14. ibid., 15 June 1568.
15. ibid., 12 June 1568: Herries to Leicester.
16. ibid., Domestic Addenda, 2 September 1568.
17. ibid., 13 March 1569.
18. This was against the Duke of Norfolk, contesting the wardship of his nieces, who prejudiced his claim to the Dacre inheritance.
19. ibid., Domestic Addenda, 13 December 1569. Declaration by John, Bishop of Carlisle, of a conspiracy to kill him and take the castle.
20. ibid., Domestic Addenda, 13 December 1569.
21. ibid., Domestic Addenda, 3 February 1570: Scrope to Hunsdon and Forster.
22. ibid., Domestic Addenda, 21 February 1570: Hunsdon to Cecil. And 20 December 1570: Hunsdon to Queen.
23. ibid, Domestic Addenda, 7 February 1593: Petition of John Meye and 11 others, the sheriff and J.P.s in the Western Marches, to the council.
24. ibid.
25. Appleby, A.B., *Famine in Tudor and Stuart England* (1978), p.36.
26. Stedman, J.O., 'A very indifferent small city'. *The Economy of Carlisle 1550-1700* (1988), pp.34-9. The returns for the parishes of St Mary and St Cuthbert include a number of rural settlements. A multiplier is used to convert households to population. The census included households within the city walls, and an estimate was used for houses in the suburbs. Large estimate variance occurs as disparate assumptions are made.
27. Appleby, op. cit., pp.183 and 134.
28. *State Papers* (1597). Complaint of William James, Dean of Durham, to Burghley.
29. Stedman, op. cit., p.167. P.R.O. S.P.12/117/83.
30. Ferguson, R.S., *Royal Charters of Carlisle*, p.xxiii.
31. Stedman, op. cit., pp.201-2. L.R.2/212 ff.129-58.
32. ibid., p.175. P.R.O. S.P.14/22/3.
33. ibid., p.162. That is, 26 per cent tanners, 10 per cent shoemakers and 7 per cent glovers.

Chapter 6

1. *Historical Commission Manuscript Report 10, Appendix Four*, 14 February 1604-5: Council to Commissioners, p.229.
2. ibid.: King to Commissioners, f3. N.D.
3. ibid., 17 May 1605: Council to Commissioners.
4. ibid., 13 September 1606.
5. ibid.
6. Also known as Bauld (Bold) Willie. The more familiar nickname of Belted Will can be attributed to Sir Walter Scott, in his 'Lay of the Last Minstrel'. Lord William was a scholar and antiquary, and the founder of a notable library at Naworth Castle.
7. The family of Dacre had ended in daughters. They were the wards of the Duke of Norfolk, who had married them into the Howard family. Lord William Howard married Elizabeth Dacre, one of the three

co-heiresses of Lord Dacre of Gilsland. It was the division of the Dacre estates between the three sisters that so riled their uncle, Sir Leonard Dacre, and led him into his ill-starred adventure of rebellion against Queen Elizabeth.

8. Ornsby, G. (ed.), *Household Book of Lord William Howard* (1878), 1603-4: Lord William Howard to Sir W. Lawson.

9. ibid., pp.423-5. 1616: 'A Paper concerning Lord William Howard and the State of the Northern Counties as regards Recusancy'.

10. Ferguson, R.S., *Diocesan History of Carlisle* (1889), pp.132-3. Bishop Snowden's address to the King, found in papers of the Dukes of Buckingham.

11. ibid.

12. Jefferson, S., *History and Antiquities of Carlisle* (1838), p.47. He is quoting from a manuscript in the British Museum: *Journal of a Tour through part of England by three officers.*

13. Nightingale, B., *The Ejected of 1662 in Cumberland and Westmorland* (1911), pp.136-7. See also Perriam, D.R., 'Demolition of Priory of St Mary's Carlisle', *C.W.* no.87 (1987).

14. *Historical Manuscripts Commission Report 10, Appendix Four*, 28 September 1640: Sir William Howard, Sir George Dalston and Sir Thomas Dacre to the High Constable of Allerdale.

15. Rushworth, J., *Historical Collections (1659-1721)*, 27 October 1640, p.1307.

16. Jefferson, S. (ed.), *Narrative of Siege of Carlisle 1644-5 by Isaac Tullie* (1840). Tullie is the principal source of evidence for the siege. Although his account is pro-royalist, he was subsequently well-disposed to the Commonwealth, and served as mayor. Tullie died shortly after the Restoration.

17. There are copies of the coins in Carlisle Museum.

18. Jefferson, *Narrative of Siege*, p.24.

19. ibid., p.44.

20. ibid., p.47.

21. *Historical Manuscripts Commission*, Report 6, p.158.

22. Mannix and Whellan, *History, Gazetteer and Directory*, p.111.

23. *Historical Manuscripts Commission Report 12, Appendix Seven*, (1890), 20 October 1651, p.20. 24. Todd, H., *An Account of the City and Diocese of Carlisle* (1697), p.26.

25. Perriam, op. cit., pp.132-3. He believes that the reduced importance of the cathedral, the decreased congregation and the poor condition of the building led to the demolition of the nave *c.*1652.

26. Nicolson and Burn, *History and Antiquities* vol. 1, pp.170-1.

27. Ferguson, op. cit., pp.xxviii-xxix.

28. 13-14 Charles II c.22 (1662).

29. North, R., *Lives of the Norths* (1826), pp.277–97.

30. Stedman, J., '*A very indifferent small city*', Appendix Four, p.376.

31. ibid., pp.304-7.

32. ibid., pp.372-4.

33. Cumbria Record Office: pp.612, 1,587, 1,691 and 1,628.

34. Todd, op. cit., pp.29-30.

35. Morris, C. (ed.), *Illustrated Journeys of Celia Fiennes 1685-1712* (1984), pp.172-3.

36. Perriam, D.R. *Carlisle in Camera* (1988), p.16.

37. Stedman, op. cit., p.356. Survey in C.R.O.

Chapter 7

1. Downie, J.A., 'Disfranchisement of Christopher Musgrave, M.P., by Carlisle Corporation in 1692', *C.W.* no. 75 (1975), p.78.

2. Hopkinson, R., *Elections in Cumberland and Westmorland (1695-1725)* (1973), pp.193-5.

3. ibid., p.187.

4. Hopkinson, R., 'The Electorate of Cumberland and Westmorland in the late 17th and early 18th centuries', *N.H.* no. 15 (1979), p.107.

5. A pocket borough was one in which the right to nominate the parliamentary representative was held by one person.

6. *Historical Manuscripts Commission Report 15, Appendix Six*, 29 Oct. 1715. Lord Carlisle MS.

7. Bishop Nicolson has been described as 'a man of great gifts, the possessor of an intellect of singular acuteness, a man of great versatility, Anglo-Saxon scholar, medievalist, antiquarian, botanist, diarist, administrator, politician; lover of a good dinner, and of good conversation, and fond of the sports of his day – hunting and cockfighting, but he was no soldier'. Bouch, C.M.C., *Prelates and People of the Lake Counties* (1948), p.317.

8. *Gentleman's Magazine*, vol. XVI (May 1746), p.234.

9. Jefferson, S., *History and Antiquities of Carlisle* (1838), pp.59-64.
10. Lewis, W.S., Smith, W.H. and Law, G.L. (eds.), *Horace Walpole – Correspondence with Sir Horace Mann* vol.3 (1955), p.165.
11. ibid., pp.165-6.
12. Mounsey, G.G., *Occupation of Carlisle 1745* (1846), p.94.
13. *Gentleman's Magazine*, op. cit., p.235.
14. Holtby, R.T., *Carlisle Cathedral* (1969), p.20.
15. Perriam, D.R., 'Demolition of the Priory of St Mary Carlisle', *C.W.* no. 87 (1987), p.142.
16. *Gentleman's Magazine*, op. cit., pp.494-5.
17. Wilson, J., *Victoria County History of Cumberland and Westmorland* vol.2 (1905), p.308.
18. Defoe, D., *A tour through the whole Island of Great Britain* (1724), p.278.
19. Hutton, B.G., 'A Lakeland Journey' (John Crofts), *C.W.* no. 61 (1961), p.292.
20. Hutchinson, W., *History and Antiquities of Carlisle* (1794), pp.659-61.
21. ibid., pp.659-61.
22. Morris, C. (ed.), *Illustrated Journeys of Celia Fiennes*, pp.172-3.
23. Prevost, W.A.J., 'A Journie to Carlisle and Penrith in 1721' (Sir John Clerk), *C.W.* New Series L XI (1961), p.202.
24. Beckett, J.V., *Landowners in Cumbria c.1680-1750* (1975), p.45.
25. Radcliffe, W., *Origin of the New System of Manufacturing called Power Loom Weaving* (1828, reprinted 1974), p.58. The main textile areas listed by him were:
a. Manchester and area within 30-50 mile radius.
b. Glasgow, including Perth, Aberdeen and much of the Highlands.
c. Nottingham, Derby, Warwick, Lichfield, etc.
d. Carlisle and environs, stretching as far as the Manchester and Glasgow areas.
26. 8 Geo.I c.14. Bank End on the Eden is halfway between the Solway and Carlisle.
27. Chartres, J.A., 'Road carrying in England in the 17th century: myth and reality', *Economic History Review*, second series XXX no. 1 (1977), pp.73-89.
28. The turnpike acts largely removed the burden of trunk roads from the parishes to bodies authorised to charge tolls, which provided an equitable means of financing road improvements, chargeable to the people who used the roads.
29. Harley, *Journey in England* (1725). Historical Manuscripts Commission: Report on MSS of Dukes of Portland.
30. *Cumberland Pacquet*, 9 May 1734.
31. Williams, L.A., *Road Transport in Cumberland* (1975), p.38.
32. Lawson, W., 'Construction of the Military Road in Cumberland 1751-58', *C.W.* new series L XXIX (1979), p.1. The equivalent modern road is the B6264 from Carlisle to Brampton, then the B6318 from Greenhead to Heddon.
33. ibid., p.118.
34. Mannix and Whellan, *History, Gazetteer, and Directory*, p.38.
35. Williams, op. cit., p.35.
36. *Cumberland Pacquet*, 15 December 1774.
37. *Universal British Directory* (1790), p.63.
38. Woodall, R.G., 'Carlisle Mails', *The Philatelist* (August 1950), p.3.
39. *Cumberland Pacquet*, 21 November 1791.
40. *Universal British Directory* (1790), p.631.
41. Bailey, J. and Culley, G., *General View of Agriculture in Cumberland* (1794), p.22.
42. Nicolson and Burn, *History and Antiquities* vol. 2, p.11.
43. Hutchinson, W., op. cit., p.659.
44. Mannix and Whellan, op. cit., p.147.
45. Ferguson, R.S., 'On the Collection of Chap-Books in the Bibliotheca Jacksoniana at Tullie House, Carlisle', *C.W.* (1896), p.5. The Pinners-up affixed their wares to walls or railings. Long-Song-Sellers pasted three yards of songs together, and their wares were carried suspended from the top of a tall pole.
46. Marshall, J.D. and Walton, J.K., *The Lake Counties from 1830 to the mid-twentieth century* (1981), p.20. Whitehaven's core of professional and married men numbered 7.6 per cent of males over 20. In Carlisle this was 5.4 per cent, and nationally 5.6 per cent.

Chapter 8

1. Jones, B.C., 'Carlisle's First Factory', *C.W.* no. 85 (1985).
2. Hutton, B.G., 'A Lakeland Journey', *C.W.* no. 61 (1961).

3. Two of these printfields are shown on the map of 1790: Lamb's, on Corporation Dam; and Donald's, in Willow Holme.

4. Barnes, J., *Popular Protest and Radical Politics 1790-1850* (1981), p.25.

5. Muggeridge, R.M., *Report on condition of Hand-Loom Weavers* (1840), pp.584–6.

6. Lysons, *Magna Britannia*, vol. 4 (1816), p.6, and Douglas Jarrold's Weekly Newspaper (October 1846).

7. Brown, J.W., *Round Carlisle Cross* (1928), p.39.

8. Radcliffe, W., *Origin of the New System of Manufacturing called Power Loom Weaving* (1828), p.60. He estimated that it required six to eight people to spin and prepare enough yarn to keep one weaver working.

9. Eden, F.M., *The State of the Poor* (1797, reissued 1966), p.60.

10. Table One: average weekly wage from Muggeridge report, p.552, and weight of 'shopping basket' and rent index from *Select Committee Report on Hand Loom Weavers* (1835), p.xxxi.

11. Muggeridge, op. cit., p.594.

12. *Carlisle Journal*, 12 June 1812.

13. ibid., 3 March 1819.

14. This was a system of outdoor relief that was adopted in Berkshire in 1795, and followed widely. Wages that were below subsistence were supplemented.

15. Pringle, *The Commissioners of the Poor Law Report*, Appendix A (1834), p.323A.

16. Jollie, F., *Directory* (1811), p.83.

17. Jerrold, op. cit., October 1846.

18. Losh quoted by Mawson, D.J.W., 'Langthwaite Cotton Mill', *C.W.* no. 76 (1976), p.168.

19. *Carlisle Journal*, 16 January 1836.

20. Mannix and Whellan, *History, Gazetteer and Directory*, p.166.

21. Bulmer, T., *History and Directory of East Cumberland* (1884), p.52.

22. *Universal British Directory* (1790), p.623.

23. William Chapman (1749-1832). An eminent engineer and friend of Watt and Matthew Boulton. He was a consultant engineer for many dock and canal schemes. Thomas Harrison (1744-1829). An architect, who studied in Rome. He designed and rebuilt many buildings, for example Chester Castle and Lancaster Castle, and built bridges, including Grosvenor Bridge, Chester, and Skerton Bridge, Lancaster. Thomas Telford (1757-1834). Widely regarded as the greatest engineer of the age, he built many major roads, canals and bridges.

24. Chapman, W., *Survey of Line of Navigation from Newcastle upon Tyne to the Irish Channel* (1795).

25. Chapman, W., *Report on the means of obtaining a safe and commodious communication from Carlisle to the Sea* (1807).

26. Harrison, T., *A Letter to the Select Committee of the Cumberland Navigation Canal* (1808).

27. Telford, T., *Report on the intended Cumberland Canal* (1808).

28. Chapman, W., *Report on the proposed Canal Navigation between Carlisle and the Solway Firth* (1818).

29. The subscriptions from the great landowners included the Earl of Lonsdale, £5,000; John Christian Curwen, M.P., £1,000; Sir James Graham, £1,000; Sir Philip Musgrave, £500. Subscriptions from the industrialists included Peter Dixon and Sons, £4,000, James and John Forster, £2,000; J.R. and J. Ferguson, £1,500; Richard and John Ferguson, £500 each.

30. Total estimated annual tonnage was 73,749. This included coal, 29,549; lime, 15,000; stone from Whitehaven, 5,000; slate, 1,500; cotton yarn, 1,500; linen from Ireland, 800; grain, 2,000; timber, 1,800; manufactured goods for export, 1,000.

31. The total population of Carlisle at this time was about sixteen thousand. It is evident that the opening ceremony of the canal must have dominated the lives of people both in the city and in a considerable part of the surrounding countryside.

32. *Carlisle Journal*, 12 March 1823.

33. Parson, W., and White, W., *History, Directory and Gazetteer of Counties of Cumberland and Westmorland* (1829), p.168. The services from the canal basin included boats to Liverpool weekly, to Glasgow regularly and to Bowness three times a week during the summer.

Chapter 9

1. The major sources for this chapter are reports by Dr. D.B. Reid, Robert Rawlinson, Sir John Walsham and Edwin Chadwick, that were published between 1840 and 1850. Full details are given in the bibliography.

2. Rawlinson, R., *Report to General Board of Health* (1850), p.91.

3. ibid., pp.54-5.

4. ibid., pp.91 and 101–3.

5. ibid., p.90.

6. ibid., p.51, quoting the *Report of the Carlisle Sanitary Association*.

7. Reid, D.B., *Report on the State of Large Towns* (1845), pp.214-5. Brown's Row was near Brown Street, which has now disappeared under the southern railway approach to the citadel station.

8. Rawlinson, op. cit., p.56.

9. Reid, op. cit., p.215.

10. Rawlinson, op. cit., p.50, quoting Dr. Murray.

11. Reid, op. cit., p.216.

12. ibid., p.215.

13. Rawlinson, op. cit., p.50.

14. Taylor, A., 'The Dukery of Carlisle', *Country Life* (31 August 1989), quoting James Losh's diary.

15. Peter Dixon built at Holme Eden (1837), his brother John at Knells (1835), Richard Ferguson at Harker Lodge (1807). The banker George Head built Rickerby House (1834). Other houses erected at this time include Brunstock House (1828-30), Castleton House (1809-11), Houghton House (c.1818) and Woodside (c.1826), occupied by James Losh.

16. John Heysham M.D. (1753-1834) settled in Carlisle in 1778, and lived there until his death. He was also a naturalist, and his observations of the district's flora and fauna were published in Hutchinson's *History of the County of Cumberland*. Heysham is buried in the cathedral, and a memorial window to him has been placed at the east end of the south aisle. See Glass, D.V., *Development of Population Statistics* (1973), where Heysham's 'Observations on the Bills of Mortality in Carlisle' are reprinted.

17. Glass, D.V., *Development of Population Statistics*, p.6.

18. ibid., p.5.

19. Henry Barnes' President's Address, at the 64th annual meeting of the British Medical Association (1896), *British Medical Journal* (August 1896), p.248.

20. Glass, op. cit., p.1.

21. ibid.

22. Young, G.M., *Portrait of an Age* (2nd edition, 1953), p.21.

23. Chadwick, E., *Report on Sanitary Conditions of Labouring Population* (1842), p.370.

24. Mannix and Whellan, *History, Gazetteer and Directory*, p.144.

25. Rawlinson, op. cit., p.64.

26. Barnes, op. cit., p.249.

27. Barnes, J., *Popular Protest and Radical Politics in Carlisle 1790-1850* (1981), pp.96–108.

28. Ferguson, R.S., *Cumberland and Westmorland M.P.s 1660-1867* (1871), p.250.

29. ibid., pp.248-50.

30. Lakeman, W.H., *Local Government of the City and County Boroughs of Carlisle 1158-1958* (1958), p.51.

31. Parson and White, *History, Directory and Gazetteer*, p.130.

32. They supported reforms that together were known as the People's Charter: universal male suffrage, equal electoral districts, vote by ballot, annual parliaments, abolition of property qualifications for members, and payment of members.

33. Hutchinson, W., *History of the County of Cumberland*, vol II (1794), p.680.

34. ibid., pp.680-1.

35. ibid., p.680.

36. Nutter, M.E., *Carlisle in Olden Times* (1835), p.26.

37. Mannix and Whellan, op. cit., pp.83-4.

38. Bouch, *Prelates and People*, pp.380-1. Quotes the report of commissioners who were appointed to enquire into ecclesiastical revenues in England and Wales, in 1835.

39. *Carlisle Journal*, 8 October 1803.

40. Wordsworth, D., *Journal* (1803), ed. W. Knight, p.164.

41. Robert Smirke was the designer of many important buildings, including the British Museum. He designed the court houses in Carlisle, the new Eden Bridge and Lowther Castle.

42. *Jollie's Directory* (1811), p.9. Jollie's complacency about the openness of the principal streets was not shared by Mannix and Whellan, who complained of the clutter of old buildings adjoining the market house in 1847.

43. Perriam, D.R., 'Demolition of Carlisle City Walls', *C.W.* (1976), p.189.

44. Parson and White, op. cit., p.14.

45. 'Old Carlisle', *Cumbrian Gazette* (1986).

Chapter 10

1. Chapman, W., *Report on cost and separate advantages of a ship canal or railway from Newcastle to Carlisle* (1824).
2. 10 Geo.IV c.72.
3. Mannix and Whellan, *History, Gazetteer and Directory*, p.40.
4. Jefferson, S., *History and Antiquities of Carlisle* (1838), pp.305-7.
5. Mannix and Whellan, op. cit., p.145.
6. *Carlisle Journal*, 18 December 1846.
7. The *Carlisle Journal* gave the figure of 930 horses, but Mr. Mould, superintendent for the contractors, was reported as saying that 10,500 horses were employed. Possibly this referred to the whole period of the contract, but if the figures are to be reconciled there must have been a horrific loss of horses.
8. *Carlisle Journal*, 18 December 1846.
9. Walton, J., 'Railways and Resort development in Victorian development in Victorian England: the case of Silloth', *Northern History* (1979), p.196.
10. *Carlisle Journal*, 29 August 1856.
11. The expenditure was authorised only for the purpose laid down in the act, i.e. railway and dock. The creation of a new town was not mentioned.
12. The central part of the line, reaching 1,200 ft. on the Pennine moors between the Eden and Ribble valleys, needed 14 viaducts, nine tunnels, embankments and cuttings to permit a fast line, with a maximum gradient of one in a hundred.
13. *Arthur's Guide to Carlisle* (1881), pp.136-7.
14. Howard, J.M., *Notes on the Railways of Carlisle.*
15. Now the co-educational Trinity School.
16. Hutchinson, W., *History and Antiquities of Carlisle*, p.659.
17. Both schools used the monitorial system, in which a single teacher taught a small number of the older and more able children, who in turn each instructed another group. Inevitably the teaching was by rote, and many groups were taught simultaneously in one large classroom.
18. Parson and White, *History, Directory and Gazetteer* (1829), p.144.
19. See Appendix Two.
20. Marshall, J.D. and Walton, J.K., *The Lake Counties from 1830*, p.243. The *Journal* was a liberal paper, and the *Patriot* was conservative.
21. ibid., p.142.
22. Mannix and Whellan, op. cit., p.147.
23. Jefferson, op. cit., p.96.
24. Whellan, W., *History of Cumberland and Westmorland* (1860), p.96.
25. The great band of rail tracks between West Walls and Denton Holme necessitated underpasses, but these, in time, proved to be inadequate. The solution was the construction of Victoria Viaduct in 1877, into which Nelson Bridge was integrated.
26. Harris, A., 'Denton Holme, Carlisle', *C.W.* no.67 (1967), p.220.

Chapter 11

1. *Commerce and Industry Directory 1989-90*: Cumbria.
2. *Local Government of City and County Borough of Carlisle 1158-1958* (1958).
3. *Carlisle Urban Area Local Plan* (Carlisle City Council, 1989).
4. *Local Government*, op.cit.
5. Williams-Ellis, C. (foreword), *Cautionary Guide to Carlisle* (1930). An especial seal of approval was given to the new, and renovated, public houses built under the State Management Scheme of 1916, and the consequent abolition of many of the old drinking dens. Management by the State was a successful answer to the notorious drink problems of munitions workers at nearby Gretna. It was only in 1975 that the industry was re-privatised.
6. Figures from N-Com. Cablevision of Carlisle Ltd. Market research in support of application for cable franchise: 1990.

Bibliography

LIST OF ABBREVIATIONS

A.J.	Archaeological Journal
B.A.R.	British Archaeological Report
C.A.	Current Archaeology
E.H.R.	Economic History Review
N.H.	Northern History

PRIMARY SOURCES

Anglo Saxon Chronicle, ed. G. N. Garmonsway (1972)
Bain, James (ed.), *Chronicles of John, Prior of Hexham* (1864)
Bain, J. (ed.), *Hamilton papers 1532-1590* (1890-2)
Bain, J. (ed.), *Border papers 1560-1603* (1894-6)
Bain, J. (ed.), *Calendar of Documents relating to Scotland 1108-1272* (1895)
Bede, *History of the English Church and People*, ed. L. Sherley-Price, (1968)
Bede, *Lives of the Saints*, ed. J. F. Webb (1965)
Bliss, W. H. (ed.), *Calendar of Papal Registers and Papal Letters 1198-1304* (1895)
Camden, W., *The Destruction of Britain*, ed. E. Gibson (1722)
Defoe, D., *A tour through the whole Island of Great Britain* (1724)
Douglas, D. C. and Greenaway, G. W., 'Richard of Hexham', *English Historical Documents*, vol. 2 (1981)
Eyton, R. W. (ed.), *Itinerary of Henry II* (1978)
Fiennes, C., *Illustrated Journeys of Celia Fiennes 1682-1712*, ed. C. Morris (1982)
Golgrave, B. (ed.), *Two Lives of St Cuthbert* (1971)
Haddon, A. W. and Stubbs, W. (eds.), *Councils and Ecclesiastical Documents* (1869-78)
Hinde, T. (ed.), *Symeon of Durham* (Rolls Service)
Howlett, R. (ed.), *Chronicles of reigns of Stephen and Henry II* (1884-9)
Leland, J., *Itinerary* (1685)
Lumby, J. R., (ed.), *Chronicon Henrici Knighton 1348-9* (1895)
Lysons D., *Magna Britannia* (1816)
Maxwell, H. (ed.), *Chronicles of Lanercost 1272-1346* (1913)
Nennius, *British History and Welsh Annals*, ed. J. Morris (1980)
Nicolson, W., *Leges Marchiarum* (1747)
Ornsby, G. (ed.), *Household Books of Lord William Howard of Naworth* (1878)
Paley, W., *Principles of Moral and Political Philosophy* (1785)
Radcliffe, W., *Origin of the New System of Manufacturing called Power Loom Weaving* (1828)
Rushworth, J., *Historical Collections,(1659-1721)*
Shirley, W. W. (ed.), *Royal letters of Henry III* (1862-8)
Stephenson, J. (ed.), *Chronicle de Mailross* (1835)
Stubbs, W., (ed.), *Benedict Abbas Gesta Hen. II, Ric. I* (Rolls Series)
Symeon, *History Dunelm Eccles*, ed. T. Arnold (Rolls Series)
Symeon, *Historia Regum*, ed. T. Arnold (Rolls Series)
Symeon, *Hist. de S. Cuthbert*, ed. T. Arnold (Rolls Series)
Tullie, I., *Narrative of Siege of Carlisle 1644-5*, ed. S. Jefferson (1940)
Tacitus, *The Agricola and the Germanus*, ed. S. A. Handforth (1970)
Young, A., *Six months tour through the north of England* (1770)
Zosimus, *History of Count Zosimus*, Oxford edition (1814)

Reports

Chadwick, E., 'Report on enquiry into the Sanitary Conditions of the Labouring Population of Great Britain', *House of Lords Political Tracts P 1172* (1842)
Chadwick, E., *Demoralisation and injuries occasioned by the want of proper regulations of labourers engaged in construction and working on Railways* (1845)

Muggeridge, R. M., Report on conditions of Hand Loom Weavers of counties of Lancaster, Westmorland, Cumberland and Part of West Riding of Yorkshire, *Parliamentary Papers* (1840)
Power, W. H., *Report to the Local Government Board on recent epidemic prevalence of fever in Carlisle and sanitary state of the city* (1874)
Pringle, Capt., *The Commissioners of the Poor Laws Report*, xviii (1834)
Rawlinson, R., *Report to General Board of Health on City of Carlisle*, (1850)
'Report on the Petition of several Weavers', *Parliamentary Papers* (1808)
'Report from Select Committee on Hand Loom Weavers', *Parliamentary Papers* (1835)
Reid, D. B., 'Report on the Sanitary Condition of Carlisle', *Second Report of Commissioners of Enquiry on The State of Large Towns and Populous Districts*, Appendix to part 2 (1845)
Select Committee Report on Railway Labourers vol. 13 (1846)
Walsham, Sir John, 'First Report on the State of the Dwellings of the Labouring Classes (no. 14), Cumberland, Durham, Northumberland and Westmorland', *Political Tracts P 1173* (1840)
Carlisle Canal Reports
Chapman, W., *Report on the means of obtaining a safe and commodious communication from Carlisle to the sea* (1807)
Chapman, W., *Report of the proposed Canal Navigation between Carlisle and the Solway Firth* (1818)
Chapman, W., *Report on the cost and separate advantage of a ship canal or railway from Newcastle to Carlisle* (1824)

DIRECTORIES AND GAZETTEERS
Arthur's Guide to Carlisle (1881)
Bailey, J. and Culley, G., *General view of Agriculture in Cumberland* (1794)
Bulmer, T., *History and Directory of East Cumberland* (1884)
Carlisle Directory (1792)
Carlisle Directory (1837)
Guide to Carlisle (1821)
Hutchinson, W., *History and Antiquities of Carlisle* (1794)
Jefferson, S., *History and Antiquities of Carlisle* (1838)
Jollie's Directory (1811)
Lyson, *Magna Britannia* (1816)
Mannix and Whellan, *History, Gazetteer, and Directory of Cumberland* (1847)
Nicolson, J. and Burns, R., *History and Antiquities of Counties of Westmorland and Cumberland vol. 2* (1777)
Nutter, M. E., *Carlisle in Olden Times* (1845)
Parson, W. and White, W., *History, Directory and Gazetteer of Counties of Cumberland and Westmorland* (1829)
Picture of Carlisle and Directory (1810)
Todd, H., *Account of City and Diocese of Carlisle* (1699)
Universal British Directory (1790)
Whellan, W., *History of Cumberland and Westmorland* (1860)

SECONDARY SOURCES
Appleby, A. B., *Famine in Tudor and Stuart England* (1978)
Armstrong, A., Mawer, A., Stenton, F. M., Dickens, B., *Place Names of Cumbria*, parts 1 and 3 (1952 and 1971)
Bailey, R. N., *Viking Age Sculpture in Northern England* (1980)
Baines, E., *History of Cotton Manufactures in Great Britain* (1835)
Baldwin, J. R. and Whyte, I. D. (eds.), *Scandinavians in Cumbria* 1985
Bouch, C. M. L., *Prelates and People of the Lake Counties* (1948)
Bunt, C. G. B. and Ross, E. A., *Two centuries of English Chintz (1750-1950)* (1957)
Cameron, K., *English Place Names* (1961)
Carlisle Corporation Officers, *Local Government of the City and Borough of Carlisle 1158-1958* (1958)
Chadwick, N. K., 'Celtic background in Early Anglo-Saxon England', *Celtic and Saxon Studies in Early British Borders* (1963)
Chadwick, N. K., *The Conversion of Northumbria* (1962)
Charlton, J., *Carlisle Castle* (1985)
Deane, P., *The First Industrial Revolution* (1965)
Dod, R. C., *Electoral Facts (1832-53)* (1853)
Duckworth, J., *Carlisle Parliaments of Edward I* (1930)
Ekwall, R., *Scandinavian and Celts in N.W. England* (1918)
Farish, W., *Notes on progress of Carlisle – an autobiography* (1872)
Ferguson, R. S., *Cumberland and Westmorland M.P.'s (1660-1867)* (1871)
Ferguson, R. S., *Diocesan History of Carlisle* (1889)
Ferguson, R. S., *History of Cumberland* (1890)

Ferguson, R. S. and Nanson, W., *Some municipal records of Carlisle* (1887)
Gatrell, V. A. C., Lenman, B., Parker, G. (eds.), *Crime and Law. Social History and Crime in Western Europe since 1500* (1980)
Glass, D. V., *Development of Population Studies* (1975)
Gosling, P. F., *Carlisle – an Archaeological Survey of the Historic Town* (1970)
Hay, D., *Albion's Fatal Tree. Crime in Society in 18th-century England* (1975)
Higham, N., *The Northern Counties to A.D. 1000* (1984)
Jackson, K., *Language and History of Early Britain* (1953)
McCalmont, *Parliamentary Poll Book* (1971)
McCarthy, M., *Carlisle – A Frontier City* (1980)
McCarthy, M., Summerson, H. R. T., and Annis, R. G., *Carlisle Castle – A Survey and Documentary History* (1990)
Marshall, J. D. and Walton, J. K., *The Lake Counties from 1830* (1981)
Mitchell, W. R. and Joy, D., *Settle-Carlisle Railway* (1979)
Mounsey, G. E., *Occupation of Carlisle 1745* (1846)
Nicolas, H., *Siege of Caerlaverock* (1828)
Nightingale, B., *The Ejected of 1662 in Cumberland and Westmorland* (1911)
Perriam, D. R., *Carlisle in Camera* 1 and 2 (1988)
Pevsner, N., *Buildings of England – Cumberland and Westmorland* (1967)
Smith, K., *Carlisle* (1970)
Stenton, F. M., *Pre-Conquest Westmorland* (1936)
Stenton, F. M., *Anglo-Saxon England* (1972)
Ure, A., *The Philosophy of manufacturers* (1835)
Williams, I., *Canu Talieson* (1938)
Willis, B., *Survey of Cathedrals: York, Durham, Carlisle, Chester* (1727)
Wilson, J. (ed.), *Victoria County History of Cumberland* vol. 2 (1905)
Wilson, P. R., Jones, R. F. J., Evans, D. M. (eds.), *Settlement and Society in the Roman North* (1984)
Ziegler P., *The Black Death* (1970)

ARTICLES AND THESES

Armstrong, W. A., 'Trend of Mortality in Cumberland between the 1780s and 1840s', *E.H.R.* (1981)
Barnes, H., 'Presidential Address', *British Medical Journal* (1896)
Barnes, J., 'Popular Protest and Radical Politics (1790-1850)', Ph.D. thesis, Lancaster (1981)
Barrow, G. W. S., 'Anglo-Scottish Border', *N.H.* (1966)
Beckett, 'Landowners in Cumbria *c.*1680-1750', Ph.D. thesis, Lancaster (1975)
Burgess, J., 'Growth of methodism in Cumbria', *N.H.* (1981)
Borsay, P., 'English Urban Renaissance. Landscape and Leisure in the Provincial Town *c.*1660-1770', Ph.D. thesis, Lancaster (1981)
Caruana, I., 'Carlisle', *C.A.* no. 86 (1983)
Caruana, I., 'Carlisle', *C.A.* no. 101 (1986)
Charlesworth, D., 'Roman Carlisle', *A.J.* (1978)
Dobson, R. B., 'Cathedral Chapters and Cathedral Cities, York, Durham and Carlisle in the 15th century', *N.H.* (1953)
Hopkinson, R., 'The Electorate of Cumberland and Westmorland in late 17th and early 18th centuries', *N.H.* (1979)
Hopkinson, R., 'Elections in Cumberland and Westmorland (1695-1785)', Ph.D thesis, Newcastle (1973)
Keeling, S. M., 'Reformation in the Anglo Scottish Border Counties', *N.H.* (1979)
Keeling, S. M., 'Church and Religion. Anglo-Saxon Border Counties 1534-1572', Ph.D. thesis, Durham (1975)
McCarthy, M. and Padley, H., 'Excavation and Finds, the Lanes, Carlisle', *Britannia* vol. xiii (1982)
McCarthy, M., 'Thomas, Chadwick and Post Roman Carlisle', *B.A.R.* Brit. Series 102 (1982)
McCarthy, M. and Dacre, J. A., 'Roman Timber Buildings in Castle St. Carlisle', *A.J.* (1983)
Spence, R., 'Pacification of Cumberland Borders (1593-1628)', *N.H.* (1977)
Spence, R., 'Backward North modernised. The Cliffords and Socage Manor, Carlisle 1611-1643', *N.H.* (1984)
Stedman, J., 'A very indifferent small city. Economy of Carlisle 1550-1700', Ph.D. thesis, Leicester (1988)
Summerson, H., 'The place of Carlisle in the Commerce of Northern England, 13th century', *Newcastle Conference* (1985)
Taylor, A., 'The Dukery of Carlisle', *Country Life* (1989)
Walton, J., 'Railways and Resort Development – Silloth', *N.H.* (1979)
Woodall, B. G., 'Carlisle Mails', *Philatelist* (1950)

Index

Adelulf, Bishop, 18–19
Aetius, 10
Aglionby family, 23
Agricola, 3, 4
agriculture *see* Carlisle, hinterland
Alexander II, King of Scotland, 19, 21–2
Alexander III, King of Scotland, 25–6
Allectus, 7
Alston silver mines, 24
American civil war, 85
Anglo-Saxon Chronicle, 13, 15, 17
Annetwell Street, Roman fort excavations, 3, 4
Antigonas Papias, 6
Antonine Itinerary, 6
Antonine wall, 3, 7
Antoninus Pius, 3
Appleby, Bishop, 34, 38
Appleby, 16
  castle, 18, 20, 33, 65
archaeological excavations, 3–8, 16
Ardderyd (Arthuret), battle of, 11
Arkwright, Richard, 78
Armstrong, William, of Kinmount ('Kinmount Willie'), 49
Armstrong family, 41
Ashley, Lord, 117
Aske, Robert, 43
Aspatria, 14, 16
Athelstan, King, 15
Athenaeum, 106, 119
Attacotti tribe, 8
'Auld Alliance', France and Scotland, 41

B.S.R.A. (Kangol), 124
Bailie Nicol Jarvis steam packet, 89
Bakhaus, John de, 22
Balliol, Edward, 33
Balliol, John, 26
Bamburgh, 15
banks and banking, 77
Bannockburn, battle of, 30
Barbarian threat to Roman Empire, 8, 9–10
Barnard Castle, 48
Barons' revolt (1215), 19, 21
Barwise family of Ilekirk, 56
Batty, Superintendent of Police, 101
Bede, 1, 8, 9–13
Bell, Andrew, 117
Bernicia, 11, 17

Berwick-upon-Tweed, 43, 53
Best, Bishop John, 46, 48
Bewcastle, 4, 11, 12, 15
Birdoswald, 11
Bishops' War (1639–40), 56
Black Death, 34–5, 38–9
Blackfriars Street, 4, 6, 8
Blamire, George, 77
bleaching of cloth, 77
Blenkinsop colliery, 107
Bolingbroke, Henry (Henry IV), 36
Bolton in Wensleydale, 47
Bonsoir Ltd, 123
border, 45
border warfare, 1, 24, 46, 67
  law enforcement (1662 Act), 59
Boroughbridge, battle of (1322), 31
Bowes, Sir George, 48
Breda, Declaration of (1660), 58
bridges,
  Caldew, 22, 72, 130
  Eden, 4, 22, 72, 104, 130
  Nelson, 121
  St Nicholas, 130
Brigantes tribe, 3, 6
British Rail, 124
  see also railways
Brough under Stainmore, 20
Brougham Castle, 33
Bruce, Edward, 29
Bruce, Robert, 26, 28, 29–30, 31–2, 33
Buchan, Earl of, 26
Buchanan, Eliza S., 128
Buck's textiles, 115, 123
building societies, 121
Burgh by Sands, 18, 29, 33
Bush Hotel, 72

Caerlaverock, 28
Caldew, river, 18, 72, 77, 121
  bridge, 22, 72, 130
Caledonii (Caledonians), 3, 4
Candida Casa (Whithorn), 10
Canu Taliesin, 11
Canute, King, 15
Cappock, Thomas, 67
Carausius, 7
Carlatton manor, 22
Carleton family, 49

Carleton manor, 18
Carlisle,
  castle, 17–18, 21–2, 24, 28, 30, 32, 35–6, 39,
    45–50, 52, 61, 67
    decayed (1250s), 25
    Mary, Queen of Scots at, 47
    Northern Rebellion, 48–9
    Tudor re-design, 43, 45
  cathedral, 16, 18–19, 22, 28, 29, 43, 47, 52, 55,
    67
    bishops, 22, 33
    destroyed in Civil War, 58
    diocese, 18–19, 20, 32, 36, 103
    rebuilt, 36, 37–8
    Renaissance influence, 41
  citizens' lifestyle, 61, 74, 119, 121–2, 124, 128–9
  city walls, 39, 50, 67, 72
    in 1697, 61
    demolished, 104
    Norman, 18, 24, 30
    repairs to, 36, 45
    Roman, 6, 8, 12
    ruinous, 35–6
  civic government,
    medieval, 22–4, 37
    16th century, 50, 52
    17th century, 58
    19th century, 103, 117
    20th century, 128
    see also charters
  Civil War coinage, 57
  condition of,
    Middle Ages, 38–9
    18th century, 68
    19th century, 91–5
  culture and recreation, 74, 76
  earls of, 70
  economy,
    medieval, 24–5, 36–7
    16th century, 52
    17th century, 60–1
    18th century, 68, 70
    19th century, Chapter 8 passim, 114–15
    20th century, 123–4
  electorate and politics, 63–4, 102–3, 116–17,
    127–8
  fires,
    1292, 22–3, 26, 37, 38–9
    1391, 36, 39
  hinterland, 52, 68, 70
  names, 14
    Luel, Carleol, 13
    Luguballia, 12
    Luguvalium, 1, 4, 6–8, 9
  'Parliament', 26, 28–9
  priory, 24, 43
  Roman, 1, 3, 4, 5, 6–7, 8

    sacked by Danes, 13
    sieges of,
      1173, 20–1
      1315, 30
      1644, 56–7
    Statute of (1307), 29
    surrendered,
      to Charles Stuart 1745, 65, 67
      to Scots 1216, 21
    townscape, 104, 118–19, 121–2
      medieval, 22, 38–9
      Tudor, 50
      Stuart, 61–2
      18th century, 68, 72, 74
      20th century, 124, 130–1
    Treaty of (1597), 49
Carlisle, Annan and Liverpool Steam Navigation
  Company, 90
Carlisle Canal, 87–90, 107–8
Carlisle Canal Company, 110–12
Carlisle, Earls of, 60, 70, 102
Carlisle Gas Light and Coke Company, 104
Carlisle Labour Party, 116–17
Carlisle and Liverpool Steam Navigation
  Company, 89–90
Carlisle Radical Workers Men's Association, 101
Carlisle Sanitary Association, 94–5
Carnaby's Folly, 74
Carr, Jonathan Dodgson, 111, 114
Carr, Theodore, 114
Carrick and Johnston textiles, 85
Carrick's, hatters, 115
Carr's of Carlisle, 114–15, 124
Carr's Flour Mills, 114, 124
Carter, Abbot of Holm Cultram, 43
Cartwright, Edmund, power loom, 81
Carvetii tribe, 6
Castle Sowerby, 22
Castle Street, 4, 6, 22
Catholic churches, 103
Catraeth (Catterick), 11
cattle trade, 60
Cavenham Foods, 124
Cecil, Sir William, 46, 48
Chadwick, Edwin, report (1842), 98–9
Chance, F.W., 117
chapbooks, 74
Chapman, W., 87–8, 107
Charles I, King, 55–6
Charles II, King, 58
charters,
  Henry II (c.1158), 24
  35 Henry III (1251), 23
  21 Edward I (1293), 23
  9 Edward II (1316), 23
  25 Edward III (1352), 34, 36
  9 Elizabeth I (1567), 50, 52

12 Charles I (1637), 52, 58, 60
16 Charles II (1664), 58
36 Charles II (1684), 58
Chartists, 101
cholera, 97
church building, 103
cinemas, 123, 128
citadel, 45, 72, 104
   Roman, 6
Civil War (1642–5), 56–8
'Civitas Carvetiorum', 6, 8, 11
Clarke Chapman, 124
Clement V, Pope, 28
Clerk, Sir John, 68
Clifford family, 43
Clifford, Henry, 1st Earl of Cumberland, 43
Clifford, Henry, 2nd Earl of Cumberland, 48
Clifford, Lord (1611), 54
Clifford, Sir Thomas, 43
Clodius Albinus, 4
coach and carrier services, 72
Cockermouth, 33, 43
cockpit, 76
coins, Anglo-Saxon, 16
Comyn, John, 28
Constantine, Emperor, 7
Constantine III, Roman usurper, 9
Constantine III, King of Scots, 15
Constantius Chlorus, 7
Corbridge, 18
Corby Castle, 107
Council of the North, 43, 50, 54
Courtaulds, 123
covered market, 122
Cowan Boyd, 124
Cowans, John, 114
Cowans Sheldon, 114, 124
craft guilds see guilds
Crofts, John, 68
Cromwell, Oliver, 58
Cromwell, Richard, 58
Crown and Mitre hotel, 72
cullery tenures, 23–4
Culloden, battle of, 67
Cumberland, Duke of, 67
Cumberland, earls of see Clifford
Cumberland Infirmary, 97, 119
Curwen family, 47
Curwen, Sir Patrick, 57
Cuthbert, St, 8, 12, 13

Dacre, Lord (fl.1513), 41
Dacre, Sir Charles, 43
Dacre, Sir Christopher, 43
Dacre, Elizabeth, 53
Dacre, Francis, 48
Dacre, Leonard, 48–9, 53
Dacre, Sir Thomas, 45

Dacre family, 23, 43, 46, 47
Dacre cross, 15
Dalman, Robert de, 22
Dalston, 15
   Hall, 56
Dalton, Robert, 50, 52
Danes, 13, 16
   see also Vikings
David I, King of Scotland, 18, 19
David II, King of Scotland, 33
de Boyville family, 23
de Tilliot family, 23
'Debatable Lands' (border), 41, 45
Defoe, Daniel, 68
Denton, John, 17
Denton, John de, 28
Denton, Richard de, 34
Denton family, 23
Denton Holme estate, 121
Denton Iron Works, 115
directories, trades and occupations, Appendices,
   2, 3, 4
disease, 95–7
   see also plague
Dispensary, 96
Dissolution of the Monasteries, 43
Dixon, Captain, 57
Dixon family, industrialists, 84–5, 87, 103, 108,
   111, 114, 116–17, 121, 124
Dixon, John, 87, 103, 110
Dixon, Peter, 84–5, 87
Dolfin, 17
Domesday Book, 15
Dormont book (1561), 50
Douglas, Sir William, Earl of, 33, 35
Drumburgh, 33
Dunmail, King of Strathclyde, 15
Dunmalloght, 33
Durand, Col., 65, 67
Durant the moneyer, 24
Durrance, Richard, 61

Eadred, Abbot, 13
Eamont Bridge, 15, 17
Eardulf, English princeps, 14–15
Eardulf, Bishop, 13
Ecgfrith, King, 12
Eden, river, 18, 21, 56, 70
Eden Fishing Board, 99
Edmund, King, 15
Edward the Elder, King, 15
Edward I, King, 19, 24, 25, 26, 28–9, 33, 36
Edward II, King, 29–33, 36, 38
Edward III, King, 35
Edward IV, King, 36
Edward VI, King, 45
Edwin, King of Northumbria, 11
Egremont castle, 33

Elizabeth I, Queen, 46, 49
Erebald, silver mine owner, 24
Errington, J.E., 110
Ethelfrith, King of Northumbria, 11
Ethelred, King, 15
Eugenius, King of Strathclyde, 15

famine (1623–4), 54
Ferguson, George, 84, 85
Ferguson, John, 84
Ferguson, Joseph, 84–5, 103
Ferguson, Richard, 77, 84
Ferguson, Richard (jun.), 84
Ferguson family, industrialists, 84–5, 111, 114,
    116–17, 121, 124
Fetherstonehaugh, Sir Timothy, 57
Fiennes, Celia, 61–2, 68
Fleming, Lord, 47
Flemings, settlers, 17, 18
Flodden, battle of, 41
Forster, Joseph, 87
Forster, Sir John, 48
fort, Roman (Flavian), 3–6
forum, Roman, 5
French prisoners, 77
French settlers, 17
friars, Franciscans and Dominicans, 19, 43
Friggate works, 85

gaols, 101–2
Geddes, Captain, 89
Gelt, battle of River, 48
General Strike (1926), 128
George I, King, 64
Gildas, 1, 9, 10
Gillesland (Gilsland), 53
Gilpin, Capt. William, 65, 67
Glasgow, John, Bishop of, 18
Glenham, Sir Thomas, 56–7
Gosforth cross, 16
Gosling Syke, 50
Gospatric, lord of Allerdale and Dalston, 15
Graham, Mrs Isa, 128
Graham, Ritchie, 41
Graham, Sir James, 102, 116
Graham family, 45, 49, 53
    transportation of, 53
Great Salkeld, 33
Gregory, Pope, 22
Guildhall, 37
guilds, 23, 24, 25, 36, 37, 52, 54, 60
Guliker brothers, 77
Guthred, 13

Habrickley, Richard, 28
Hadrian, Emperor, 3
Hadrian's Wall, 3–4, 7, 8
Hales, Sir Charles, 52

Halfdan, 13
Halton, Bishop John, 26, 28, 30
Handleys, carriers, 72
handloom weavers, 77–84
Harcla, Andrew de, 30–2
Hargreaves, James, spinning jenny, 78
Harley, Lord, 70
Harrison, Thomas, 87
Harthacanute, 15
Haschenperg, Stefan von, 43, 45
Head, G.H., 110
Henry I, King, 18, 19
Henry II, King, 19, 20, 24
Henry III, King, 19, 22, 25
Henry IV, King, 36
Henry VII, King, 41, 43
Henry VIII, King, 41, 43
Herries, Lord, 47
Hetherington family, 48
Heysham, Dr, 95–7, 99
Hicks, John, 70
Highhead castle, 33
Highmore House, 67
Hill, Rowland, 72
Hispanus, Cardinal Petrus, 28
Historia Brittonum, 1, 11
Hodgson, R. and W., 77
hogback tombs, 16
Holm Cultram abbey, 20, 21, 23, 24, 26, 28, 29,
    31, 36, 43
Holme Head works, 84–5
Holme weaving factory, 81
Holy Trinity Church, Caldewgate, 30, 38
Honorius, 9, 10
horse racing, 74, 76, 130
hospitals, 97
House of Recovery, 97
Housing Acts (1890, 1919), 124
housing conditions, 91, 93
housing development, 119, 121–2, 124
How, John, 63
Howard, Lord William, 53–4
Howard, Charles, 57
Howard, John, 101
Howard, Sir Philip, 57
Howard, Philip Henry, 102, 116
Howard, William, 63
Howard family, 63, 70
    see also Norfolk, dukes of
Hudson Scott, 115, 124
Hundred Years War, 33, 36
Hunsdon, Lord, 48, 49
Hutchinson, W., 68

industrial estates, 124
Industrial Revolution, Chapter 8 *passim*
Inglewood forest, 23, 24, 36, 39
Inquests (1535), 41

Inquisition (1344), 39
Irton cross, 15

Jackson, Thomas, 67
Jacobite rebellions,
    (1715), 64–5
    (1745), 65, 67
James III, King of Scotland, 41
James IV, King of Scotland, 41
James VI and I, King of England, 49, 53, 54
James II, King of England, 58–90
James, William, 102
Jefferys, Chief Justice, 58
John, King, 19, 21–2
John Laing and Sons, 115
John Lewis Partnership, 124
Jordan Fantosme, *Chronicle*, 21

Kay's flying shuttle, 78
'Kinmount Willie' (William Armstrong), 49
Kirkby, John de, 33–4
Kite, Bishop, 41
Knighton, Henry, 34
Knollys, Sir Francis, 46
Knox, John, 45

Lacy, Sir Antony de, 32
Laing and Sons, John, 115
Lancaster, Earl of, 31
Lancaster, Joseph, 117
landowners in Carlisle,
    c.1300, 8, 23–4
    c.1600, 54
Lanercost Priory, 23, 24, 26, 28
Lanes,
    archaeological site, 4, 5
    development, 5, 130–1
Langrigg, William de, 28
Langthwaite mill, 84–5, 87
Langwathby manor, 22
Lascelles, Sir Thomas, 25
law and order, 99–102
'laws of the marches', 45
Lawson, Wilfred, 56
leather trade, 52
leper hospital (St Nicholas), 30, 33, 38
Leslie, David, 56
Lewyn, John, 36
library,
    public, 130
    subscription, 74, 106
Liddel,
    barony of, 18, 23
    castle, 20
Liddesdale, 45, 48
Lindisfarne, 12–13
Linstock,   castle,   26,   28
    manor, 18

literacy,   18th   century,   74
    19th century, 118
Locke, Joseph, 110
lodging houses, 93
Lollicus Urbicus, 3
Lonsdale, earls of, 102
Lonsdale, James Lowther, 1st Earl of, 63–4, 64–5,
    70
Losh, James, 85, 95
Lowther, Sir James, 76
Lowther, Sir John, 59
Lowther, Richard, 46
Lowther, Sir William, 64
Lowther family, 63, 76
    see also Lonsdale, earls of
Lowther, 16
Lucy, Lord, 33
Lucy, Thomas de, 34
Luguvalium, Luel, Carleol *see* Carlisle, name of

McAdam, John, 70
McAlpin, Thomas, 114
Macready, William, 74
Maeatae tribe, 4
Magna Carta, 21
Magnentius, 8
Magnus Maximus, 9
mail services, 72
Main Guard house, 62, 74
Malcolm I, King of Scotland, 15
Malcolm III, King of Scotland, 15
Malcolm IV, King of Scotland, 20
Mallerstang castle, 33
Margaret of Anjou, Queen, 36
market hall, 122
Marsden power loom manufactory, 81
Marston Moor, battle of (1644), 56
Mary, Queen of Scots, 45, 46–7
Mary I, Queen, 45
Maryport, 70, 87
Matilda, Queen, 19
Mattinson, John, 100
Mauclerk, Bishop, 19
Maxwell, Lord, 45
mendicity society, 81
Merks, Bishop Thomas, 36
Meschin, Sir Ranulf, 18, 20
Metal Box Company, 115, 124
Methodism, 76, 103
Meye, Bishop John, 49
Middleton, George, M.P., 128
Milne, J., 95
mint, 24
Mitchell, A.P.V., 124
Mons Graupius, battle of, 3
Moot Hall, 24, 62
Morpeth, Lord, 58
mortality rates, 95–7, 99

Morton Sundour, 115, 123
moss troopers, 59, 67
motor bus services, 127
Muggeridge report (1840), 78, 80
mule spinning, 78
Municipal Corporation Act (1835), 103
Musgrave, Sir Christopher, 59, 63
Musgrave, Sir Edward, 54
Musgrave, Sir Philip, 100
Musgrave family, 23, 47, 63
'mushroom elections', 63–4

N.E. Industries, 124
Nadin, Joseph, 101
Napoleonic wars, 78
Naseby, battle of, 57
Naworth castle, 33, 48, 53
Nennius, 1, 9, 11
Nestlé, 124
Netherby, 4
Neville, Charles, 6th Earl of Westmorland, 47–8
Neville family, 43
Newburn church, 18
Newcastle-upon-Tyne, 17–18
newspapers and journals, 118
    Carlisle Patriot, Carlisle Journal, 74
Newton Arlosh, 33
Nicholson, Bishop, 65
Ninian, St, 10–11
Norfolk, dukes of, 43, 48, 49, 76
Norfolk, dukes of, *see also* Howard
    North, Roger, 59–60
North, Sir Francis, 59–60
Northern Rebellion (1568), 47–9
Northumberland, earls of *see* Percy
Northumbria, kingdom of, 11–12, 13, 14

occupational structure,
    16th century, 52
    17th century, 60–1
    18th century, 74
    19th century, 115
    20th century, 123
occupations,
    1790–1901 Appendices, 2, 3
    1921–1951 Appendix, 4
Oglethorpe, Bishop Owen, 46
Orme, Henry, 70
Osnaburghs, type of linen, 77
Oswald, 11
Oswy, 11–12
Otho, papal legate, 21
Otterburn, battle of, 35
Owain, 11
Owen the Bald, of Strathclyde, 15

Paley, William Appendix, 5
Palmer, John, 72

Patrick, St, 10, 11
Pattinson, John, 58
Pattinson, Thomas, 61, 65, 70
Paulinus, Archbishop of York, 11
Peel, Sir Robert, 100
pele towers, 33, 67
penny post, 72
Penrith, 16, 22, 50, 53, 59, 65
Percy, Bishop Hugh, 103
Percy, Henry, 6th Earl of Northumberland, 43
Percy, Thomas, 7th Earl of Northumberland, 46,
    47–8
Percy family, earls of Northumberland, 23, 43,
    54
Petilius Cerealis, 3
Petriana, 3, 6
Petteril, river, 18, 99
Picts, 8, 9–11
picture houses *see* cinemas
Pilgrimage of Grace, 43, 47
Pirelli, 124
plague, 34–5, 38, 49–50, 57, 61
    see also Black Death
police force, 100–1
poll tax (1377), 39
Poor Law Amendment Act (1834), 80–1
population explosions,
    16th century, 49
    19th century, 77–8, 100
population statistics (1763–1981), Appendix 1
Port Carlisle *see* Carlisle canal
Porter, Hinde and Porter, 115
poverty, 80–1, 83–4
praetorium, Roman, 5
Pratchett Bros., 115, 124
Preston Pans, battle of, 65
printfields, 77
priory, Augustinian, 18
probate returns, 52, 61
public baths, 122

Quakers, 76
Quo Warranto Edward I (1292), 23

Raegnald, 14, 15
railways, 123, 124, 127
    British Rail, 124
    Caledonian Company, 110–11, 113, 115
    Carlisle-Lancaster, 108–10, 113
    Carlisle-Maryport, 107–8, 113
    Carlisle-Newcastle, 85, 107–8, 110, 112
    Carlisle-Port Carlisle, 110–12
    Carlisle-Settle, 112–13
    Carlisle-Silloth, 110–13, 127
    Citadel station, 113
    east coast route (LNER), 108, 111
    Glasgow and South Western, 113

London and North Western Railway (LNWR), 108, 115
Midland, 113, 115
navvies, 110, 113
North British, 111–12
North-Eastern Railway Company (NERC), 108
west coast route (LNER), 108, 113, 131
workshops, 114, 115
Ravenna Cosmography, 6
Rawlinson, R., report, 91, 93, 99
Ray, James, 67
reading room, 119
Rederech, King of Britons, 11
Redness Hall (Guildhall), 37
Redness, Richard, 37
Reform Acts (parliamentary),
(1832), 102
(1867), 116
(1918), 127
(1929), 128
Reformation, 41
registration of births and deaths, 97
Reid, Dr., report (1845), 91, 93–4, 97
reivers *see* moss troopers
religion, 76, 103
Rheged, 1, 11, 12
Rhun, 11, 12
Richard, Earl, 18
Richard I, King, 36
Richard III, King, 36–7, 38
riots,
city, 100–1
railways, 110
Ripon, Treaty of (1640), 56
river transport, 70
road transport, 70–2, 127, 130
Rose castle (bishops' palace), 26, 29, 31, 33, 65
Rosegill, Robert, 22
Rothbury, 18
Roxburgh, 21
Ruthwell, 12, 15

St Alban's church, 38, 50
St Cuthbert's church, 8, 38, 74
St Mary's church *see* Carlisle, cathedral
St Nicholas leper hospital, 30, 33, 38
Salkeld, John de, 38
Salkeld, Sir Francis, 59
Salkeld, Prior Lancelot, 43
Salkeld family, 47
Salkeld manor, 22
saltpans, 24
Saxon cemetery, 16
Scaleby, 33
schools, 117–18, 128
Scotby manor, 22
Scotland,

Act of Union, 64
kingdom of, 17, 19–20, 24
trade with, 24
Scotsdyke, 45
Scott, Benjamin, 115, 117
Scott of Buccleuch, 49
Scott Lamb, 77
Scott, Walter, 104
Scottish Church Assembly, 55–6
Scrope, Henry le, Lord, 46, 47, 48, 49, 50
Scrope, Sir Galfrid de, 32
sculpture, Dark Age, 12, 15–16
Senhouse, Prior, 41
Serjeant, Andrew, 28
Severus, Emperor, 4, 6
sewage disposal, 91–5, 99
Shaddon mills, 85
shambles, 24, 74
Sheldon, Edward, 114
shopping development, 130–1
Shrewsbury, Earl of, 47
Sihtric, King of Northumbria, 15
Silloth, 110–12, 114
silver mine, Alston, 24
Siward, Earl, 15
Skinburness, 28
Slater, Richard, 26
slaughterhouses, 94
Slee, Prior Christopher, 43
slums, 91–5
smallpox, 95–6
Smirke, Robert, 104
Snowdon, Bishop, 54
social status and life expectancy, 97–8
Solway Firth, 1, 3, 7, 11, 13–15, 17, 20, 24, 29, 35
Solway Moss, battle of, 45
Spears, General, M.P., 128
Spedding, Mr., political agent, 63
Speenhamland system, 80
Spencer, Henry, 28
sport and recreation, 74, 76, 128, 130
Stainmore, 17
Standard, battle of the (1138), 20
Stanegate, 7
Stanwix, Thomas, 63
Stanwix, isolation hospital, 50
Stead McAlpin, 114, 115, 124
steam navigation, 89–90
Steel, Mr., water company chairman, 99
Stephen, King, 19, 20
Stephenson, Robert, 114
Stephenson, Brassey and MacKenzie, 110
Stilicho, 9
Stradling, Sir Henry, 57
Strathclyde, kingdom of, 1, 10, 11, 14, 15, 17
Stuart, Charles (young Pretender), 65, 67

Stuart, James (old Pretender), 64–5
Syde, Thomas, 61
Symeon of Durham, 12, 13, 14

Tacitus, 3
Teasdale and Company, 115
telephone exchange, 123
Telford, Thomas, 70, 87–8
temple, Roman, 5
Test Acts (1673 and 1678), 58
Testa, William, 29
Testamenta Karleolensis, 39
textile industry 70, 114–15, 123 and Chapter 8
    passim
theatres, 74, 106, 128, 130
Theodoric of Bernicia, 11
Theodosius, 8
Thompson, Thomas, 61
Thurston, Archbishop, 18
Tile Tower, 36, 62
timber platform, 4–5
Tite, Sir William, 113
Todd, Hugh, 17, 18, 39, 58, 61
Town Hall, 72
Towton, battle of, 36
Trajan, Emperor, 6
trams, 123, 125, 127
transport, 70
    see also Carlisle canal; railways; road transport;
    trams
Tullie, Isaac, 56–7
Tullie House, 4, 5–6, 61, 62, 72, 122, 128, 130
turnpikes, 70–1
Tylliol, Peter, 39
typhus, 96–7

United Biscuits, 124
university, proposed, 54
Urien, 11
utilities,
    electricity, 123, 127
    gas, 104, 127
    sewage disposal, 91–5, 99
    street lighting, 74, 104
    water, 93–4, 99, 127

Valentinian, 8
Vaux, Robert de, 21
Vespasian, 3
Victoria foundry, 115
Vikings, 1, 9, 14–16, 17
Vipond, Robert de, 22
Viyella, 124

Wade, General George, 65, 70
wages, weavers', 80
Wagga, reeve of Carlisle, 12
Waldegrave, Bishop, 103
Wallace, William, 26, 28
Walter, Prior, 18
Walter of Hereford, Master, 36
Warkworth, 18
Wars of the Roses, 36
Warwick, earl of (1338), 33
water supply, 93–4, 99, 127
Waterloo foundry, 115
Waugh, Chancellor John, 67
weavers, handloom, 77–84
Welton, Bishop Gilbert, 22, 33, 38
Wesley, John, 76
Wetheral Priory, 23, 24
Wharton, Sir Thomas, 45
Whitehaven, 76
Whithorn (Candida Casa), 10
Whittingham, 18
William the Aetheling, 18
William II (Rufus), King, 17–18, 61
William III (of Orange), King, 59
William the Lion, of Scotland, 20–1
Wilson, Captain, 65
Wilson, Prebendary, 67
Wittering, Robert, 26
wool trade, 24
Wordsworth, Dorothy, 104
workhouses, 104

York, 3, 13, 14

Zosimus, 1, 9